# PEOPLE AND TECHNOLOGY IN THE WORKPLACE

NATIONAL ACADEMY OF ENGINEERING

Commission on Behavioral and Social Sciences
and Education

NATIONAL RESEARCH COUNCIL

NATIONAL ACADEMY PRESS
Washington, D.C. 1991

**NATIONAL ACADEMY PRESS** • 2101 Constitution Avenue, N.W. • Washington, D.C. 20418

The study summarized in this report was supported with funds from the National Academy of Engineering Technology Agenda Program.

**Library of Congress Cataloging-in-Publication Data**

People and technology in the workplace/ National Academy of
    Engineering [and] Commission on Behavioral and Social Sciences and
    Education, National Research Council.
        p.    cm.
        Proceedings of a symposium organized by the National Academy of
    Engineering and the Commission on Behavioral and Social Sciences and
    Education, National Research Council.
        Includes bibliographical references and index.
        ISBN 0-309-04583-5
        1. Technological innovations—Economic aspects—United States—
    Congresses. 2. Employees—United States—Effect of technological
    innovations on—Congresses. 3. United States—Manufactures—
    Technological innovations—Case studies—Congresses. 4. Medical
    technology—United States—Case studies—Congresses. 5. Office
    practice—Automation—Case studies—Congresses. I. National
    Academy of Engineering. II. National Research Council (U.S.).
    Commission on Behavioral and Social Sciences and Education.
    HC110.T4P46 1991
    338'.064'0973—dc20                          91-29624
                                                        CIP

Printed in the United States of America

## SYMPOSIUM PLANNING COMMITTEE

GERALD NADLER (*Cochair*), IBM Professor of Engineering Management, Professor and Chairman, Department of Industrial and Systems Engineering, University of Southern California

EDWARD O. LAUMANN (*Cochair*), Dean of Social Sciences, University of Chicago

ROBERT M. ANDERSON, JR., Manager, Technical Education Operation, General Electric Company

ALDEN S. BEAN, Center for Innovation, Management Studies, Lehigh University

HARVEY BROOKS, Professor of Technology and Public Policy, Emeritus, John F. Kennedy School of Government, Harvard University

ROBERT L. KAHN, Research Scientist, Institute for Social Research, University of Michigan

SARA B. KIESLER, Professor of Social Sciences and Social Psychology, Department of Social and Decision Sciences, Carnegie Mellon University

W. RICHARD SCOTT, Professor of Sociology, Stanford University

# Preface

The competitive position of U.S. manufacturing and service industries in world markets has been of growing concern to managers, scholars, and policymakers since the 1970s. As has always been true when greater efficiency and higher productivity are desired, managers have turned to new, sophisticated workplace technologies. New technologies, however, have not proved to be a panacea for all the problems of productivity.

In a series of reports and symposia, the National Academy of Engineering has explored several facets of the problem of productivity and technology. Such experience has led to increasing awareness among managers and researchers that solutions to fading competitive ability cannot be found in a mythical black box of technology. In fact, any important technology has profound human consequences, both positive and negative, which often remain unplanned or unanticipated. Consequently, it is often the organizational and human factors that either facilitate or constrain the ability of firms and workers to adopt and implement new technologies. We concluded that there was a need to review what is known about the relationship between human resources, organizational decision making, and the characteristics of new workplace technologies to understand what improvements are possible in how those technologies are adopted and how leaders are trained to manage the process.

To address these issues, the National Academy of Engineering (NAE) and the National Research Council Commission on Behavioral and Social Sciences and Education (CBASSE) jointly convened an advisory committee with representatives from industry and academia. Through a series of very stimulating and challenging meetings, they planned the symposium "Designing for Technological Change: People in the Process," held on March 13 and 14, 1989. The symposium brought practitioners such as plant managers, hospital administrators, engineers, computer analysts, human resource specialists, and union leaders together with social and behavioral scientists from sociology, psychology, economics, organizational behavior, and industrial engineering. Rosabeth Moss Kanter, Harvard Business School Professor, as well as author and consultant, opened the symposium by presenting a model of successful technology adoption characterized by "four Fs: focused, fast, flexible, and friendly." The participants then examined relationships between human resources, workplace organizations, and new technologies by using case studies of technological change from diverse environments. Concurrent sessions of case presentations relied on the experience of practitioners and on social science analysis from respondents. Summary discussion sessions at the end of both days drew on the diverse expertise of the participants, further exploring the cases and related social science research and addressing more fully their implications for technological and organizational strategies.

The symposium produced a rich set of case studies, which form the core of this volume, illustrating the successful implementation of new technologies, as well as the problems that were overcome, in three areas: manufacturing facilities, medical settings, and offices. In addition, Andrew Van de Ven from the University of Minnesota, Paul Adler from Stanford University, and Tora Bikson and J. D. Eveland at the RAND Corporation, summarized the available research on technological change for each area, thus providing a broader context for the individual case studies. Kanter's piece expands the discussion beyond microlevel project changes to larger questions of organizational structures and interorganizational cooperation. From all of this diverse material, the symposium chairs Gerald Nadler, University of Southern California, and Edward Laumann, University of Chicago, and staff associate Brigid O'Farrell prepared an overview, summarizing information for managers who are considering adopting new workplace technologies and for researchers trying to bridge the gaps in conceptual and practical knowledge. This symposium and this volume are important also because they extend NAE's efforts to collaborate with other groups concerned with different aspects of technological change. This effort is the first joint activity undertaken by NAE and CBASSE, and it could not have been completed without such collaboration and I would like especially to thank Suzanne Woolsey and Robert Caplan, current and former executive directors of CBASSE, for their interest and commitment to this project.

Many people contributed to the success of this symposium and to the publication of this volume. Special thanks are due to co-chairs Edward Laumann and Gerald Nadler and the other members of the symposium committee (listed on page *iii*). In addition there are a number of staff members and fellows who have worked to make this project a success. In particular, I would like to thank Brett Hammond, Janet Muroyama, Michele Rivard, Anastasios Sioukas, Carey Gellman, Jay Ball, and Bette Janson, who all made valuable contributions in different phases of planning the symposium or moving the publication forward. Dale Langford and Bruce Guile have been involved with the project all along, and Brigid O'Farrell provided the insight and energy to bring the manuscript to completion.

ROBERT M. WHITE, *President*
National Academy of Engineering

# Contents

## 2
# MEDICAL TECHNOLOGIES

## 3
# OFFICE AUTOMATION TECHNOLOGIES

# PEOPLE AND TECHNOLOGY IN THE WORKPLACE

People and Technology in the Workplace. 1991.
Pp. 1–14. Washington, D.C:
National Academy Press.

# Designing for Technological Change: People in the Process

EDWARD O. LAUMANN, GERALD NADLER,
AND BRIGID O'FARRELL

The papers in this volume, and the symposium on which it is based, reflect the work of managers and union representatives, engineers and consultants, professors, and practitioners. Despite their common interests in the implementation of new technologies, these groups do not often meet and talk together. There are language barriers across the groups as well as within; there is no more automatic understanding, much less consensus, among sociologists and psychologists than among managers and engineers from the same industry or even the same firm. There is tension because of conflicting goals and expectations: the theoretical interests of scholars versus the day-to-day concerns of managers; the technological priorities of engineers versus the human resource priorities of personnel managers and labor leaders; underlying values of autonomy or control, individualism or collaboration.

Nowhere were these differences more obvious than among the advisory group planning this symposium. As we struggled with the questions, recognizing our diverse backgrounds and experiences, we began to bridge these gaps by using a common perspective—the human element. This is a focus that is both narrow and broad. The focus is narrowly on the role of people in the process of implementing existing technology—not technological innovation itself or the myriad of other factors that are also important in implementation such as product mix, financing, quarterly earnings, or government regulation, although these are certainly touched on in the chapters that follow. The focus is broad in that the issues related to human resources address people employed at all levels of an organization (from secretary and production worker to chief executive officer); in three different technological settings (manufacturing, medical, and office); in organizations of all sizes in both the public and private sectors (from three support staff members in a nonprofit organization to 3,000 employees in a manufacturing plant to more than 30,000 employees in a government agency).

To facilitate a useful exchange of information among these groups, the advisory committee developed a set of questions to guide both the development of the case studies and the discussions that followed. While each organization has its own unique elements, we found these questions (see the box below) helpful in thinking about common themes that could assist people who are contemplating technological changes in their organizations. They form the core of an ongoing process of planning and problem solving, which facilitates converting what we know about designing technological change into practice.

This summary and the chapters that follow were guided by, and expanded on, these questions. The case studies provide concrete examples of what worked and what did not work. The overview chapters in each section place the case examples in a larger conceptual framework and enable some generalizations about the success factors within specific areas. The opening chapter expands the discussion beyond microlevel project changes to larger questions of organizational structures and interorganizational cooperation.

Out of this diversity emerge some common views on what is known about people and the implementation process, enabling us to offer some ideas for organizations considering the adoption of new workplace technologies. There is also some agreement on what we do not know, thus suggesting areas of research needed to bridge gaps in conceptual and practical knowledge. This chapter provides a summary of what we, as engineers and sociologists, as well as cochairs and staff of the symposium, perceive to be part of the problem and several factors that have major effects on adoption of new technology. While we take responsibility for this summary, we also wish to acknowledge our special debt to the symposium planning committee as well as to the many other participants we consulted in this process.

## THE PROBLEM

New technologies have long been part of the American workplace. Never before, however, have the innovations been as fre-

---

**QUESTIONS TO CONSIDER WHEN DESIGNING TECHNOLOGICAL CHANGE**

I. A SNAPSHOT: What is the current structure of the organization (flat, hierarchical, centralized, decentralized, line of business, profit centers, etc.)? What areas would new technology change? What would a new structure look like?

II. THE PROBLEM: What problem(s) or opportunity, external as well as internal to the organization, are the technological changes supposed to solve?

III. SELECTION OF THE TECHNOLOGY AND ORGANIZATIONAL APPROACH: How is the technology designed and selected (capabilities, potentials, limitations, internal/external expertise)? What organizational factors are being considered (size, decision making, work force characteristics)? What are the key organizational changes planned?

IV. TRANSITION/HOW ACHIEVED: How will the technology be implemented, especially considering such organizational concerns as training, negotiation, and worker input and control? How is responsibility divided and what incentives are provided for change? Who gains and who loses during different phases of implementation? What are the likely effects on employees and on business performance? How are problems, set backs, resolved?

V. FUTURE ISSUES/EVALUATION: Were there surprises and how were adjustments made by managers, technical experts, and workers? After implementation, what challenges remain? What did the organization learn from the experience that could be useful in the future?

---

quent and as generally accessible. Technology enabling the flow of information and materials from homes to offices, factories, world capitals, and remote villages has transformed the way products are made and services delivered. At the same time, however, there is increasing recognition that new technologies are often underused or inefficiently used, particularly in manufacturing. As Adler discusses in his overview chapter, for example, the proportion of machine tools that are numerically controlled is less in the United States (40%) than Japan (67%) or Germany (49%). These utilization problems are linked to declining productivity in the increasingly global economy as well as to deteriorating product and service delivery at home. While clearly many businesses continue to innovate and grow, problems such as these might be avoided by learning from the experiences in the manufacturing industries.

One factor that has emerged in the reassessment of the complex process of technological implementation is the role people play in the process. Although technology is often considered a product of science, mathematics, and engineering, any piece of hardware is part of a larger system, including the individual and organizations that apply the science and engineering, build and operate the machinery, ensure a smooth flow of inputs to and outputs from the system, and determine the strategic importance of the desired change to the organization, whether it be improved productivity, reduced costs, or better service delivery. Technology is fundamentally an organizational and human endeavor linking what is theoretically possible to what happens in the laboratory, in the design shop, in the operating room, in the office, or on the plant floor.

Recognition of this factor, however, is relatively recent. Historically, engineers have assumed that implementing technology means that people will adapt and learn to use the new equipment. This approach has been reinforced by social scientists studying worker satisfaction, motivation, and organizational structures to better understand and improve the relationship between people, technology, work, and improved performance and productivity.

The implementation of new technology most often has been explained and shaped by theories in which work was divided into small tasks with clearly defined responsibilities and standards of acceptable performance based on low levels of employee skill and motivation. Management roles were highly specialized, and authority was reinforced through sharp status hierarchies. Labor and management relations have for the most part been hostile.

Emphasis on the individual fit well into large bureaucratic organizations where breaking down work into its smallest components and having strict rules and regulations were critical to turning out the mass production products. Collective action was discouraged, collaborative efforts were not rewarded, internal competition was fierce. New technology was often associated with the "deskilling" of jobs and job loss. The pyramid structure set the competitive framework for management, and a strong resistance to unions led the way for nonmanagement workers. The manufacturing model led the way for government bureaucracy and the burgeoning service sector in both public and private institutions.

Today more than ever the successful introduction of technology is tied to the understanding of existing organizational structures as well as employee perceptions and expectations. Underlying these changes is a shift in basic assumptions about people from ones of limit and control to trust and cooperation, reflected in each of the overview chapters. For example, Kanter's identification of four characteristics of successful technology adoption, "the four Fs: focused, fast, flexible, and friendly," Adler's development of a dynamic model of technological change, Van de Ven's revision of Roger's basic innovation model to reflect organizational complexities, and Bikson and Eveland's emphasis on the implementation process all incorporate these changed assumptions through discussion and documentation of increasing employee responsibility, decreasing management control, and designing technologies that people can understand and adapt to their work situation.

This shift is complex and there are no easy answers for managers considering the use of new technologies. Yet out of the combined research, case studies, and discussions at the symposium it seemed to us that six factors emerged related to people's involvement in the process that are important to consider in designing the implementation of new technology in any organization: leadership, employee involvement, training, incentive systems, organizational structures, and technological characteristics. Together these factors form the culture of the organization, which can either facilitate or discourage technological change and the implementation process.

## LEADERSHIP

Innovations can come from any level in an organization, but leadership is necessary to implement changes. Leadership for technological change can come from managers, executives, professionals, and union leaders. In most organizations the decision to invest in new technology appears to be primarily a management decision, with professional or technical consultation, although there are some joint labor/management initiatives. Depending on the scope of the technology and its organizational implications, the case studies provide examples of decisions that rest with office managers, unit directors, district or division managers, vice presidents, chief executive officers, or the board of directors. Even in relatively flat organizational structures a person or relatively small group of people initiate the change, commit the resources, and establish the cultural framework for implementation.

The significant role of committed and involved leaders was noted in all of the cases presented at the symposium. For example, in the Ambulatory Care Unit case, the board of directors and trustees were fully committed to the project and to the resulting organizational changes and provided the necessary support throughout. Leaders develop the shared vision and goals and effectively communicate them throughout the organization. They provide not only the necessary financial support during the change process but also psychological support to project and middle-level managers who implement the technology and to the employees who are the ultimate users.

Leaders also make or allow the organizational modifications necessary to accommodate the change and the transition process. They create the mechanisms for employee participation, training, incentive schemes, organization design and structure, as well as technology choice and development. In all the automated manufacturing cases, for example, leaders supported employee training, work process redesign and improvement, and changes in the incentive schemes so that employees would be stimulated and engaged by the process.

Sometimes a change in one level of leadership is necessary to motivate, accommodate, or guide the change. In the Shearson Lehman case, new leaders were chosen to identify the main purposes and goals and methodically guide the technological changes to accomplish these goals. In this case, the new leader communicated a clear vision of a successful application of new technology and made the structural changes that made success possible: new personnel, new incentive schemes, new organizational structures. There was a high cost, however, in personnel, and many people lost their jobs. This is in contrast to the Boeing case, where efforts were made to involve the current employees, or the United Way case, where building on the expertise of the current staff was one of the primary goals.

Basically, leaders set the cultural context within which people implement technological change. If this means more shared decision making and flatter organizational structures, it also means a change in the role of the leader, perhaps requiring the leader to give up some control and authority and work in a collaborative structure that has not been common in U.S. organizations. There is a fine tension here between leaders initiating change and controlling the resources for implementation while at the same time delegating authority and involving people at all levels of the organization. How leaders resolve this tension, as well as the very practical ways in which they communicate goals, build trust, and delegate authority are in need of further research.

## EMPLOYEE INVOLVEMENT

Employee involvement appears to be an important but not clearly defined concept in the implementation process. It becomes more important as the technology advances more quickly and facilitates user feedback in what Adler calls the dynamic model of technology. Bikson and Eveland report that participative decision making in all aspects of the implementation process is a strong predictor of successful transition to new computer-based tools. This approach assumes that organizational members have ideas and skills that make them a valuable resource and they can build on and improve the technology being introduced.

The case studies provide several examples of employee participation. First, in the Boeing case a major planning meeting was designed to gather employee input into the plant design from all levels, including production workers, union representatives, and supervisors. In another example, at the *Los Angeles Times*, editorial and production staff were assigned to the new technology project on a full-time basis and a wide-ranging and rotating advisory committee was established to provide first-hand use feedback rather than technological feedback from the computer department. Consolidated Diesel provides an example in which an entirely new organization was established. They had the opportunity to hire employees who desire to participate in decision making. A fit with the participative culture was determined by peer as well as management interviews. Research at Rochester Methodist Hospital underscored the importance of involving first-line supervisors, in this case head nurses, in the design and implementation process.

The opposite of employee participation is of course resistance. Van de Ven provides a summary of why people resist change: "They resist change when the need is not well understood, it is imposed from above, perceived as threatening, seems to have risks that are greater than the potential benefits, and interferes with other established priorities." Because people tend to reject solutions they did not create, when they actively participate in the decision-making process they develop a sense of owning the change they helped develop. Consequently, tensions, uncertainties, and insecurities are alleviated and replaced by commitment to realization and functionality of the project. Interestingly, Bikson and Eveland were more likely to find resistance in the organization rather than in the employees. They report "countless examples of individuals doing old tasks in new ways and doing new tasks they

would not have anticipated when they entered their current jobs."
Organizations, however, were reluctant to recognize changes in
employees' skills, tasks, or standards with changes in job titles,
job descriptions, or pay.

Employee resistance due to fear of job loss is a reality, however,
as demonstrated in the Shearson Lehman case. Adler finds that
this is often the source of union resistance to changes, and this
fear was certainly the perception, if not the reality, in the United
Way case. Adler and Kanter also find, however, that trust can be
developed even in the face of layoffs if goals and information are
honestly shared with employees, and humane efforts are made to
relocate employees who must be let go.

Resistance may also be related to the deskilling of jobs or decreases in the level of control and responsibility. The Neonatal
Intensive Care case provides an important example. The technology was successfully implemented and babies' lives were saved.
Yet there was and continues to be staff resistance to the new
technology because the responsibility and control of the medical
staff were shifted to other medical professionals without staff
involvement in the decision.

Although employee participation is generally seen as a factor
contributing to successful technological implementation, there is
also a fundamental problem defining what employee participation
in decision making actually means and reconciling employee participation with the reality of job loss, deskilling, or reduced responsibility. More research is needed to explore the meaning of
participation—for example, what is the degree of control over outcomes—to describe the political and psychological dimensions of
participation, and to analyses of linkages among all these aspects.
Providing everybody with the opportunity to participate can also
become costly if it involves endless inconclusive discussions that
do not come to closure in concrete actions. Further efforts are
needed to better understand the most cost-effective roles at various stages of the change process (e.g., evaluator or generator of
ideas) and in various positions in the organization (e.g., middle
manger, design engineer, consultant, shop-floor worker, financial
analyst).

## TRAINING

From the research reviews in this volume to the participant
discussions at the symposium, training is noted as an important
aspect of implementation. While there is continuing debate about

the overall effect of technology on job skills, in those cases where technology clearly upgrades the skills, for example, see Adler's discussion of the CAD/CAM jobs, training is necessary. Related organizational changes may also require new management techniques emphasizing cooperation and support. Bikson and Eveland's findings in office automation may also be widespread, however. The importance of learning support for effective computer use was widely acknowledged but rarely manifest in organizations. Most of the organizations in their research provided brief beginning-level training, but then users were expected to progress with little besides self-instruction.

Several of the cases presented here required job redesign, whereby employees' jobs are altered to include a greater variety of tasks and to require more autonomy in decision making. Workers were required to act rather than react as they acquired skills in many jobs and learned to plan effectively how to convert knowledge and ideas into action. Managers had a more supportive role, acting as teachers and resources rather than as authoritative directors. At Consolidated Diesel Company, for example, a training center was established where each employee received 28 weeks of training between 1982 and 1987. Training encompassed not only courses on work methods and technology but also on communications, finance, group dynamics, and conflict resolution.

Assessment of training needs requires a thorough evaluation of current and projected skill levels of the work force and the jobs. Measuring skill levels and designing successful training programs, however, are developing areas of expertise. There are few packaged programs that will apply to any situation. Several research questions emerge: What are the trade-offs between training and replacement of employees; for example, increased motivation and training costs of current employees versus costs and the political impact of firing and hiring? What skills are needed by managers to drive the adoption of new technologies? Does training in these skills actually improve the process? What is the relationship between project success and different training approaches given varying skill levels in managers and employees?

Measurement of skill levels of employees as well as of job variety, task authority, and other job-related variables at the national level is also needed. This would allow for comparative studies over time between industries. Better measurement of current and projected skill levels and training needs are necessary for realistic and effective educational reforms as well employment planning on individual, organizational, and national levels.

## INCENTIVES

Incentives and rewards are an inherent part of organizational structure. They include both the external rewards such as increased pay, promotions, and job titles, as well as intrinsic rewards such as job satisfaction or autonomy. These systems can be used to encourage the development as well as the implementation of technological change. They must also be adjusted to reflect real changes in skill levels and responsibility brought about by new technology. In general, awards to individuals are expected to increase the number of completely new work processes or products and the number of ideas for improvement. Group awards on the other had are expected to shorten the time needed for innovation implementations and to increase the number of incremental innovations or small improvements on existing work processes or products.

Reward structures work better if they ensure equal pay for equal work and the same types of special benefits to all employees who contribute to productivity improvement. Shearson Lehman, for example, modified its salary and bonus system to facilitate and encourage collaboration between end-users and data processing professionals. Both groups were able to receive similar bonus pay for outstanding results.

Adler presents an interesting case of an auto plant (New United Motor Manufacturing, Inc., NUMMI) where new, technology-facilitated jobs were broken down into smaller parts and time pressures increased well beyond the standards of the old system. Yet workers appeared satisfied. He accounts for this by the fact that workers themselves were involved in setting the standards and all were aware of the common plantwide goals they were working toward. He suggests that managers need to rethink some of the basic assumptions about employee motivation and satisfaction as new systems are brought into existing organizations.

Underlying the discussion of rewards and incentives are three areas of tension: short-term versus long-term goals; allowing for mistakes; and subjective performance appraisals. As the case studies ably demonstrate, the larger the proposed change, the more time will be involved. While clear targets can be set for measuring accomplishments, there must be time for errors, reassessments, and plan adjustments. A major criticism of U.S. industry in general has been the emphasis on short-term goals, especially in comparison with Japanese industry. Managers responsible for implementing major technological innovations will be hard pressed to meet the standard weekly, monthly, or even yearly targets with any precision under a short-term philosophy that does not foster risk taking and allow for making mistakes.

No matter how much an organization professes that it wants change, if managers' and employees' career decisions are based on short-term measurements, there is likely to be little progress. The core of the *LA Times* case, for example, took more than seven years. Yet admitting to error in year six and virtually starting over with new software did not stop the project, which ultimately resulted in a successful new system.

The reward system cannot be separated from the personnel evaluation system that informs it. One problem is that the judgments involved in evaluation systems that put a premium on innovation may be inherently more subjective than systems dependent on more easily measurable performance indices. Subjectivity in personnel evaluation is often perceived, and sometimes rightly so, as putting more power in the hands of managers and supervisors at the expense of the technical and nonmanagement workers.

Many questions remain unanswered in developing appropriate reward systems to support implementation. For example, what rewards are more appropriate for an idea generator and technological implementer, both of whom play a significant role in the total solution? What happens in pay-for-knowledge systems when employees have learned all the necessary skills? How does an organization continue to motivate employees? How have long-term benefits been recognized and long-term incentives been institutionalized?

## ORGANIZATIONAL STRUCTURE

Organizational structure provides the context in which all of the above factors operate. It encompasses both the formal rules and regulations, and accompanying organizational charts, as well as the informal associations, methods, and procedures that govern daily work lives. In mature industries, rules and procedures are desirable in order to avoid continually revisiting problems that have been solved. These same codified rules and procedures, however, can predispose workers and managers to a myopic view that overlooks opportunities for innovation. Thus, there is potential conflict between static and dynamic efficiency. Rapid technological improvement requires a flexible and fluid organizational structure that risks insufficient control and unnecessary error in more mature operations. Conversely, requirements for error-free mature operations may conflict with the innovative behavior needed for continuing improvement. This conflict in the life cycle of organizations is not new and must certainly be recognized in developing structures and people that will encourage innovation, while maintaining that which is necessary for the ongoing operation of the organization.

Flexibility in organizational structure is a theme throughout this volume and the symposium, beginning with Kanter's opening remarks highlighting the importance of flexibility at the work unit level, across work units, and in the innovation project itself. A major strategy to increase flexibility is to develop flatter organizational structures, with fewer layers of management, thus reducing the hierarchy of the traditional management pyramid. The development of the traditional structures has been well documented, including a fierce competitiveness among managers and teams to secure the relatively few positions at the top.

To some extent a change in the structure of many organizations occurred in the 1980s through downsizing. As part of the increased global competitiveness, extra layers of management have been stripped away, and the number of unemployed managers is at a record high. Flexibility, however, requires that not only the number of managers but also the actual layers of management in the pyramid be reduced. This reduction is most often accompanied by a decrease in the number of job titles, while the jobs themselves may be enlarged and enriched in scope. Decreasing the layers of control increases communication and the flow of information across departments and groups, while also making the organizations more complex, differentiated, and decentralized. All of these changes call for new working arrangements and related training (discussed above).

Most of the cases presented show that flexibility through a shift to participative management is a significant factor in successful technological change. For example, in the Bio-Synthetics case the organizational structure was redesigned, leaving it only three levels of management. This shift was also easier when the organization was new, as in the Boeing and Consolidated Diesel cases.

Questions remain about when and what new structures are most effective. How can companies make a successful shift when they are not starting new? Who are the key decision makers in the reorganization process? What are the appropriate changes in organizational structures for various changes in the environment? Which organizational design, by function, product, or something else, is more adaptable to uncertainties?

## TECHNOLOGY

Finally there is the question of technology. Selecting and adopting technology is a complex process that must be based not only on technological alternatives but also on organizational strategy and ideology as well as social system considerations. It is generally recognized that deciding to implement state-of-the-art technology simply for the sake of using the best available processes may not bring about the expected benefits. Technology must be matched with the problem to be solved. The Forest Service case describes a very large organization systematically balancing these needs with the technology available; in this case, not a particular technology, but a set of integrated technologies to be implemented nation-wide. The *LA Times* case offers an interesting contrast. When the process started there was no satisfactory technology available, so newspaper employees worked with a computer company to develop their own software. After several years this did not yield a workable system. By then, however, a new technological package on the shelf could be adapted to meet their needs.

As noted by Adler, many engineers have "idiot-proofed" their innovations, making it virtually impossible for the user to inter-act or offer suggestions to adapt the technology to meet their specific needs. This lack of confidence in users and distrust of people other than the developers has outlasted its usefulness. It is time to move beyond the "black box" concept of technology where users do not really understand the technology but must learn to work with it. Bikson and Eveland find user participation, including working with systems designers to be the most effective way to link complex tool development to substantive task performance.

Affordable and proven technology can be carefully adapted to suit the needs of the people who will work with it. In the manu-facturing area, for example, the Boeing case illustrates technologi-cal design that is going through iterations to accommodate the decisions that are made on the way work will be organized, such as in groups. At International Bio-Synthetics, technology was designed to fit the needs of the employees as they themselves defined them. In office automation, students at the United Way built a system based on input by the employee users. As both the technology and the organizations evolve, the developers and de-signers of the technology can take these changes into account. According to one participant they must "design for surprises."

Who should participate in selecting the solution, expert or user? When should experts on technology participate, in generation or implementation?  What is the relative effectiveness of different approaches to implementing technology; for example, is it more effective for an organization to start as a centralized system and to allow decentralization or to start with islands of automation and try to integrate them later.  What steps can be taken to ensure that technology will be flexible, modifiable, and expandable? Finding the best fit among technology, organization, and people is an evolving process informed by experience and ongoing research to answer these questions.

## CONCLUSIONS

In sum, the implementation of technology is a complex process that may facilitate or require organizational change or both.  Underlying the calls for flexibility, user input, and cooperation is a fundamental shift in the assumptions about people, theories of management, and technological design.  Employee roles, at all levels, are expanded rather than minimized, and this means increasing autonomy and responsibility.  Managers give up control and become resources encouraging cooperation and trust rather than authoritarian guards.  Engineers move from designing black boxes to designing interactive technologies that change and develop over time.

The human resource factors identified here as contributing to or hindering successful implementation are not meant to be exhaustive, nor are the remaining questions.  Rather they highlight important issues discussed in detail in the remainder of this volume and provide valuable information to engineers, managers, labor representatives, and social scientists who are designing, implementing, and studying technological changes so important to future U.S. development and growth.  This symposium and this volume underscore the need for continuing cooperation and exchange among the people involved in technological innovation as they grapple with converting what we know into daily practice while continuing to resolve unanswered questions.

People and Technology in the Workplace. 1991.
Pp. 15–56. Washington, D.C:
National Academy Press.

# Improving the Development, Acceptance, and Use of New Technology: Organizational and Interorganizational Challenges

ROSABETH MOSS KANTER

Implementation of technological innovation rests largely on readiness for change, and change is not always received positively.

One view of change was satirized by comedian Woody Allen. In an "all-purpose commencement speech," he wrote that at this point in history, humanity faces a crossroads. "One path leads to despair and utter hopelessness; the other to total extinction. Let us pray that we have the wisdom to choose the right one." Allen was expressing the way that many people view change in organizations: Whichever path we take is going to be equally dreadful.

The other view of change is exemplified by a true American hero, Seymour Cray, founder of Cray Research, and an inventor largely responsible for America's lead in supercomputers. Cray, an avid sailor, would build a new wooden sailboat every year. At the end of the season, he would destroy it so that he could build a better one the following year without being limited by his previous mistakes. Cray offers a very different perspective on change— that change means continuous improvement, opportunities to keep mastering new skills using new ideas and new tools.

How do we build environments in which change is not only accepted but embraced, Seymour Cray-style, rather than rejected, Woody Allen-style? To find answers, I argue that we must look to macro as well as micro factors—to the organization itself and to the relationships between organizations. The human factors in change, I submit, are only part of the equation; the other part is the relationships between organizational actors that are encouraged or constrained by the organizational context.

## THE NATURE OF INNOVATION: WHAT IS KNOWN

There is already a great deal of knowledge about how to make change work effectively at the work unit or project level, knowledge available for decades, including pioneering research at the University of Michigan after World War II. For the acceptance of change it is important that there is a shared vision or shared goals to which people are committed; there is participation of the users in the process of implementing change; there is ample training so that people acquire the skills; there are transition periods to ease people in where the new and the old exist side by side; and there is ample communication and humane redeployment if the implementation of new technology costs jobs or creates displacement.

This knowledge has been accumulated and supported by decades of thoughtful research at the micro level. So, why is it that America sometimes lags in the implementation of technology, including technology invented here?

Perhaps the answer lies beyond the project level, beyond the work unit, and beyond the micro process. Instead, we need to look at the relationships between work units, at total organizational relationships and systems, and at interorganizational relationships if we are truly going to understand the context for the implementation of new technology. Such macro-level system variables augment process models of innovation development and adoption.

There is also a great deal of research evidence about the broad kinds of organizational circumstances in which different types of innovations flourish. Product innovations are more likely in new entrant organizations, and process innovations in established ones. Product innovations are more common in earlier stages of a product's history; process innovations in later stages (Abernathy and Utterback, 1978). Technological innovations are more frequent when resources are scarce (Kimberly, 1981). Evolutionary innovations (modest, incremental changes) are more likely in organizations that are more formalized and "centralized"; more revolutionary innovations in organizations that are more complex and "decentralized" (Cohn and Turyn, 1984).

A great deal is also known about the ways in which innovating organizations come to resist change as they move through their life cycles. Many of America's most successful companies have gone through a life cycle similar to the product life cycle, getting locked into a "mature product" mode of operation. They began as innovators, then grew to be giants in their markets. They need new products to continue to grow, but their organizational structure has become inappropriate. Innovation tends to center on incremental nonproduct features; groups feel proprietary about their products and suboptimize; and financial measures emphasize short-term bottom-line and sunk costs. But in a dynamic environment, assets quickly become liabilities (e.g., banks thinking of their branches as assets, and, therefore, buying more bricks and mortar instead of electronic banking with remote service centers; or tire manufacturers in the early 1970s investing in plants to manufacture cross-ply tires, and, therefore, slow to recognize the shift to radial tires) (Bennett and Cooper, 1984). Of course, sometimes it is wise to wait, since new technology is often inferior in quality to the old and initially finds a limited use in a handful of specialty niches or segments. While newer firms can more easily afford to absorb the risk of untried technologies and have fewer sunk costs or established interest groups to contend with, older organizations may become more cautious.

While these broad relationships between type of innovation and the organizational life cycle are interesting, they are too general to guide research and practice on the implementation of innovation, and they do not account for the reasons some organizations—even older ones—implement new technology better than others.

Thus, we need a new model that links implementation of new technology to organizational variables. Six characteristics of innovation must be taken into account.

1. *The innovation process is uncertain.* The source of innovation or the occurrence of opportunity to innovate may be unpredictable. The innovation goal may involve little or no precedent or experience base to use to make forecasts about results. Hoped-for timetables may prove unrealistic, and schedules may not match the true pace of progress. "Progress on a new innovation," Quinn (1979) wrote, "comes in spurts among unforeseen delays and setbacks. . . in the essential chaos of development." Furthermore, anticipated costs may be overrun, and ultimate results are highly uncertain. Indeed, analysts have variously estimated that it takes an average of 10 to 12 years before the return on investment of new ventures equals that of mature businesses (Biggadike, 1979);

7 to 15 years from invention to financial success (Quinn, 1979); and 3 to 25 years between invention and commercial production (Quinn, 1985). These data make clear the importance of appropriate top management commitment and support. At the same time, it is equally important that top management not kill "experiments" or fledgling new activities with overattention—e.g., too much reporting—or let them flourish without criticism or opposition because of premature publicity (see Mason, 1986, on the latter point).

2. *The innovation process is knowledge-intensive.* The innovation process generates new knowledge intensively, relying on individual human intelligence and creativity and involving "interactive learning" (Quinn, 1985). New experiences are accumulated at a fast pace; the learning curve is steep. The knowledge that resides in the participants in the innovation effort is not yet codified or codifiable for transfer to others. Efforts are very vulnerable to turnover because of the loss of this knowledge and experience. There need to be close linkages and fast communication between all those involved, at every point in the process, or the knowledge erodes.

3. *The innovation process is controversial.* Innovations always involve competition with alternative courses of action. The pursuit of the air-cooled engine at Honda Motor, for example, drew time and resources away from improving the water-cooled engine. Furthermore, sometimes the very existence of a potential innovation poses a threat to vested interests—whether the interest is that of a salesperson receiving high commissions on current products, or of the advocates of a competing direction. (Fast, 1979, for example, argues that "political" problems are the primary cause for the failure of corporate new venture departments.)

4. *The innovation process crosses boundaries.* The creation and use of innovations are rarely, if ever, contained solely within one unit. First, there is evidence that many of the best ideas are interdisciplinary or interfunctional in origin—as connoted by the root meaning of entrepreneurship as the development of "new combinations"—or they benefit from broader perspective and information from outside of the area primarily responsible for the innovation (Kanter, 1983a; 1988). Second, regardless of the origin of innovations, they inevitably send out ripples and reverberations to other organizational units, whose behavior may be required to change in light of the needs of innovations, or whose cooperation is necessary if an innovation is to be fully developed or exploited. Or there may be the need to generate unexpected

innovations in another domain in order to support the primary product, like the need to design a new motor to make the first Apple computer viable.

5. *The innovation process often changes work relationships and hierarchical arrangements.* This shows up, for example, in the resistance of supervisors to change. Klein (1984) identified five groups of resisters in a study of the implementation of employee involvement in eight manufacturing plants: unbelievers (who reject the concept itself); status seekers (who fear losing prestige); skeptics (who doubt the sincerity and support of upper management); equality seekers (who feel bypassed); and deal makers (who had developed a base of power under the old system).

6. *The conditions for origination and invention are different from the conditions for adoption and diffusion.* Successful invention may occur in isolation; successful diffusion depends on the quality of linkages to other activities. Whereas creation and development—production of the innovation model—can occur with few resources, little visibility, modest coalitions, and the isolated activity or relatively small teams, use of the innovation is a different matter. If creation is an *intensive* process, diffusion is an *extensive* process. Use requires many other people, activities, patterns, and structures to change to incorporate the innovation. It is not surprising, then, that innovations are more successfully transferred, commercialized, or diffused where the organization or market is already receptive to the idea and prepared for its use. (See Kanter, 1988, and Leonard-Barton, 1988, for more evidence and analysis.) This is almost tautological. Where there is stronger organizational commitment in the development process, signified by funding, visibility, coalition support, and so forth, there are more "side bets" placed on the idea (i.e., staking of reputations on the outcome) as well as greater sunk costs. Thus, there will be more pressures to use the innovation in more ways and make it more central to the organization's strategy. Organizational arrangements will already have begun to bend in anticipation of the successful development, often through negotiations among departments—the "logical incrementalism" by which new strategies are adopted (Quinn, 1980). Perhaps this is why evidence indicates that successful new ventures in large corporations are more likely to be the ones sponsored by operating line executives rather than by corporate executives (Hobson and Morrison, 1983); the line-sponsored ventures are already closely connected with implementors.

Thus, if innovation is *uncertain, fragile, political,* and *imperi-*

*alistic* (reaching out to embrace other territories), then it is most likely to flourish where conditions allow flexibility, feedback, quick action and intensive care, coalition formation, and connectedness. Innovation proceeds through a set of cycles of adaptation (Leonard-Barton, 1988). It is most likely to grow in organizations that have integrative structures and cultures emphasizing diversity, multiple structural linkages both inside and outside the organization, intersecting territories, collective pride and faith in people's talents, collaboration, and teamwork. The organizations producing more innovation have denser networks that link people in multiple ways and encourage them to "do what needs to be done" within strategically guided limits, rather than confining themselves to the letter of their job. Such organizations are also better connected with key external resources, including other organizations as collaborators, and operate in a favorable institutional environment.

Recent field research in over 80 companies has examined the emergence of an organizational and managerial paradigm that embraces these characteristics (Kanter, 1989a; 1989b). In general, the conditions favoring implementation of new technology can be summarized under the rubric of four "Fs." Organizations that are successful users of new ideas are more focused, fast, flexible, and friendly. Each of these "Fs" suggests hypotheses or research questions that might shed light on ways to improve the application and acceptance of new technology.

## FOCUS: STRATEGY, RESOURCES, REWARDS

My first major proposition is that greater organizational *focus* in the mix of an organization's businesses and activities, backed by appropriate rewards, supports investment in and effective implementation of new technology.

### The Business Mix

There has been a great deal of discussion recently, among analysts of corporate strategy, about the relative merits of diversified versus focused organizations. An emerging conclusion is that organizations in fewer lines of business with those lines more closely related are much more successful than organizations that are highly diversified. Mainstream economic literature has long produced mixed results, showing some benefits to unrelated diversification, but recent work tends to support the new proposition (Montgomery, 1985; Montgomery and Thomas, 1988). The reasoning is similar to that for individuals: It is very difficult to be on top of all the things you need to do if you're distracted by too many demands, too many requirements, too many unrelated things. Thus, the idea of *focus* in corporate strategy is coming back into vogue. Twenty years ago, the conventional wisdom urged companies to diversify—keep many eggs in many baskets, have a large portfolio of many different businesses or activities, as a hedge against change. The "portfolio" or "holding company" approach—in which each part stands alone and needs to be different in order to compensate for the weakness of other parts—has been increasingly discredited. Sometimes the delegitimation of the diversified conglomerate has occurred for defensive reasons: avoiding the administrative costs of managing diversity or the vulnerability to takeovers engendered by the ease with which the business units can be unbundled and sold at a premium. However, the quest for focus and synergies also comes from growth goals, especially in global technology companies, which face brutal, fast-paced competition, and thus must transfer intelligence and innovation across the boundaries of business units and countries. *Focus* permits the attainment of critical mass and sustained competence.

Porter, for example, examined the track record of 33 *Fortune* 500 conglomerates with respect to their acquiring businesses that were unrelated to their core business (Porter, 1987). Over a 30-year period, those conglomerates divested a high proportion of all the things they bought: about 60 percent of all their unrelated acquisitions. It was interesting to look at who was high and who was low on that list. Lowest on the list were Johnson & Johnson and Procter & Gamble, companies that have a clear focus in their businesses. They bought the fewest unrelated businesses, and they tended to sell the fewest—under 15 percent of what they bought. Indeed, P&G is known today for some of the world's most advanced manufacturing plants in terms of social as well as technological systems; its experimentation was aided by a strong and integrated manufacturing function. At the high end were CBS and RCA, which bought many different businesses and sold close to 90 percent of them. Did this effort weaken the companies? Consider subsequent events: RCA has disappeared into GE, and CBS has become part of the Tisch empire.

In terms of the mix of businesses involved in the corporation, then, having a clear focus can provide a strategic advantage in a rapidly changing environment in which strength may come from a concentration of resources in building and enhancing a critical business competence. The *focus* hypothesis may hold true inside a corporation as well; successful departments may be the ones with clear strategy and awareness of their critical competence.

If focused organizations are better able to concentrate on their key skills, they may be more likely to want to make the investments in the kind of technology that will augment those key skills. Thus, implementation of critical technology may occur more effectively in more focused entities. Companies in many different businesses may face many different success factors and, therefore, fragmentation in technology as well as in resource allocation, so that development and use of any particular innovation does not gain sufficient support. Research supports this hypothesis. For example, as one study showed, successful new products in the electronics industry were likely to be close to the firm's areas of expertise, close to the main business area of the firm, and influenced by corporate reputation. It made no difference whether basic research was in-house or outside or whether the firm needed to establish new marketing channels (Maidique and Zirger, 1985). Relatedness to the focus was more important than the origin of the ideas.

Thus, corporate strategy is clearly a key to whether or not organizations are good at adopting and using new technology. Technology will be acceptable if it is seen as part of the competitive advantage of the firm and, therefore, will get resources and attention. Effective adoption and use of technological innovation require a strategic decision that this innovation should get resources allocated to it, resources necessary to exploit its potential. For product and technical process innovations, and even for some organizational innovations, the greatest financial requirements begin after the model has been developed. Thus, the nature of the strategic decision process and how top management is linked to the innovation project is another critical structural element in an innovation's success or failure (Burgelman, 1984).

At the transfer point, when resources to exploit an innovation are allocated, visible and well-connected projects already aligned with the organization's strategic objectives are likely to fare better. In turn, the degree of investment the project gets as it is moved into commercialization, routine production, or institutionalization affects its prospects for success as an ongoing product or practice. "Thinking small" and not providing adequate investment are often identified as a reason for new venture failures (Drucker, 1985). Research on the first four years of operation of 117 corporate ventures in established markets in manufacturing found that the "winning" ventures initially set higher market share objectives, had R&D spending levels twice those of the other ventures in the first two years, and had marketing expenditures about 1.5 those of the other ventures in the same period (Hobson and Morrison, 1983).

## The Activity Mix

The business portfolio is one area in which focus plays an increasingly important role; another is the mix of services. Many companies are rethinking the management of ancillary services— support services that help in the production of the company's goods or services but that are very different in the skills required. There is beginning to be a displacement of support activities from internal departments staffed by employees to marketlike arrangements with outside contractors and specialist organizations. In one interesting case in a midsize, high-tech company, the corporate librarian set up the library as a profit center and then an entrepreneurial venture, moving from employee to entrepreneur while doing the same work. As employee she was buried in an administrative hierarchy; as entrepreneur, she is on contract to her former employer and active as a resource to other companies as well. On a larger scale, Eastman Kodak recently contracted with IBM to run its management information systems department so that Kodak could tap IBM's expertise while focusing its own management attention on Kodak's core businesses.

Some firms are demonstrating that it is possible to operate effectively even with most activities performed by independent contractors, if computer linkages permit coordination, as a cluster of British examples show. About two-thirds of the work of the F.I. Group, one of the U.K.'s largest software systems houses, is performed at the homes of part-time free-lancers; about 400 clients at a time are served from about 800 sites. Furthermore, F.I.'s work itself increasingly replaces the entire in-house programming department for client companies (Collins, 1986). Rank-Xerox tried a similar organization of work, turning employees into independent contractors (Judkins, West, and Drew, 1985). Handy (1989) asked a multibillion-pound British company's managers to determine what work could not be subcontracted; the answer was only "the chief executive and his car phone."

Indeed, "producer services" (e.g., accounting, recordkeeping, or janitorial work performed for organizations on a contract basis) is one of the fastest-growing occupational categories in America, and many small companies have emerged to supply such services.

This trend could have great implications for determining which companies are more likely to adopt and accept new technology. For example, focused small firms that sell services to giant corporations may be more likely to invest in new technology to improve that service than the giant corporation for which the service is peripheral. The focused firm, furthermore, is more likely to create a sense of pride in their people so that their people embrace new technology that will help them do their job better.

Consider the case of ServiceMaster, a highly profitable company that provides cleaning and related support services to hospitals, school systems, and other institutions, exporting services to Japan as well as other countries (Heskett, 1987). ServiceMaster has an R&D budget for the application of new technology. Because of the organization's single-minded emphasis on providing the most cost-effective janitorial services, it is constantly investigating the use of new tools. As a consequence, technology is seen by employees not as a threat to be resisted, but as a force to be embraced because it allows them to do their work more effectively and, therefore, gain more of those service contracts that keep the company in business.

Thus, more focused organizations engaged in a less diverse mix of activities may be more likely to allocate resources for new technology that augments core strengths. At the same time, focus means a clear set of priorities that guide the actions of everyone at every level. Perhaps the most important task of leaders is to convey these priorities throughout the ranks in a meaningful and inspiring way. Komatsu, a Japanese company that came from behind to challenge Caterpillar's world dominance in earthmoving equipment, set a series of yearly improvement goals that were transmitted to everyone. These "themes of the year" made it possible for the power of the entire corporate team to be concentrated on just those factors that would help the company succeed; energy was not wasted on unproductive projects. Such focus provides the discipline to march in the same direction while enabling people to operate autonomously.

## Rewards

Focus is also important at another level, at the level of behavior. Here, reward systems of an organization play an important role. Reward systems direct attention to particular activities, thus helping determine responses to change.

Some observers argue that many American companies are not providing sufficient rewards and recognition for innovation. Innovation requires risk, and risk requires reward. In Foster's (1986) study of companies (2/3 of which were under $100 million in annual revenue), those weak in idea development also had a very weak innovation incentive program. The companies fell into three groups: innovation realists, innovation dreamers, and innovation ignorants. Innovation realists had financially significant incentives, specific and measurable innovation goals for performance, and the incentives were doled out on a relatively objective basis. The financial incentives were created in novel ways in these companies, and they were significant enough to get managers away from their daily routines and interested in innovation. But token incentives got token results. Leonard-Barton (1988) also demonstrated the impact of reward system misalignments in reducing incentives for users to accept technology innovations.

In general, the greatest disparity between what managers value and what they find in their workplace lies in the area of rewards. In a 1988 survey of 171 top managers and 212 middle managers by the American Productivity and Quality Center, 91 percent rated as important "recognition when I've done a job well," 89 percent "pay clearly tied to my performance," and 85 percent "good, fair performance measures"; but these factors existed for only 55 percent, 50 percent, and 39 percent of the managers, respectively. At the same time, job security was considered much less important, and more managers (68 percent) had generous benefit programs than valued them (54 percent).

Executives themselves are increasingly concerned that traditional reward systems direct attention away from innovation. It is a common critique of large U.S. corporations that reward systems lead managers to focus on measures of profitability such as ROI (return on investment), thereby creating an incentive to keep investment low, or on such measures of "responsibility" as the size of their staff. In a recent discussion with a large group of executives from some 75 companies about the problems of U.S. competitiveness, the consensus was that traditional pay systems bear a major share of the responsibility for the "decline" of U.S. industry. The typical job grading system assigns more points, and, therefore, more base pay, to jobs with more responsibility for more people and more assets—in effect, the size of the empire people have managed to construct. At the same time, measuring performance on the basis of return on investment tends to focus people away from long-term capital investment and toward keeping expenses down right now by letting the equipment age and letting the work force go untrained.

In leading companies, reward systems, including the determination of pay, are being reconstructed in order to focus people's attention on key success factors rather than on the preservation of tradition or territory. There is a quiet revolution in pay philosophy in the United States, as organizations move away from paying people for status or rank in the organization and toward paying people for contribution or performance (see Kanter, 1987, 1989a, chapter 9).

This shift in rewards has implications for whether or not people embrace change. When people are paid on the right performance basis—e.g., bonuses at higher levels or gain-sharing at lower levels—they have an incentive to seek productivity-enhancing technology because they share in the returns to the company's investment in that technology. Even nonmonetary recognition is important in this respect (see, e.g., Derra, 1989). Thus, I suggest also that researchers look at the focus that is being introduced through reward systems as one of the keys determining whether organizations adopt and use new technology.

A longer-term horizon encouraged by an innovation focus in rewards is important to counter the shorter-term bias reinforced by career systems that tie increases in rewards to promotion in a hierarchy. Promotion-based reward systems can have three negative consequences. First, in many companies, managers may get more credit for decisions than they do for implementation, and follow-through or follow-up is neglected when frequent mobility to "better" or "higher" jobs is the only way for people to increase their earnings in an organization. This tends to create instability in leadership, shorter-term views, and incentives to make bold strokes like equipment purchases without incentives to make sure the equipment is used effectively through the duller, less glamorous, and longer-term work of implementation. Second, a two-class system is reinforced; whereas managers move in and out frequently and may wish to make changes to demonstrate leadership, workers with limited mobility remain in place through the turnover of managers and may resist changes sought by "temporary" managers. Finally, tying managerial rewards to promotion encourages a proliferation of hierarchical divisions, and hierarchy (as we shall see shortly) creates barriers to timely and speedy implementation of new technology.

In contrast, there is persuasive evidence that performance-based pay is associated with better organizational performance. A study of compensation survey data for the period between 1981 and 1985, including more than 16,000 top- and middle-level managers in over 219 business units and firms, examined differences in firm compensation strategy. The smallest organizational effects were at the level of base pay; the largest, on bonus levels and eligibility for long-term incentives. Overall, greater contingency of pay in the form of bonuses and long-term incentives was associated with better firm performance. An increase of 10 percent in the ratio of bonus to base pay was associated with 21 to 95 percent greater return on assets; an increase of 10 percent in the number of managers eligible for long-term incentives was associated with a 17 to 20 percent better return on assets (Gerhart and Milkovich, 1989).

A clear focus, then, supported by systems that drive behavior toward the focus, may be an important factor in the development and use of new technology.

## FAST:  TOWARD MULTIPLE, SPEEDY INNOVATIONS

My second "F" for success in the new environment is *fast*. U.S. organizations are beginning to realize that they have to move faster because of a comparative disadvantage with respect to some foreign competitors (Jaikumar, 1986). For example, studies show that in some areas of manufacturing Japanese firms implement new process technology about four times as fast as U.S. firms, thus gaining a temporal advantage in putting their investing addition to the value of the technology in terms of raising productivity. Similarly, Clark's study of 24 car projects (11 Japanese, 5 United States, 8 European) found that Japanese companies took about one-third as much time on average to engineer a new car during the mid-1980s as U.S. companies, so that Japanese cars could arrive on the market some two years faster, on average, than new U.S. models (Clark and Fujimoto, 1988).

Speed is a function of the capacity to innovate—to generate ideas and move them through the system. Organizational variables are key factors in nurturing innovation, beginning with the "first mover" advantage:  translating ideas into innovations before others to master an environment that is constantly changing.

### Willingness to Be First

Organizations often benefit from the first mover advantage. Otherwise the company is always trying to catch up rather than defining the terms of the game. Empirical research supports this proposition.  For example, analysis of 119 new corporate ventures in the Strategic Planning Institute's STR4 data base found that early entrants achieved superior market shares and competitive advantages over later entrants (Miller, Gartner, and Wilson, 1989).

Success in a rapidly changing environment involves the willingness to take the risk of being the pioneer.  Thus, companies that emphasize innovation work on being ahead of the competition and attempt to use all their skills from every functional area to provide a new source of strategic advantage.  For example, American Airlines used information technology to get a clear first-mover advantage.  It placed the American Sabre System in travel agencies to help them make reservations by computer; American flights appeared first.  (Later, this advantage was reduced by legal action.)  American has been first in a number of areas, including marketing innovations (frequent flyer programs) and human resource innovations (two-tier wage systems).

By being first, the organization gains both the opportunity to reach and secure the customer before the competition and the experience that permits improvement while others are still farther down the learning curve.  It also gains control through shaping the innovation rather than responding to someone else's version.  Thus, being the first mover is one way that small companies can sometimes steal the march on big companies, gaining an advantage in the use of new technology because of greater speed of action.  Less red tape and better communication and collaboration may allow smaller firms to act more quickly.  One of the most dramatic examples of this type of advantage involved Ocean Spray Cranberries, the first U.S. company to apply a new packaging technology, the paper bottle (aseptic packaging).  This was a well-known technology in Europe but was not used in the United States.  In the early 1980s, the European manufacturers approached large U.S. food companies about the technology; one of them was interested enough to set up a committee to study it!  Ocean Spray heard the same presentation, committed the next day, signed a deal by the end of the week, and obtained an 18-month exclusive license.  For 18 months, Ocean Spray had a *de facto* monopoly; market share shot up.

## Channels for New Ideas

How was Ocean Spray able to move so quickly?  Leaders had explicitly asked employees to be scouts for new technology.  People at the middle level, including engineers, saw that part of their job was to bring new technologies with potential applications to the attention of management. There was a forum for discussions between upper management and employees to discuss technological developments with implications for Ocean Spray products. At one of those forums, a middle-level engineer brought the new packaging to the attention of top management. Therefore, they were ready when the presentation was made.

That organizational style, asking all employees to seek new technology, may also make average employees more receptive to the thought of change than in organizations where change is simply imposed upon them. My recent research has documented various methods by which organizations encourage and fund what I call "newstreams." Intensive cases have been developed on eight types of new idea programs, some of which encourage people at middle and lower levels to develop ideas that become seeds for projects that may be implemented on a wider scale. The programs involving ideas bubbling up from the ranks tend to involve smaller-scale, more incremental innovations than those in which the corporation acts as a venture capitalist to invest in big new businesses; but the smaller-scale, up-from-the-ranks programs tend to be the most successful in terms of rapid return on investment, the fastest in implementation (often because of modest project scope), and the most enduring (Kanter, 1989a).

Thus, it is important to have a flow of new ideas to encourage every department and all employees to think about innovating in their own areas as well as in others. Special support and encouragement may be necessary to help fragile new ideas see the light of day (and sometimes even a special "greenhouse" or "incubator" in which to house the project). A portfolio of experimental concepts under development—all funded at relatively low levels until they prove themselves—ensures that the company can continue to be an innovator. Vehicles such as Ohio Bell's Enter-Prize Program can drive the search for innovations by encouraging employees to come forward with ideas, facilitating the formation of project teams, and protecting such "newstream" projects in their infancy. More than 60 employee projects have helped Ohio Bell make major product introductions and modest but useful improvements in productivity. At Teleflex, a midsize manufacturer, a New Venture Fund in operation for almost 20 years (funded with $\frac{1}{2}$ percent of sales) has helped provide set-aside funds for experiments not yet ready to be funded by operating budgets; perhaps 80 percent of the company's current products have received benefits from one of those experiments.

AT&T's new venture program shows how much potential is there to be tapped in an organization. Several years ago, just before the 1984 divestiture of local telephone companies, AT&T quietly put in place a program by which they would seek employee ideas. They would screen the ideas and choose a few for which the employee suggesting the idea would receive considerable funding to run the projects and, in some cases, run new business ventures in the middle of AT&T. They expected to fund a dozen or so projects out of maybe 50 to 100 ideas that would be submitted. They did not publicize the program; they just wanted to try it. Consequently, without publicity and with the expectation of receiving fewer than 100 of these ideas for new businesses, extensions of existing technology, or other innovations, they began the program. More than 2,500 ideas were submitted in the first year.

## Communication Links

The third aspect of moving fast is communication linkages. The diffusion and application of innovations involves the transfer of knowledge and information and thus is influenced by the type of connection between all the players involved at each point. Some Japanese firms implement some kinds of technology more quickly than their U.S. counterparts because they are more likely to use cross-functional teams, build overlapping relationships between functions and between stages of the process, and stress communication that bridges the gap between specialties or functions. For example, fast-cycle companies such as Toyota encourage people to think of themselves as part of one integrated system and to know how their own jobs relate to rest of organization. Work is organized around small, self-managing multifunctional teams; cycle times are tracked throughout the organization; and learning loops are built into the organization so that everyone is informed about customers, competitors, and internal operations (Bower and Hout, 1988).

Overall, as Clark's work shows, communication processes account for a major share of the difference between speedy and slow development systems in the auto industry. In slow systems there is a formal bureaucratic process with uncertain completion times; in rapid ones there is direct, informal communication. In rapid systems, orders for the next step are placed before the final release of the previous one; in slow systems, development is a sequential activity in which each step has to wait for completion of the last. Speedy organizations also have projects of narrower scope than slower ones; therefore, mounting projects that are less complex to manage—preferring many smaller, more incremental projects to a few big ones (Clark and Fujimoto, 1988). In general, in faster development systems problem solving is quicker, and change is constant, but projects are divided into smaller, more manageable increments.

When all those involved in designing and implementing new technology work in parallel, the approach has been described as resembling a rugby match more than a relay race. A multidisciplinary team stays with the project from start to finish, and later steps are begun while earlier ones are still being finished. Japanese researchers Takeuchi and Nonaka credit this method for the speed at which Japanese companies such as Honda, Canon, NEC, and Fuji Xerox bring new products to market (Uttal, 1987). On the other hand, bottlenecks are likely to develop when the group responsible for one phase hands off to another group with whom communication is indirect or poor.

The importance of the quality of connections shows up again and again. A survey of 158 products in the electronics industry, half successes and half failures, made clear that conventional "external factor" explanations (state of the economy, foreign competition, and lack of funding) were not major contributors to product failure. But one of the most important differentiators was coordination of the "create, make, and market" functions (Maidique and Zirger, 1985). Successes were also more likely to be better matched with user needs, developed by teams that fully understood user needs, and accepted more fully by users, perhaps as a function of more active marketing, including efforts to educate users. The successes were technically superior and introduced to the market earlier than the competition (Maidique and Zirger, 1985).

If communication across functions is fundamental, then perhaps we should not even use the term "R&D" anymore, but instead "R&D and M&M&S"—one phrase to connect research, development, manufacturing, marketing, and sales. Bringing together autonomous teams that comprise all of those functions and have total project responsibility can improve both the speed of implementation and the receptivity of the organization to change. A Honeywell division, for example, had been notoriously late and over budget with new products until it formed "Tiger Teams" of everyone from engineering to marketing, housed in their own building, with the instruction simply to "get the job done"; speed went up,

and cost came down.  Similarly, Hillerich and Bradsby, manufacturer of Louisville Slugger baseball bats, typically took three weeks
to complete a bat until the company reorganized the factory, moving
from highly specialized batch work (such as sanding) to teams
that manufactured complete bats.  Both machines and people "re-
tooled" so that they could turn quickly from one job to another.
Baseball bats could then move through the factory in about a day.
Case after case shows the superiority of cross-functional teams
for speed.  At the Xerox East Rochester Skunk Works, an independent cross-functional team developed and commercialized the first
new copiers in years to immediately gain a high share of the
Japanese market.  The team took about *half* the time of the usual
product development process at Xerox because of the Skunk Works
system; the group was in business almost as though they were
independent entrepreneurs.  After the project had succeeded, however, the team was broken up and put back in their functional
departments; now the development of enhancements to the original product has slowed to the usual product development pace—
twice the time of the "independent" cross-functional team. To
capitalize on such lessons, Corning Glass views innovation as a
total organizational problem that requires the cooperation and
interaction of many different people, both inside and outside the
company, at many different levels (*Intrapreneurial Excellence*,
1986).  Technical personnel are sent on sales calls or occasionally
assigned to areas other than their own, dealing with problems of a
completely different nature than the ones they usually confront,
to stimulate their thinking and to build relationships that improve cross-functional communication.

Communication may be influenced by physical space as well as
by organizational and technical matters.  Collocation is one important part of developing the cross-functional teamwork necessary for rapid development and application of innovation.  For
this reason, significant projects may get quasi-independent status,
with a team separated out from the rest of the organization in its
own place (such as a "greenhouse" or "incubator"), so that all
functions are represented, and all communicate as part of one
large team. For example, Honda develops cars in a self-contained
subsidiary that conducts all R&D, including field tests, in one
large room without partitions; meetings are convened in the center.

Similarly, Steelcase, which had been lagging behind competition in innovation, built a new Corporate Development Center
for designers and engineers in an attempt to stimulate and nur-

ture creativity. Opened in 1989, the new facility was conceived as a prototype facility promoting an "integrative workplace" (Kanter, 1983a). Features included areas allowing unplanned, spontaneous contacts and information exchange between disciplines; looser layouts promoting tinkering with both the physical environment and the administrative and social features of work groups; and spaces encouraging use of a collaborative and overlapping product development process instead of a linear one. Spaces are designated as "caves" for privacy, neighborhoods for related activities, and town squares for the whole community. There are marker boards at coffee-break stations so that people can sketch ideas to see what passersby think. Perhaps more practically, the facility brings together everyone involved in product development (designers, engineers, marketers) under one roof.

### Dismantling Territorial Rivalries and Status Barriers

One barrier to more collaboration and communication across functions and across business units is cultural. A management style that I call "cowboy management" (Kanter, 1989a) has been hurting U.S. industry by stressing competition, rivalry, and contention over cooperation (e.g., the popular idea that R&D is improved by "performance shoot-outs" between competing teams). This is the essence of high noon at the O.K. Corral, making heroes out of leaders who "shoot from the hip" and "fire before aiming." In some U.S. companies the communication gap caused by "cowboy" attitudes was traditionally so great that colorful metaphors were used to describe it: the array of "smokestacks" at Ford or the "elevator mentality" at Westinghouse. Both described the independence of each specialty and the need to send messages up to the very top of each tower rather than building direct links between the people at lower levels with a common goal. Speed is reduced by communication blocks, then, but also by "hostility" to "foreign" ideas or outputs from another group. Furthermore, incentives and rewards have discouraged cooperation by stressing success in one's own discipline alone or within one's own department; career success meant a ride up the elevator or a rise through the chimney.

Barriers to cross-function and cross-level communication still exist even in organizations that would like to learn to break them down. I recently visited a facility of a large manufacturer that had acquired an information systems company a few years earlier, in part to learn something about a faster-moving, more entrepreneurial style so that the giant, too, could implement change more quickly. Once the two companies were merged and operating in the same site, parent company managers were restricting some of the open communication that supported the information systems company's entrepreneurial capability. The younger, vibrant company had been accustomed to frequent informal gatherings across levels and department functions at the end of the work day. There would be casual talk about what is going on, or a group would go out to have a beer together, as is common in Silicon Valley. Parent company managers stopped this practice. Why? I was told that "They are afraid that we will go to a bar together after work, and we might say something proprietary that a competitor will overhear." Given the isolated location of the facility, this was highly unlikely. Strikingly, in Silicon Valley, where, in fact, competitors do sit in bars and listen to conversations at other tables, the practice of informal gathering continues. So something else underlay this. My observations showed that the "something else" was the threat to the hierarchy. The information monopoly of managers, one of their signs of status and importance, was undermined by a free flow of information at lower levels. Rank and status in an organization are thus among the biggest barriers to change.

The reluctance of managers to give up traditional hierarchical status and power became clear in observations of a leading heavy-equipment manufacturing company that is moving aggressively against foreign competition (Kanter, 1989b). With the concurrence and help of top management and consultants, the product development process was reorganized to increase speed, quality, and cost-effectiveness; this required much closer collaboration between engineering, manufacturing, and other functions as well as with external suppliers. The company moved from a highly segmented process to one involving integrated project teams drawn from component divisions, functional departments, and external suppliers. Among the significant implications were overlap between areas of responsibility, collocation of some technical and manufacturing people, assignment of full-time liaisons from the functional areas to the larger development teams, and direct team contact with higher levels of the company.

For the engineering managers at higher ranks, these changes were experienced as loss of power. They felt they were losing control over their people because they did not always know what their people were doing, and yet they still thought they would be expected by upper echelons to know. They no longer had sole input into performance appraisals; there were other voices from other functions—some more knowledgeable about the people's project performance. New career paths were opening that reduced the importance of pleasing these managers in order to move up the functional line; technical people were taking a turn in the factories. Moreover, the engineering managers were often bypassed as their people interacted directly with decision makers in the company and in the suppliers' organizations. Their people sometimes had contact with powerful people the managers did not, including division executives and senior corporate staff, and some of those so-called subordinates sat in on high-level strategy meetings to which their managers were not invited.

At first the vice president and chief engineer shepherding the changes thought the resistance of his managers to the new process was just the normal noise associated with any change. Then he began to realize that something more profound was happening. The traditional hierarchy was being shaken at its foundations; traditional notions about the role and power of managers were being challenged; and it was not clear what was taking their place.

Status barriers influence the acceptance of new technology as well as the ability of groups to communicate. A 1983 survey on the use of office automation was revealing in this regard. Almost 1,000 matched pairs of managers and secretaries in information-intensive businesses were included in the study; despite positive views about the idea of office computers, their use was still limited. What accounted for the limited use? As I scrutinized the data, I found social considerations rather than technical considerations influencing the amount and direction of use (Kanter, 1983b; 1986). Patterns of use could be understood in terms of traditional office relationships. While technology itself may be a neutral tool, its users are people who are arrayed in social space in particular ways and bring to their organizations particular conceptions of their roles and relationships.

In the early stages of new technology, it is possible to pretend that social roles don't need to change; one simply uses the tool and imposes upon it existing organizational structures. But eventually it becomes clear that new technology often changes social relations—and, indeed, often requires these changes to be fully implemented. The secretaries studied wanted to *change* their role, to become a part of the team, to take on more challenging and responsible assignments. The managers wanted to *maintain* current roles and, in some cases, even increase the distance by using automation to eliminate rather than increase communication with office workers. In addition, managers did not necessarily want to use the equipment themselves.

Whenever a traditional culture that respects the wisdom of age encounters a new way of life, it is generally the young that learn it faster. Whenever a group exists in a state of constant and continuous change, the knowledge of the most recently educated is the freshest and most valid, and that means the young. So in a reversal of status, the young teach the old—just as the children of immigrants taught English to their parents, and today 13-year-old computer programmers are starting businesses to teach their elders. Until the new knowledge is stabilized or widespread, a group faces this threatening situation: "lower status" members who are superior in knowledge to "higher status" ones. In most workplaces, the people closest to office automation and the ones most likely to learn it first are the secretaries. But the secretaries, according to the survey, are likely to be younger than their managers, female, and newer to their organizations. Thus, it may seem like status reversal to some managers to learn about office automation.

The most status-conscious organizations are the most likely to resist new technology, losing productivity potential in the process. Organizational life is not fully "rational," then, not fully subject to the logic of efficiency. Social roles must be redesigned in order for the potential of new technology to be realized. But this poses grave challenges to hierarchical organizations.

Kiesler (1986) observed the hierarchy-disrupting effects of electronic communication. Wherever computers are available, she argued, people tend to use them as general-purpose tools to gather and distribute information and talk with others—whether or not that was the principal reason for their installation. For example, the Defense Department's large computer network allowed research computers at many locations to share computing resources located at only a few sites. Soon most of the traffic was not computer to computer but researcher to researcher. It helped them form communities of people who exchanged reports, ideas, computer programs, gossip, and travel plans without reference to hierarchical standing. The result of these systems, Kiesler says, is remarkable freedom to communicate free of status barriers because (a) no tangible artifacts (like paper) are necessary, (b) any format is possible, and (c) people are less bound by convention or the need to create a good appearance. An information system's "distribution lists" are also democratizing, since anyone can easily get more information to more people, thereby creating new groups in the organization with new forms of social interaction. One product developer used an electronic mail message to ask for suggestions about adding a feature to a product and sent the request to a distribution list reaching hundreds of people in his organization. Within two weeks he got back more than 150 messages that cut across geographical, departmental, divisional, and hierarchical boundaries—including messages explaining why the assignment was a crummy idea in the first place.

Many traditional status-derived buffers disappear under the new information/communication technology, permitting greater person-to-person access, again regardless of organizational position. One of my research assistants was having trouble getting by the secretary of the president of a software company. When she got a busy signal on the secretary's phone one day and was routed to the electronic message center, she punched in the numbers of his direct line, leaving him a voice-mail message. He returned her call immediately.

Unless the organizational hierarchy is changed, and status relationships reconceived, it will be difficult to develop and implement new technology quickly. For this reason, some progressive organizations are not only removing communication barriers as they build and collocate cross-functional teams but also striving to remove status barriers. At least two leading U.S. banks—traditionally very status-conscious institutions with very tall hierarchies—are trying to eliminate officer titles (e.g., the many kinds and levels of vice presidents) in favor of broad descriptions of work activities.

## Commitment

The final factor enabling organizations to move fast is high levels of employee commitment that produces sheer hard work. Change always requires above-and-beyond effort; companies that implement innovation quickly count on employee goodwill.

For example, Magaziner and Patinkin documented how the Korean company Samsung came from obscurity in the late 1970s (selling only 1,460 microwave ovens in a 5,000,000-unit oven market) to being the world's largest manufacturer of microwave ovens in 1989. Samsung's advantages included investment in "better minds," not just better technology; low-wage workers; willingness to wait for payback; dedicated employees at every level; and unity of purpose and goal. But the most crucial factor in Samsung's success was the employee dedication. When the company got its first order from J.C. Penney, the authors relate, I. J. Jang, the senior production manager for microwave ovens, "started with an empty factory and a delivery date only months away. His senior people often began at dawn, worked until 10:30 p.m., took a brief nap, and went to work for the rest of the night. Even Jang's boss, Park—one of the highest executives at Samsung—kept the same hours. There was only one sign of privilege—a few cots scattered around the factory. The executives got those; the others grabbed their naps in chairs" (Magaziner and Patinkin, 1989, p. 87). The common motivating factor was their desire to help their country move from being a third world nation to a modern productive power. Samsung's employees felt personally responsible for "planting seeds for the country and the company" and were willing to settle for low wages because they knew that in the long run their entire nation would benefit from their hard work.

Overall, being fast results from cross-functional collaboration and communication, a flow of ideas (and idea entrepreneurs who are willing to bring them forward), and a base of commitment to the organization because speed is also a function of people's willingness to overcome inertia and resistance.

## FLEXIBILITY: THE USE OF RESOURCES

The third "F" for success in the new environment is *flexibility* in the use of resources. Three kinds of flexibility are relevant to the change process: at the work unit level, across work units, and in the innovation project itself.

### Work Systems

Rapid change and intense competition mean that people at every level of the company need to be more flexible, drawing from a broader range of skills, with more open-ended assignments that permit them to solve problems rather than be concerned about jurisdictions. Thus, they are more easily redeployed in the service of another task or project as circumstances change—and they manifest less resistance. People who are more skilled can perform a variety of tasks and be directed by fewer managers in a flatter structure; together with their team, they can take more responsibility for improvements in job performance; and because of their greater responsibility, they feel more "ownership" of innovation.

At the work-unit level, the evidence is compelling: Flexible work systems in which the definition of people's jobs is broader tend to be much more conducive to embracing change. For years, the prototypical U.S. production job was very narrow and specialized and valued efficiencies of repetition over problem solving; in effect, thinking was considered a form of error. Today, the imperatives of industry and the growth of the service sector have led to a revaluing of problem solving. Increasingly, we want people to think; we want them to make decisions about quality; and we want them to understand the purpose and results of their labor. It was not always necessary for workers to understand more than the mechanics of the immediate task at hand. Charles Brown, the former chairman of AT&T, once told me about a visit to a Western Electric telephone equipment plant; he spoke to an immigrant woman on the line who thought she was making irons—she thought she worked for *General* Electric. That epitomizes the human results of a narrow, specialized division of labor. Narrowly defined jobs with clear distinctions between territories create an incentive to guard the territory rather than to learn and change. Consider this quote from a blue-collar worker in a traditional, bureaucratic company: "I know what innovation means. Innovation means I am going to lose my job." He went on to say that the design of his job gave him little chance to learn skills for a new one.

In contrast, when General Motors started the New United Motor Manufacturing, Inc. (NUMMI) plant in Fremont, California, with Toyota as joint venture partner, one of the concessions sought from the United Auto Workers union involved the number of job classifications. Under GM management, there had been more than 30 separate classifications for one major production area; in a similar Toyota plant, there were just 3. Similarly, Procter & Gamble has some of the most advanced manufacturing technology in the world, especially on the social system level. In one state-of-the-art plant, for example, there was one job classification: technician. Everyone was called a technician, assigned to a team that has responsibility for that part of the factory. Pay was determined on a skill basis in a pay-for-knowledge system. For each new job learned, pay increased. Recently, about 75 percent of the people in the plant were at the highest pay level. In addition, there was profit sharing, providing workers a "piece of the action" for what they helped produce, the ultimate in pay-for-contribution. This type of work system has been impressively cost effective. Costs are about half of what they are in the traditional P&G factories; productivity is much higher; and quality is

also much higher. Perhaps most striking, however, is flexibility—the ability to learn and use new technology—which is so
high that when the company was changing the manufacturing
system worldwide for an important product, hundreds of technicians from the new work system plants served as consultants to
help other plants learn how to develop the work system that allowed them to adapt quickly to new technology. Procter & Gamble
has not only created a one-time acceptance of technology through
this flexible work system, they have also created a learning organization that knows how to embrace change.

At the work-unit level, then, job design can help or hinder
flexibility. For the effective adoption of innovation, organizations
need people attuned to results and to learning more skills rather
than guarding narrow territories against change.

### "Desperately Seeking Synergies"

Innovation is aided also by collaboration across work units in
the pursuit of new ways to combine their resources to produce
mutual benefits. One of the key findings from research about innovations is that innovation generally requires teamwork from
more than one area. Unless it is very narrowly focused on the concerns of only one function, innovation cuts across areas and requires more people to cooperate (Kanter, 1983a). Thus, organization
structure, especially the interface between and among work units,
plays a crucial role in determining the use of new technology.

Collaboration is one of the most challenging kinds of flexibility
for corporations but has the highest potential payoffs: for example, joint marketing between divisions A and B, or a product
package joining components from units that traditionally sold their
wares separately, or the procurement staff for one business unit
helping another business unit find a supply source for a new venture. Corporations are realizing that internal competition, which
set divisions or departments against one another in hostile rival-
ries, must be replaced by collaboration if the corporation is going
to maximize the value of having all those units under one roof.
In-house competition undermines goal achievement, which leads
groups to emphasize defeating their rivals instead of strong task
performance. It can drive out innovation and lower performance
standards, a counter-intuitive finding (Kanter, 1989a).

Thus, many companies are now—to parody a popular film title—
"desperately seeking synergies" (Kanter, 1989a, chapter 3). Synergies are not attained in theory because there is a theoretical fit on

paper between parts of a business, but in practice—through active collaboration and the capacity to move resources around the company, to combine them in new ways to tackle new opportunities. The new quest in U.S. business is to seek ways to make the whole worth more than the sum of the parts, and to find the greater value by combining resources. Why, for example, should each unit decide to have its own unique computer system? What is the justification for independent decisions on the part of independent business units when a collaborative effort could reduce costs for the whole organization and perhaps even produce a better system?

At American Express the search for synergies was part of chairman James Robinson's "One Enterprise" campaign, an effort to balance the autonomy and results consciousness of entrepreneurial business units with the willingness to share information, staff, systems, or programs across units. In that way, the "whole" is indeed worth more than the sum of the parts. Project teams drawn from diverse divisions might tackle corporationwide issues, such as quality or the contract for telephone services; one business might use the services of another, such as data processing; referrals of marketing leads may flow across division boundaries; or the experts in one unit might be temporarily deployed to another to help solve new problems. Thus, some companies actively encourage organizing to find synergies. They champion the cause from the top, provide forums to help managers identify opportunities outside their own areas, offer incentives and rewards for teamwork, make resources available for joint projects, and promote relationships and communication to help people know each other across diverse areas. All of this helps people to perceive that their fate is shared and they can help one another. Jack Welch, CEO of General Electric, considers GE's ability to transfer "best practices" across the company one of its key strategic capabilities.

## Project Flexibility

In addition, flexibility is also a requirement for the success of technological change. Innovations often fail to proceed as planned, but instead to encounter unexpected roadblocks or obstacles that require replanning and redirection if the innovation is ever to be produced. Cost overruns and missed deadlines are common because of the inherent high uncertainty of the development process. For example, in one pharmaceutical company the ratio of actual to expected cost of new products was 2.11; the ratio of actual to expected time was 2.95 (Mansfield et al., 1981).

Numerous cases in numerous fields illustrate the unpredictable nature of innovation and, therefore, the need for flexibility in order to persist with a project. Projects cannot be launched and ignored—as though the resources could be doled out and that's that; change of any kind, development of the new, and implementation of innovation require constant management vigilance. Because of the likelihood that pitfalls and problems will arise between idea or strategy and results, a truth of management (if not of life) is that "everything looks like a failure in the middle." In nearly every innovation project, doubt is cast on the original vision because problems are mounting and the end is nowhere in sight. Resources have been expended without the ability to demonstrate when there might be a return.

There are four main sources of this "vulnerability of the midstages," well illustrated by numerous small-scale innovations (Kanter, 1983a) as well as large efforts such as the IBM 360 development (Bower, 1988):

- *Forecasting problems.* The project runs out of time or resources because of overoptimistic forecasts ("it's costing $40 million—now $50 million—now $60 million . . ."), themselves a function of the enormous uncertainties inherent in innovation and change.
- *Unexpected obstacles.* The project hits bottlenecks, technological roadblocks or "unscheduled developments"—which mostly could not have been foreseen because there is no experience base to know they might be there.
- *Critics surface.* Although there may be resistance at all stages, resistance is likelier once the project is well under way and looks as if it might succeed, because then the threat changes from an intellectual matter to a tangible matter—hey, this might actually happen.
- *Working teams lose momentum.* Change is, after all, hard work, and results are not instantaneous or guaranteed. After the euphoria of beginnings, when awareness of a special mission is highly motivating, middles can seem like an endless series of disappointments and thankless tasks.

To overcome such vulnerabilities, it is helpful to have good leadership, including top management champions and project managers that remain dedicated to the project and willing to commit extra resources, deal with critics by continuing to sell the vision, and support shifts of tactics. It is not enough to deal with setbacks by providing additional time and resources—a "grace" period in which the project team can try to complete the assignment; there should be an active attempt to discover what went wrong, to ask what has changed, and to learn from mistakes (see, e.g., the studies in Van de Ven, Angle, and Poole, 1989). Flexibility is the most important issue:  to allocate new resources, to mount secondary projects to remove the unexpected roadblocks, to renew the spirit of the working team, and to rethink the approach in light of the learning that emerges.  Thus, as Quinn (1985) found across three countries, multiple approaches, flexibility, and quickness are required for innovation because of the advance of new ideas through random and often highly intuitive insights and because of the discovery of unanticipated problems. Project teams need to work unencumbered by formal plans, committees, board approvals, and other "bureaucratic delays" that might act as constraint against the change of direction.

Furthermore, innovations often engender secondary innovations, a number of other changes made in order to support the central change (Kanter, 1983a). As necessary, new arrangements might be introduced in conjunction with the core tasks.  Methods and structure might be reviewed, and when it seems that a project is bogging down because everything possible has been done and no more results are on the horizon, then a change of structure or approach, or a subsidiary project to remove roadblocks, can result in a redoubling of efforts and a renewed attack on the problem.  This is why Van de Ven (1986), among others, argued that distinctions between technical and organizational innovations lack utility; in practice, one often entails the other.  Indeed, restructuring of the organization often occurs during the innovation process, including joint ventures, changes in organizational responsibilities, use of new teams, and altered control systems (Schroeder et al., 1986). Of course, there is a danger that intervention to save a project might actually hurt it. New projects, especially those involving high technology, are prone to cost overruns—but desperation measures to stop a hemorrhage of funds can so cripple a project that it can't succeed (Davis, 1985).

Flexibility is an organizational rather than a purely individual variable.  Those organizations that permit replanning, give the working team sufficient operating autonomy, and measure success or allocate rewards for results rather than adherence to plan are likely to have higher rates of innovation production than those that do not.  Because of the inherent uncertainty of innovation, advance forecasts about time or resource requirements are likely to be inaccurate; it is difficult to budget or to forecast when lacking an experience base, and this situation exists by definition in the case of a new idea. The GTE telemessenger, an electronic mailbox, was almost aborted when the project manager's first market test failed because he had not brought in the results he promised. He then went through several rounds of argument to get an original "15 days to fix it" extended to two months (Powell, 1985). Replanning ultimately led to a highly profitable revenue stream. Requiring commitment to a predetermined course of action interferes with the flexibility needed for innovation.

Finally, flexibility also means the willingness to take and use good ideas from any source, rather than looking only to one's own experts. A survey of *Fortune* 500 companies found that firms with the largest number of successful new ventures tended to have an external, market-driven focus and were more acquisition oriented than they were R&D oriented. They sought a variety of ways to grow and did not demand that ideas come only from within (Klavans et al., 1985).

## FRIENDLY: INTERORGANIZATIONAL COLLABORATION

The fourth "F" for success in the new environment is *friendly*. What I mean by "friendly" is the ability to build collaborative rather than adversarial relationships with all the other organizations with which the company deals—in effect, partnerships. Interorganizational relationships play a role in the spread and use of new technology. Joint ventures and strategic alliances are sometimes considered a fad of the 1980s, but behind any fad is genuine substance. Although a long-established form, joint ventures are now forming with increasing frequency; there is more diversity in the age, industry, and nationality of the corporations involved; there is an increasing frequency of joint ventures between big and small firms and an increasing variety of functions performed (Pisano et al., 1988). Such alliances and partnerships are means for organizations to stretch their capacity while sharing the risks, to gain new competence or a window on new technology, and to improve quality or implementation speed. Therefore, partnerships play an ever-larger role in the introduction and use of new technology.

### *Stimulating New Uses for Technology*

The desire to bridge the gap between organizations can be the stimulus for identifying new uses of technology. Consider these examples involving the use of information systems. I have already mentioned American Airlines' Sabre System for travel agents. In an even closer collaboration, Security Pacific Bank put terminals in the hands of car dealers to help sell more car loans along with more cars. The shared system permits the dealer to check on a loan and financing package immediately, evaluate the customer's credit rating, put together a deal on the spot, and have the necessary paperwork delivered seconds later. Then information and packages for ancillary services, such as insurance, can also be provided. For the dealers, the advantage is a faster, more efficient process; for the bank, the advantage is that it gains information as well as customers. In another realm, Nichols Institute, a California-based medical testing company, has developed systems to link hospitals to their testing laboratories to provide information helpful in the interpretation of test results.

## Capability Expansion

Second, partnerships can be useful in the implementation of new technology when they expand the capabilities of the companies involved in the alliance. A good example of this is the venture between Hercules and Montedison, two chemical firms. Montedison was Italy's largest chemical company and had come up with a fantastic new polypropelene plastic process that saved 30 percent on electricity use and 90 percent on steam use during manufacture. Montedison, however, had a very weak position in the global market—it had only 17 percent of European market share and none of the U.S. market. Hercules, on the other hand, was the dominant U.S. polypropelene producer and had the largest share of the global plastics market, but was very weak in process technology. These two companies were ideal partners for a joint venture in this field. Himont, a joint venture with 50-50 ownership, was the result of their collaboration, and it quickly became the world market leader in polypropelene plastics, combining Montedison's technological prowess with Hercules' marketing expertise (Gomes-Casseres, 1989).

The companies that have received the greatest benefits from alliances are those whose main commitment has been to learning (Hamel et al., 1989). For example, NEC invests less in R&D as a percentage of revenues than any of its major competitors, yet NEC is the only company in the world with one of the top positions in three separate industries: telecommunications, computers, and semiconductors. NEC has used alliances to leverage its internal

R&D in the last 20 years. But if alliances are viewed merely as cost- and risk-reducing ventures, then they may become "little more than sophisticated outsourcing arrangements" (Hamel et al., 1989).

## Organization-Spanning Technology

Third, the use of some technology, not only by its nature but also by its origin, does not rest on issues *within* work units but on relationships *between* organizations. Some technology is difficult to use without redefining cross-organizational relationships to become closer, more "friendly." For example, just-in-time inventory systems cannot be used effectively without friendly relationships with suppliers and without interlinked systems. Clearly, this involves a more complex issue than getting a single work unit to accept change. Redefining the nature of the relationship between organizations is one of the major frontiers for understanding how to encourage the implementation and spread of new technology. Significant involvement of suppliers in product development is among the reasons Japanese automakers have shorter lead times for product development than their U.S. counterparts (Clark and Fujimoto, 1988).

In addition, sometimes the conditions necessary to support innovation lie outside of the control of a single organization and therefore *require* interorganizational collaboration for use of new technology. Labor-management partnerships can facilitate the acceptance of new technology. Pacific Bell created what its leaders call a "business partnership" with its major union, the Communication Workers of America, to support the implementation of new technology in the workplace (Kanter, 1989a). The partnership was designed to develop collaborative forums for discussing how both parties are going to deal with the technological change they foresaw and the implications of such change for jobs and job displacement. The partnership forums led to a version of pay for performance through profit sharing, substituting for an automatic cost-of-living increase. More important, they developed the social infrastructure—a system of retraining and career counseling—that would allow the company to deploy their human resources much more flexibly. This would in turn allow them to implement new technology much more quickly, with active collaboration from local union presidents because of their involvement in the decision and the planning.

Similarly, the implementation of computer-integrated manufacturing (CIM) in a unionized plant at Allen-Bradley required union collaboration. Management went to the union leadership and explained the situation, the fact that the plant was going to be automated and that their own engineers were going to design and build the plant. They needed the union's permission, which they received, and then asked for volunteers to train to be operators of the plant. The volunteers were given an aptitude test, and the four top scorers were chosen to be the operators. The maintenance people, the machinery-building people, and the several operators were all part of the same bargaining unit, getting full union support. The hardware and software designers were from different divisions, and at first it was hard to get them to work together and to work under tight controls. But eventually, with union help, the collaborative approach eased the tensions (Avishai, 1989).

Government is another institutional force affecting the development and use of new technology. Because of cooperative relationships with government officials, Merck was able to get FDA approval for a new drug in less than half the time it normally takes, through an informal process of working closely with the regulators on every step of the process. More formal public-private or business-government partnerships also help the effectiveness of innovation. For example, Massachusetts has had many important programs for technology transfer and diffusion of innovation across organizations. The Machine Action Project was a partnership between the state and a network of machine tool companies, all vulnerable to foreign competition; one result was a collaborative training program to spread skills in the uses of new technology, allowing the companies to move into profitable, specialized market niches as low-cost commodity production moved offshore. Similarly, a Massachusetts Center of Excellence on applied technology involves business leaders, union leaders, and educators in the state to plan how new technologies can best be disseminated so that people are educated about them in advance, gain needed skills, and therefore, greet them with minimum resistance.

The government's role as a "partner" is to remove barriers to use of new technology and to set conditions fostering innovation. "Fertile fields" include the following kinds of features, associated with entrepreneurship in the form of start-ups as well as innovation in established organizations:

• Close proximity and ample communication between innovators and users
• A more highly skilled, professionalized, cosmopolitan work force

- A flow of new technical ideas from R&D centers
- A more complex, heterogeneous environment that encourages innovation as an uncertainty-reduction strategy (Kimberly, 1981)
- Channels of communication for exchange of innovation ideas
- Competition from entrepreneurial new companies, in turn benefiting from the availability of venture capital
- More interorganizational interdependence and integration (Pierce and Delbecq, 1977)
- Public encouragement of new ideas as social goods

Certainly the more direct role played by governments in other countries has to be noted. Although most attention has focused on Japan, Korea also deserves mention. In the success of companies like Samsung, the Korean government played an important role; it gave tax rebates, subsidized utilities, built industrial parks, and gave low-interest loans, all as incentives to produce. Samsung managers met often with government officials to discuss strategy and projects (Magaziner and Patinkin, 1989).

### "Bridging" Organizations: Mechanisms for Technology Transfer

Finally, diffusion or transfer of technology may require the development of new organizations to bridge the gap. Even if the technology exists, there must be organizational arrangements that convey it from developers to users—in short, interorganizational linking arrangements. Even where the United States leads in invention, it may lag in technology transfer. For example, a 1979 study showed that universities employed 13 percent of R&D scientists and engineers, spent 16 percent of R&D funds, but held only 2 percent of all patents (Udell et al., 1979). There was thus a gap between idea development and transmission of basic research into useful, commercializable, or transferable products or services.

But new models are emerging. In the medical field, Nichols Institute has developed a collaborative model for technology transfer that has helped bridge the gap between academic laboratory research developments and widespread applicability to the patient population. The company was founded in 1971 as a specialized endocrine laboratory, later adding specialized testing procedures in genetics, toxicology, oncology, and immunology. Technology transfer is managed through the Academic Associate program, involving leading academic researchers in direct supervision of the use of their developments at the Nichols laboratory. A relationship is established between the Associate, his parent institution, and Nichols Institute. The institute is a potential source of support for basic research by returning a percentage of revenues from the applications to the university's basic research and development fund. Academic Associates keeps a foot in both worlds, directing the transfer process at Nichols Institute while maintaining their responsibilities at the university level. Closely linked with the academic world, Nichols Institute Academic Associates have been quick to respond to new technology when it arises. In 1988, Nichols Institute provided diagnostic testing for more than 3.5 million patients, using 1,350 assays (tests), and returned more than $1.75 million to universities to support basic research.

The transfer or diffusion issue should be conceptualized as a continuum. At one extreme, there is perfect identity between the developers and the ultimate users, so the innovators are essentially producing the innovation for themselves, to their own specifications, with foreknowledge that they will be using whatever it is that they make. Organizations can come close to replicating this condition in customized development work for specific clients already internally committed to use, in which client representatives actually sit on the development team. In this case, transfer or diffusion is nonproblematic; it is an inevitable part of successful development.

At the other extreme, there is little or no connection between developers and those to whom the innovation could potentially be transferred, nor is there an established transfer process. There is high uncertainty (an information issue) and controversy (a political issue) about what the next step is to get anyone to use the innovation, who should take this step, whether there are customers for the idea, and whether anyone does or should want the innovation.

A variety of interface or bridging structures can reduce both the uncertainty and the controversy, thus making it more likely that successful transfer will occur. One method for diffusing new ideas is to establish a group whose formal responsibility is to move new ideas into active use (Engel et al., 1981). Members serve as active agents of diffusion, managing the process by which the realized idea is transferred to those who can use it. Part of their mandate is to gather the information to make systematic the process of getting the innovation to users.

Inside organizations, such bridging structures might take the form of product managers, whose job is to manage the successful entry of a new product into the marketplace. In this role they draw on every function in the organization that might contribute, from continuing work on the design, to the manufacturing process, to the sales effort. In the case of organizational or work innovations, the bridging structure might be a transition team or "parallel organization" (Stein and Kanter, 1980) that concentrates on the change process as a management task in and of itself.

Agents of diffusion may also exist outside the organization. Indeed, it can be argued that external agents are even more important in diffusion than champions inside the organization, for they add real or imagined legitimacy to the idea. This is why Rogers and Shoemaker (1971) found contact with consultants such an important part of the diffusion of innovation. What is important is not only the cloak of respectability in which the external party clothes the innovation but also the communication service provided. Thus, Walton (1987) found that the diffusion of work innovations in shipping was aided in eight countries by formal organizations set up to study and write about those innovations. They served as a necessary communication channel to transfer innovations to other users.

How well organized the environment is for the transfer of ideas can account for how rapidly a particular innovation is diffused. By "organized" I mean the ease with which those with common interests can find each other, and therefore how easily connections can be made between innovations and users. Thus, the existence of conferences, meetings, and special interest associations should all be valuable in diffusing innovations, even product innovations, which have to be brought to the attention of specific groups. Again, this can occur within as well as outside a particular organization. 3M and Honeywell both organize a large number of internal conferences and "idea fairs" to connect ideas with those who can use them or help take them the next step.

Trade associations, professional organizations and societies, and specialist consulting organizations are among those groups serving this purpose more broadly. The Food Marketing Institute, trade association for grocers and supermarkets, was largely responsible for facilitating the spread of universal price codes on packages from manufacturers and hence the spread of scanners in stores.

### Complexities of Collaboration

The difficulties of interorganizational collaboration should also be noted, because they require change inside the organizations entering into them (see Kanter, 1989a, chapter 6). The role of partnerships varies, but they may necessitate profound accommodations from the organizations entering into them. A major contract IBM recently won with Ford for office automation required that IBM and Ford engineers work together on a single team to design the system. (One can ask why Ford's secretaries were not also on the team!) Having the user and the supplier on the same team, not simply to adapt technology but to design it and develop it for the needs of the organization, involves dramatic changes. IBM, formerly known as a very closed company, had to learn to share proprietary technical information with a customer in order to win the contract. Similarly, many computer companies now have a management consulting arm or an organizational consulting arm because they realize that unless they get inside their customers' organizations to promote change, they are not going to sell any more equipment.

One way organizations cope with the risks inherent in sharing ideas is by creating an ownership structure that safeguards investments and aligns incentives for cooperative behavior. A study of 195 collaborative arrangements in biotechnology (comparing collaborative arrangements for R&D with those involving technology transfer, supply, marketing, manufacturing agreements) shows that equity is more likely when R&D is involved, because of its inherent uncertainty. That is, because it is difficult to transfer knowledge across boundaries, difficult to specify in a contract all contingencies in advance, and possible that valuable unanticipated side benefits will ensue, then some financial ownership helps bind parties to one another. Equity is also more likely when collaboration encompasses multiple projects and less likely when there are more potential collaborators. Because of higher hazards, equity is more likely when collaboration crosses national boundaries (Pisano, 1989).

But reaching outside does not have to dilute the strength of bonds inside the organization. Take the case of Banc One, one of the most profitable and innovative bank holding companies in the United States. Feelings of commitment and pride, of belonging to a strong community, are engendered by such elements of Banc One culture as the company song ("18,000 People Who Care"), Banc One College for managers, a video magazine, and a large travel budget that keeps managers in frequent contact. Yet Banc One does not hesitate to go outside to form partnerships with other companies—with Merrill Lynch for a banking and brokerage product and with EDS for a financial data processing venture, balancing internal teamwork with external teamwork. Indeed, one can argue that organizations with stronger internal identity and cohesion may make more effective collaborators with other organizations. Union-management partnerships have been found to work better, for example, when both the union and the company have clear goals and strong leadership (Kanter, 1983a, chapter 9).

Overall, then, a "friendly" stance on the part of organizations is the final factor contributing to effective development and diffusion of new technology. Partnerships among organizations can stimulate new uses for technology as well as extend the capabilities of each of the organizations entering into the relationship. Furthermore, collaborations among organizations may be necessary to enable the use of new technology by a single organization because many others (e.g., stakeholders such as suppliers, unions, or government regulatory agencies) may control some of the conditions necessary for making the changes the new technology requires. And technology transfer may be enhanced by the formation of bridging organizations that help connect developers of technology to its users.

## CONCLUSION

The case studies in this volume will help augment knowledge about innovation at the level of the work unit and project-level implementation of change. But I have suggested here that it is important to enlarge our understanding of the circumstances favoring the development and use of new technology by exploring a research frontier, at the macroorganizational level. The domains roughly circumscribed by my four "Fs"—strategy and goals, organizational design and corporate form, hierarchical and cross-work-unit relationships, and interorganizational relationships—may be the most critical areas to examine, as they define the context for the use of new technology. "Perfect" management of innovation projects may not be enough unless organizations are designed to facilitate technology development, use, and transfer. Organizations that are focused, fast, flexible, and friendly may be necessary conditions for more effective technological changes.

I have suggested a large number of hypotheses, based on my own field research and findings from the research literature, about the strategic and organizational factors favoring technological innovation. In light of the rapid changes and faster pace of the global economy, such organizational factors are matters not only of academic interest but of urgent practical significance. America's technological leadership is diminishing at the same time that American organizations require the improvements in productivity or quality that new technology may bring. Thus, awareness of the strategic and organizational issues I have raised can help us begin to awaken the sleeping giants of industry and even teach them to dance.

## REFERENCES

Abernathy, W. J., and J. M. Utterback. 1978. Patterns of industrial innovation. Technology Review 80(June/July):41–47.

Avishai, B. 1989. A CEO's common sense of CIM: An interview with J. Tracy O'Rourke. Harvard Business Review 67(January-February): 100–117.

Bennett, R. C., and R. G. Cooper. 1984. The product-life cycle trap. Business Horizons 27(September/October):7–16.

Biggadike, E. R. 1979. Corporate Diversification: Entry, Strategy and Performance. Boston, Mass.: Harvard University Press.

Bower, J. L. 1988. IBM 360: Giant as Entrepreneur. Harvard Business School Case #989003.

Bower, J. L., and T. M. Hout. 1988. Fast-cycle capability for competitive power. Harvard Business Review 66(November/December):69–76.

Burgelman, R. A. 1984. Managing the internal corporate venturing process. Sloan Management Review 25(Winter):33–48.

Clark, K. B., and T. Fujimoto. 1988. Lead time in automobile product development: Explaining the Japanese advantage. Harvard Business School Working Paper #89-033.

Cohn, S. F., and R. M. Turyn. 1984. Organizational structure, decision-making procedures, and the adoption of innovations. IEEE Transactions on Engineering Management EM31(November):154–161.

Collins, E. 1986. A company without walls: an interview with Steve Shirley. Harvard Business Review 64(January-February):127–137.

Davis, D. 1985. New projects: Beware of false economies. Harvard Business Review 63(March/April):95–101.

Derra, S. 1989. Honoring the stars of research. Research and Development 31(August):49–52.

Drucker, P. F. 1985. Innovation and Entrepreneurship—Practice and Principles. New York: Harper & Row.

Engel, J. F., D. T. Kollat, and R. D. Blackwell. 1981. Diffusion of Innovations. Pp. 472–481 in Corporate Strategy and Product Innovation, R. R. Rothberg, ed. New York: Free Press.

Fast, N. D. 1979. The future of industrial new venture departments. Industrial Marketing Management 8(November):264–273.

Foster, W. 1986. Innovation success quality #4: Innovation incentives. Intrapreneurial Excellence 1(November):9.

Gerhart, B., and G. T. Milkovich. 1989. Organizational differences in managerial compensation and financial performance. Cornell University School of Industrial and Labor Relations Working Paper #89-11.

Gomes-Casseres, B. 1989. Joint ventures in the face of global competition. Sloan Management Review. (Spring):17–26.

Hamel, G., Y. Doz, and C. K. Prahalad. 1989. Collaborate with your competitors and win. Harvard Business Review 67(January/February): 133–139.

Handy, C. 1989. The Age of Unreason. London: Business Books Ltd.

Heskett, J. L. 1987. Servicemaster industries. Harvard Business School Case #9388064.

Hobson, E., and R. Morrison. 1983. How do corporate start-up ventures fare? Pp. 390–410 in Frontiers of Entrepreneurial Research, J. A. Hornaday, J. A. Timmons, and Karl H. Vesper, eds. Wellesley, Mass.: Babson College Center for Entrepreneurial Studies.

*Intrapreneurial Excellence.* 1986. Innovation: A cornerstone at Corning. October:1–3.

Jaikumar, R. 1986. Post-industrial manufacturing. Harvard Business Review 63(November/December):69–76.

Judkins, P., D. West, and J. Drew. 1985. Networking in Organizations: The Rank-Xerox Experiment. Aldershot, England: Gower.

Kanter, R. M. 1983a. The Change Masters. New York: Simon and Schuster.

Kanter, R. M. 1983b. Office Automation and People: A New Dimension. Report to Honeywell. Minneapolis, Minn.: Honeywell Corporation.

Kanter, R. M. 1986. Computers should be head tools, not hand tools. Management Review April 13–14.

Kanter, R. M. 1987. From status to contribution: Organizational implications of the changing basis for pay. Personnel (January).

Kanter, R. M. 1988. When a thousand flowers bloom: Structural, collective and social conditions for innovation in organizations. Research in Organizational Behavior 10:169–211.

Kanter, R. M. 1989a. When Giants Learn to Dance: Mastering the Challenges of Strategy, Management and Careers in the 1990's. New York: Simon and Schuster.

Kanter, R. M. 1989b. The new managerial work. The Harvard Business Review 67(November/December):85–92.

Kiesler, S. 1986. The hidden message in computer networks. The Harvard Business Review 64(January/February):46–60.

Kimberly, J. R. 1981. Managerial innovations. Pp. 84–104 in Handbook of Organizational Design 1, W. H. Starbuck, ed. New York: Oxford University Press.

Klavans, R., M. Shanley, and W. M. Evan. 1985. The management of internal corporate ventures: Entrepreneurship and innovation. Columbia Journal of World Business 20(Summer):21–27.

Klein, J. A. 1984. Why supervisors resist employee involvement. Harvard Business Review 62(September/October):87–95.

Leonard-Barton, D. 1988. Implementation as mutual adaptation of technology and organization. Research Policy 17:251–267.

Magaziner, I., and M. Patinkin. 1989. Fast heat: How Korea won the microwave war. Harvard Business Review 67(January/February):83–92.

Maidique, M. A., and B. J. Zirger. 1985. The new product learning cycle. Research Policy 14(December):299–313.

Mansfield, E., J. Rappaport, J. Schnee, S. Wagner, and N. Hamburger. 1981. Research and innovation in the modern corporation. Pp. 416–427 in Corporate Strategy and Product Innovation, R. R. Rothberg, ed. New York: Free Press.

Mason, P. A. 1986. Managing internal corporate joint ventures: A process approach. Unpublished Doctoral Dissertation, Columbia University.

Miller, A., W. Gartner, and R. Wilson. 1989. Entry order, market share, and competitive advantage: A study of their relationships in new corporate ventures. Journal of Business Venturing 4(May):197–210.

Montgomery, C. A. 1985. Product-market diversification and marketing power. Academy of Management Journal 28:789–798.

Montgomery, C. A., and A. R. Thomas. 1988. Divestment: Motives and gains. Strategic Management Journal 9:93–97.

Pierce, J. L., and A. L. Delbecq. 1977. Organization structure, individual attitudes and innovation. Academy of Management Review 2:27–37.

Pisano, G., M. Russo, and D. Teece. 1988. Joint ventures and collaborative arrangements in the telecommunications equipment industry. Pp. 23–70 in International Collaborative Ventures in U.S. Manufacturing, David Mowery, ed. New York: American Enterprise Institute for Policy Research.

Pisano, G. 1989. Using equity participation to support exchange: Evidence from the biotechnology industry. Journal of Law, Economics and Organization 5(Spring):109–126.

Porter, M. 1987. From competitive advantage to corporate strategy. The Harvard Business Review 65(May/June):43–59.

Powell, J. 1985. Bootstrap entrepreneurs at GTE telemessenger. GTE Together (Winter).

Quinn, J. B. 1979. Technological innovation, entrepreneurship and strategy. Sloan Management Review 20(Spring):19–30.

Quinn, J. B. 1980. Strategies for Change: Logical Incrementalism. Homewood, Ill.: Irwin.

Quinn, J. B. 1985. Managing innovation: Controlled chaos. The Harvard Business Review 63(May-June):73–84.

Rogers, E. M., and F. F. Shoemaker. 1971. Communication of Innovations: A Cross-Cultural Approach (2nd ed.). New York: Free Press.

Schroeder, R., A. H. Van de Ven, G. Scudder, and D. Polley. 1986. Observations leading to a process model of innovation. Discussion Paper #48. Management Research Center, University of Minnesota.

Stein, B. A., and R. M. Kanter. 1980. Building the parallel organization:

Towards mechanisms for permanent quality of work life. Journal of Applied Behavioral Science 16:371–388.

Udell, G., K. Baker, and R. Colton. 1979. Stimulating and rewarding innovation: the innovation center program. Research Management 22(July):32–38.

Uttal, B. 1987. Speeding new ideas to market. Fortune (March 2):62–66.

Van de Ven, A. H. 1986. Central problems in the management of innovation. Management Science 32:590–607.

Van de Ven, A. H., H. Angle, and M. Poole. 1989. Research on the Management of Innovation: The Minnesota Studies. Cambridge, Mass.: Ballinger.

Walton, R. 1987. Innovating to Compete. San Francisco: Jossey-Bass.

# 1

## *Automated Manufacturing Technologies*

People and Technology in the Workplace. 1991.
Pp. 59–88. Washington, D.C:
National Academy Press.

# Capitalizing on New Manufacturing Technologies: Current Problems and Emergent Trends in U.S. Industry

PAUL S. ADLER

Numerous industries in the United States have been slow to capitalize on new manufacturing technology. Consider these examples.

- The United States has only one-third as many robots as Japan (Flamm, 1986).
- Use of basic oxygen furnaces and continuous casting in the steel industry has spread much more slowly in the United States than in other countries (Office of Technology Assessment, 1980).
- The proportion of machine tools that are numerically controlled is less in the United States (40 percent) than in either Japan (67 percent) or Germany (49 percent) (Collis, 1987).
- Once the commitment is made to install new process equipment, U.S. firms take longer to get up and running than Japanese firms—in the case of flexible manufacturing systems (FMS), 2.5 to 3 years and 25,000 work hours versus 1.25 to 1.75 years and 6,000 hours (Jaikumar, 1986).
- U.S. firms fail to exploit the new technologies' capabilities; in the FMS case, U.S. systems typically produce 10 parts versus 93 in Japanese systems (Jaikumar, 1986).
- Moreover, U.S. industry tends to do poorly at the process of continuous incremental improvement that has been perfected in some Japanese companies as *Kaizen* (Imai, 1986). Two of three Japanese employees submit suggestions to save money, increase efficiency, or boost morale versus only 8 percent of U.S. workers.

The Japanese make 2,472 suggestions per 100 eligible employees versus only 13 per 100 eligible employees in the United States (*Wall Street Journal*, 1989).

This chapter argues that underlying these symptoms is a deeper malady: U.S. industry is having difficulty shifting from a static to a dynamic model of management. In the static model, innovations such as the introduction of computerized equipment were slow to develop and, once installed, modifications were discouraged or prohibited. When technologies develop at a more rapid pace, a more dynamic model is needed that facilitates more frequent technological change and encourages a process of continuous improvement at all levels of the organization.

This chapter identifies key problems and emergent trends in industry's efforts to meet the challenge of this new model. The tone is one of urgent concern: the United States is not doing well thus far. Productivity growth is still slower than it was in the first two decades after World War II and slower than that of our major trading partners. The manufacturing sector has seen an improvement since 1979, but Japan is still outpacing the rate of increase in our labor productivity, and our balance of trade is still in serious deficit. Since the United States is becoming more deeply embedded in the world economy, performance relative to our trading partners is progressively more important to our living standards. These trends in performance spell stagnant living standards and increasing desperation for those trapped at the bottom of the income scale. Even middle-income Americans feel a growing sense of frustration when they see how little progress they have made over the last two decades.

Such a state of affairs has many roots, and the performance of manufacturing firms is but one of them. Despite the importance of the social, political, and macroeconomic factors that contribute to the problems, this chapter addresses these broader factors only where they touch directly on the conduct of business. This focus does not imply that business alone is to blame for our current predicament; only that it has much to contribute to resolving it.

Since the elements of this story are numerous and complex, an organizing framework is used here to classify these impediments and trends. The framework highlights six general areas of concern: technology, skills, procedures, structure, strategy, and culture. Each of these elements is discussed in turn, beginning with the major problems and then the more hopeful signs in U.S. manufacturing.

One key trend in each area is the increasing recognition that people—executives, supervisors, engineers, workers, union officers—play critical and interrelated roles in the process of dynamic change. The three case studies that follow provide practical examples of manufacturing firms introducing technological and organizational changes that are mutually supportive, involving consumers, suppliers, and employees in the process. In these cases we see how the effective implementation of new technologies—an automated storage and retrieval system at the Boeing Company (Gissing, in this volume), a distributed process control system at International Bio-Synthetics, Inc. (Hettenhaus, in this volume), and an automatic in-process gauging system at Consolidated Diesel Company (High, in this volume)—both required and facilitated related changes in areas such as employee skills training, hierarchical management structures, and the culture of the plant floor.

While each organization developed its own approach, one theme central to all of them was the development of horizontal and vertical collaboration. Teamwork, for example, was actively reinforced through changes in worker rotation procedures at International Bio-Synthetics, new training facilities at Consolidated Diesel, and early union and management involvement at Boeing. These cases illustrate various combinations of the problems and trends discussed and elaborated on in this chapter, and their implications for people and technology in the future development of manufacturing industries.

## TECHNOLOGY

The current state of technology itself creates some important impediments to its implementation. Most notable are the lack of standards and continued inflexibility:

• Lack of widely accepted standards impedes data communication between subunits using different systems. Even when CAD workstations are being used, drawings are recreated many times in the subunits, a process that is both costly and error-prone. One equipment vendor polled its customers (mainly in metalworking) and found companies typically recreated the geometry of their drawings five times between development and delivery, usually at stages such as layout, styling, drafting, finite element analysis, manufacturing documentation, numerical control (NC) programming, and development of installation and service manuals (Automation Technology Products, 1985).

• Despite the promise of programmable flexibility, manufacturing technologies are still too inflexible to allow the introduction of new product designs into manufacturing without extensive disruption. The installed base of equipment in U.S. industry is not as computerized as it could be, and those that have pushed ahead aggressively with computer control have found that it requires a great deal of engineering overhead to achieve the promised flexibility.

These technology bottlenecks must be seen in the context of the specific technical demands of the manufacturing environment (National Research Council, 1988). Because time is often of the essence, systems that are too slow will not be used, no matter how much more efficient they are in specially designed benchmarking tests. Change in products, processes, technology, markets, and competition directly constrain the usefulness of rigid but otherwise elegant systems. Further, the enormous complexity of modern manufacturing systems overwhelms many information systems. It is not uncommon for the memory requirements of the manufacturing information system to be one or even two orders of magnitude greater than the rest of the business's computer systems combined.

These technological limitations are progressively being surmounted. The emergent trends can be classed in six categories (Institute for Defense Analyses, 1988):

• *Information capture.* In design, an increasing number of companies are making the commitment to develop a common product-definition data base from which different subunits can all work. In manufacturing, sensor-based control of equipment has been identified as a key research topic by the National Science Foundation.

• *Information representation.* This is primarily a problem of standards, and several initiatives are under way in the area of engineering specifications to permit the use of information by different hardware and software systems, for example, the Department of Defense Computer-aided Acquisition and Logistics Support program and the Product Data Exchange Specification effort.

• *Data presentation.* The bottlenecks here are being surmounted with important progress in graphics, 3-D and solid modeling, videoconferencing, and high-speed printing.

• *Data manipulation.* Here developments are progressing at a rapid rate in such areas as finite element analysis, continuous fluid dynamics, and discrete event simulation.

• *System environments.* Surrounding the preceding four elements is the system environment that ensures the integration of disparate tools, controlled sharing of information, tracking of design information, configuration control, and monitoring of the design process. In this domain, several competing efforts to develop system environments are currently under way.

• *Enabling technologies.* Underlying all these activities is the development of enabling technologies such as object-oriented programming, expert systems, and relational data bases.

The current state of technology constrains not only major process innovations but also the continuous improvement process. Most automated systems are not designed to accommodate the inevitable process of tool adaptation and extension. The model that underlies most system design assumes that the user will adapt to the system. Rarely is consideration given to the ways in which users will adapt the system to their local needs (Brown and Newman, 1985). Continuous process improvement is stunted, however, when users cannot form a mental model of the inner working of the tools they use. Such models are particularly important for dealing with situations in which the system does not perform as expected—the user needs to be able to assess whether the problem resulted from a system malfunction or from the procedure employed.

Having characterized some general technological problems and trends in manufacturing, it is important to understand better which segments seem to be leading and which lagging in the technology area. Our knowledge of the ecology of technological innovation is spotty, but two general comments are in order.

First, we should note that the Department of Defense has played an important role in funding research and development and in encouraging, even forcing, the pursuit of some technological opportunities in products (such as new materials), processes (such as automated assembly), and improvement procedures (such as the IDEF methodology). It is unclear how many of these innovations spill over into the civilian sector.

Second, there seems to be an inordinately large gap between the technology efforts of industrial firms for whom these new opportunities are imperatives and the efforts of those for whom these new opportunities are merely options for increasing profitability. Economists are accustomed to assuming that opportunities to increase profits should (other things being equal) be just as powerful a stimulus for technological change as the imminent threat of going out of business, if only because one need not presume superhuman insight on the part of managers to assume that they understand that ignoring opportunities will sooner or later lead to crisis. But there seems to be a considerable difference in behavior between firms in the two different situations.

A recent study of computer-aided design/computer-aided manufacturing (CAD/CAM) experiences in printed circuit boards (PCBs) and in aircraft hydraulic tubing between 1980 and 1987 (Adler, 1990a) found technological integration efforts to have been disappointingly weak. One of the most promising elements of CAD/CAM is the possibility of linking design and manufacturing data bases so that the factory can be "driven" from the design data. In the manufacture of both PCBs and hydraulic tubing, this had been technically feasible for at least a decade prior to the study. But one-third of the electronics businesses that were contacted for the survey had not yet established any direct linkage between their CAD and CAM systems, even though PCBs were a major component of their products and most had well-developed stand-alone capabilities in CAD and CAM. While the other PCB manufacturers and all four of the sampled aircraft companies had some capability for downloading data from design data bases to manufacturing, none had developed a good set of guidelines to ensure that the data were actually usable, and none had developed a two-way communication link so that manufacturing could pass design revision suggestions directly into the design data base. Where it is a matter of using CAD/CAM to enhance efficiency in manufacturing or design, evidence is accumulating that even in high-tech industries, the United States is lagging behind international competitors.

By contrast, some other industries, such as very-large-scale integration (VLSI) semiconductors or complex metal contouring, have been much more aggressive in using CAD/CAM integration opportunities. But these more aggressive industries are characterized by intense competitive pressure to deliver products whose complexity demands CAD/CAM integration. Where firms are faced with an undeniable imperative, management appears much more willing to commit the resources needed to master new technology opportunities.

The results of a recent survey by Arthur Young & Company are sadly eloquent: surveying 378 visitors to a factory automation trade show in November 1987, they found that middle managers and engineers disagreed strongly with the common assumption among senior executives that advanced process technology was being applied widely. The extent to which technology is being applied to manufacturing is "vastly lower than that generally assumed" (*Aviation Week and Space Technology*, 1988). Future research could usefully focus on going beyond this anecdotal evidence on the ecology of technological innovation and compare the U.S. ecology with that of other industrialized nations.

## SKILLS

According to Denison (1985), education and learning on the job accounted for 26 percent and 55 percent, respectively, of U.S. productivity growth between the 1929 and 1982—a far greater contribution than capital investment, improved resource allocation, or economies of scale. The current supply of skills, however, does not facilitate adaptation to new technological opportunities.

The United States graduates and employs proportionately fewer engineers than several of its competitors (National Science Board, 1987, Table 3-15) and employs proportionately fewer in nondefense and development (rather than research) activities. Not surprisingly, managers are much less likely to have technical backgrounds (*American Machinist*, 1985). These weaknesses in engineering skills are compounded by even more serious weaknesses in the skill base of the nonengineering work force.

The quality of our formal schooling is relatively weak. The United States has the highest functional illiteracy and drop-out rate of the advanced industrial nations (Thurow, 1987). The vocational education system is widely seen as being of "limited effectiveness" (Dertouzos et al., 1989). Under-funded community colleges are left to fill the gaps. As a result, in international comparisons, U.S. 10-year-olds ranked eighth in science knowledge, while 13- and 17-year-olds ranked even lower (International Association for the Evaluation of Educational Achievement, 1988). Bishop (1989) argues convincingly that these results do not reflect greater societal diversity. Even the best U.S. schools are significantly behind the performance of the top-tier schools in such countries as Japan, Taiwan, England, Canada, and Finland.

Apart from these contextual features of U.S. society, industry does not seem to have formulated a clear understanding of its skill needs, nor has it done enough to meet some of these needs itself. U.S. industry invests considerably less than other nations in developing skills. According to a recent study by the Commission on the Skills of the American Workforce (1990), fewer than

200 firms in the United States invest more than 2 percent of their payroll on formal training, while leading foreign firms invest up to 6 percent. At the high end, very few firms support an apprenticeship program—in any given year of the last decade, the entire U.S. labor force included only some 300,000 registered apprentices, of whom more than 60 percent were in the building trades (U.S. Department of Labor, 1987). At the low end, an intolerable percentage of the work force is functionally illiterate and innumerate.

The quality of the skill formation system is an important competitive handicap when automation raises the skill requirements of the work force. This proposition raises two questions, however. First, there is some debate as to whether workers' current skills— low as they may be in comparison with other countries—are really inadequate given the modest level of skills required by most jobs. Indeed, Rumberger (1981) documents some level of overeducation in the work force. But his analysis shows that this overeducation is restricted to the high end of the educational scale. The skills in which the work force is most deficient are rather elementary ones: basic statistics for statistical process and control activities, problem-solving skills for quality improvement efforts, interpersonal skills for teamwork, and so forth. In this area there is much to learn from our trading partners' educational and training systems.

Second, there is an ongoing debate about whether the increasing automation level of industry will, over time, tend to alleviate or aggravate the skills deficiency problem. This debate is in large measure subsumed under a broader debate about the overall direction of industry's skill requirements. Singelmann and Tienda (1985) analyzed the occupational and industrial structure of the economy in recent decades and found that from 1970 to 1980, both industry shifts and occupational shifts within industries were in a skill upgrading direction. Spenner (1988) reviewed the available statistical and case-study research on skill trends over the past few decades; he concludes that substantive complexity has probably increased somewhat since World War II, both in the content of specific occupations and in the mix of occupations in the labor force.

These analyses are retrospective; future-oriented analyses suggest that upgrading in skill requirements may accelerate. If skill requirements are driven by automation, and if the rate of change in process technology accelerates as many predict, then the skill formation challenges faced by industry may grow rather than diminish. Singelmann and Tienda forecast that even though the shift toward services (which—notwithstanding a common mis-conception—has had an upgrading effect on skill requirements) will slow down over the next decades, the intraindustry trends in occupational structure will continue to create an upgrading pressure.

The recent report by the Commission on the Skills of the American Workforce (1990) makes a stronger point—one that parallels the thesis advanced in the preceding section on technology: even if industry is not currently experiencing any widespread skill short-ages, and even if technological and demographic projections do not suggest any future massive skill shortages, evidence is accu-mulating that the current skill level of the industrial work force leaves the United States less able to derive competitive advantage from new technologies than our competitors.

Apart from this extensively debated if poorly documented ques-tion of skill *levels*, there is the question of changing *types* of skill required within occupations to implement new process technolo-gies. Recent research on CAD/CAM highlights several emergent trends in the key occupational categories (Adler, 1990a):

- *Design engineering.* The introduction and integration of CAD/CAM considerably broadens the task of the design engineer. With CAD, the designer can access other parts of a design being worked on by other designers, and a much higher level of design optimi-zation is expected. With CAD/CAM integration, plant equipment is driven directly from the design data, so the manufacturability of product designs becomes much more important; as a result, a higher level of manufacturing knowledge is often expected of the designer. The automated design tools themselves are often diffi-cult to master. They require quite new approaches to the design process at the individual cognitive level. Finally, because the design software is constantly evolving, an ability to absorb new methods on an ongoing basis becomes more important (Majchrzak et al., 1987; Wingert et al., 1981).
- *Design and drafting technicians.* Design automation can re-duce the need for design and drafting personnel (for a given output level), since some human tasks are eliminated; many managers extrapolate from this to assume that automation will reduce the skill requirements of the remaining technicians. However, the limitations of these systems and the emergence of other higher-level design and drafting tasks typically make a reduction in skill requirements infeasible. Design technicians in CAD/CAM envi-ronments usually need higher levels of abstract problem-solving

capability and computer expertise, and CAD/CAM integration requires a greater understanding of the manufacturing constraints summarized in producibility design rules. These skill increases outweigh the reduced requirements in manual drawing skills. As a result, most drafting managers are shifting their recruiting criteria upward, demanding at least an associate degree (Allen, 1984; Jerahov, 1984; Majchrzak et al., 1987; Marchisio and Guiducci, 1983; Salzman, 1985; Senker and Arnold, 1984; Tucker and Clark, 1984).

• *Manufacturing workers.* Automation seems to be increasing workers' skill requirements in almost all categories. The key factor behind the general trend toward higher skills is the greater speed of automated processes. As one manager of a PCB assembly plant put it, when speeds for inserting components progress from 5,000 to 12,000 units per hour, and when some of the newer machines operate at 120,000 units per hour, "the consequences of not thinking have gone way up" (Adler, 1990a). CAD/CAM also encourages upgrading of maintenance skill requirements: traditional mechanical, hydraulic, and electrical skills need to be supplemented by electronics expertise. Furthermore, as the span of automation—the integration within a single system of previously separate operations—increases, the need for multicraft maintenance people appears to be increasing (National Research Council, 1986).

• *Manufacturing engineering.* This is perhaps the function in which skill upgrading is most dramatic. The proportion of degreed people tends to grow considerably with CAD/CAM: in one PCB shop surveyed, the proportion grew from 40 percent in 1980 to 68 percent in 1986; in another, the proportion grew from less than 15 percent in 1976 to 100 percent in 1986 (Adler, 1990a). The main impetus is the need for manufacturing engineers who can understand and program the new CAM systems; and CAD/CAM integration means that manufacturing engineers need to develop a rigorous characterization of the manufacturing process and of its producibility constraints. For organizations accustomed to promoting their manufacturing engineers from the shop floor, the change is dramatic.

• *System development engineers.* The development of new tools for manufacturing and design engineering has until recent years been the task of more experienced manufacturing workers and design engineers. This was sufficient as long as automation opportunities in design and manufacturing environments were limited. With the development of computer tools, new computer skills are needed to drive the process improvement effort, and specialized systems development departments are created. Even firms that plan to buy rather than to develop their own automation software find that both systems maintenance requirements and the value of customizing their software drive them to establish and maintain significant staffs of highly skilled systems developers (Traversa, 1984).

To complete this analysis of skills for CAD/CAM, it should also be noted that automation has tended to increase, rather than reduce, the share in the overall employment of the more skilled categories. As firms invest more in CAD/CAM, the ratio of drafters to design engineers is typically reduced, and the ratio of system developers to system users has typically risen (Adler, 1990a).

There are naturally some factors that can modify the strength of the skill upgrading trend. At any given time, the level of skills in a company or an industry will depend on many characteristics of the product and factor markets, business strategies, and institutional context. But the aggregate data suggest that these factors do not reverse the upgrading trend on a sustained basis. The reason is not hard to see. While an increase in the automation level applied to a given task might in some instances reduce skill requirements, automation typically leads (a) to further automation and (b) to changes in product characteristics. Typically, both of these dynamic effects have in turn strong skill-upgrading effects—employees must be able to support and adapt to this dynamic change—and these effects usually far outweigh any static deskilling effect.

Skills are a critical factor not only in cases of major technology innovations but also in continuous improvement. The lack of problem-solving skills is a key handicap. Statistical skills are an important element of these problem-solving capabilities. Japanese manufacturing operations have derived great benefit from the statistical skills of their blue-collar workers, since this enables them to mobilize these workers in the quality improvement process rather than rely exclusively on more expensive quality engineers. Developing coaching skills for first-line supervisors and manufacturing engineers is another important element needed to motivate and organize problem-solving activities on the part of blue-collar employees.

The firms that are more actively pursuing the opportunities associated with continuous improvement appear to invest considerable resources in training for all levels of personnel in problem-solving and group processes. They also appear to encourage a greater degree of cross training since a broader view of the production process facilitates collaborative problem solving (Suzaki, 1987).

## PROCEDURES

If the skill base of the organization is the underlying condition for the effective use of new technologies, the proximate cause for many of the implementation deficiencies is often slack in the procedures that specify how people are supposed to use the technology.

Research in the International Motor Vehicle Program at the Massachusetts Institute of Technology found that procedural mechanisms such as Just-In-Time inventory control and Statistical Process Control accounted for a much higher proportion of the variance in assembly plant productivity than did the level the automation. MacDuffie and Krafcik (1989) distinguished plants with a "lean" procedural system—characterized by small repair areas, low inventories, teamwork, despecialized quality control, and employee involvement—from plants with a "robust" system having the opposite characteristics. Analyzing the quality and productivity levels of the 47 assembly plants in Asia, the United States, and Europe, they showed that plants with low automation levels and robust procedures performed worst; but high-tech/robust plants performed about the same as low-tech/lean plants. In other words, the payoff to material technology is greatly enhanced by the more careful design of the procedural context of its use—the "organizational technology."

The relative importance of procedures is even more visible in the large segment of U.S. manufacturing that takes the form of the job shop rather than the assembly line. The typical part in the typical machining shop is being worked on only 2 percent of the time it spends there. The rest of the time is spent in transport or waiting (95 percent) and in setup or other necessary nonmachining time (3 percent) (Hutchinson, 1984). Clearly, material technology that accelerates this work time can have only a modest effect in relation to changes in the organizational technology that accounts for so much queue time.

A similar logic is found in the engineering universe. After the introduction of CAD/CAM, for example, drawings often sit idle, waiting to be worked on, just as long as they did in paper form. Certainly we can find cases where rapid new product introduction is the overriding concern, and important efforts are devoted to minimizing the wait, transport, and setup times experienced by "designs-in-process" (to use the manufacturing analogy). But at the other extreme, the processing of engineering changes (ECs) in both the civilian and military aircraft companies studied in Adler (1990a) took an average of five months of calendar time unless expedited. The estimated average critical path of these ECs was about 48 hours, including redesign, retooling, revising plans, and reviews. The ratio of work time (48 hours) to calendar time (5 months × 20 days/month × 8 hours/day) equals 6 percent—not much better than the job shop (Hutchinson, 1984).

A variety of other procedures in areas such as finance envelop operations and often function as impediments to effective use of new technology. Financial justification procedures may be too myopic. Financial analysis of investment proposals for flexible manufacturing systems, for example, often allow no credit for inventory savings or the faster time-to-market or improved quality (Kaplan, 1986). The tools for financial evaluation are also often poorly implemented (Hodder and Riggs, 1985). Manufacturing performance measures often act as a disincentive to undertake process innovations that will disrupt, even if only briefly, production schedules (Kaplan, 1983).

The role of procedures in the continuous improvement process is currently the object of an unannounced and confused but important debate. The assumption that has predominated among organization theorists and many practitioners is familiar: bureaucratic rules, narrowly prescribed roles, high degrees of formalization—in a word, proceduralization—are inimical to the learning that enables continuous improvement. To create a learning environment conducive to continuous improvement, it is commonly assumed that a more flexible, organic approach, with minimal proceduralization is needed. Autonomy is seen as the key to learning. This has been one of the main criticisms of Taylorism as a philosophy of job design: critics argue that learning is stunted when each gesture composing a task is analyzed scientifically, and everyone performing that task must employ the same prescribed sequence.

Recent experience with Japanese-owned plants in the United States, however, has posed a serious challenge to this consensus. At plants like New United Motor Manufacturing, Inc. (NUMMI), the joint venture between General Motors and Toyota located in Fremont, California, the production system can best be described as "Taylorism intelligently applied." The Toyota system of standardized work as described by Monden (1983) and Schonberger (1982) is indeed very close to Taylor's ideals. The work is regimented in its minutest gestures in a way that most industrial engineers have only dreamt was possible. This system is not without its critics among the NUMMI workers. But my own interviews at NUMMI with supporters among the workers as well as critics (see summaries in Adler, 1990b) leads me to conclude that even the critics are basically enthusiastic about the system—despite the fact that everyone in the plant agrees that the work pace is faster than what they had been used to under GM management. The criticisms are, with few exceptions, directed at what workers see as flaws in the implementation of the standardized work system, not at the system itself.

How can one explain the workers' enthusiasm for such intense proceduralization and such low levels of autonomy in deciding how to perform their own job on a lot-to-lot and day-to-day basis? One hypothesis can, I believe, be easily refuted: that NUMMI workers are particularly compliant because of their painful experience of unemployment during the period between the shutdown of GM-Fremont and the opening of NUMMI. If the workers had returned to a traditionally managed plant, productivity, quality, and morale would have rapidly returned to their traditional abysmal levels.

One important factor in the workers' support for standardized work is that they set the standards themselves. Workers actively participate in establishing the standards; indeed, the plant has no work standards engineers. Moreover, workers are encouraged to refine these standards to improve safety and quality and to reduce waste. This is clearly an important factor—participation is its own reward. But these standards, once established, are to be respected down to the tenth of a second. If these procedures were the alienating chains that conventional theory assumes they are, then the participation-driven enthusiasm would not last for long.

My interviews at NUMMI lead me to believe that another factor is at play here: workers are enthusiastic about the proceduralization of their work because they recognize the resulting standards as the most effective way of doing the job. The Toyota system taps into two motivation sources that have been accorded too little attention by managers and researchers: first, the desire for excellence, the instinct of craftsmanship, the desire to see a job well done; and second, the recognition in psychologically mature workers of what Freud called the "reality principle"—the understanding that either the plant constantly improves its performance or, independent of whether the managers are mean or nice, competitors will take its market.

Three decades ago, Gouldner (1954) suggested that bureaucracy's effectiveness may vary with the manner in which its rules and procedures are arrived at, and that "negotiated" bureaucracy may prove to be an effective form of organization. This idea gradually disappeared from view, perhaps because subsequent generations of researchers in industrial sociology and organizational behavior have been more struck by the prevalence of bureaucracies that are not negotiated and that represent efforts to ensure the compliance of a recalcitrant work force. The Toyota system of standardized work shows procedures in a novel light: they are not necessarily instruments of domination; they can be elements of productive technique recognized by participants as being in their own interests.

Recent findings reported in the literature of organization theory support these ideas. Podsakoff et al. (1986) confirm for both professional and nonprofessional employees the results found for professionals by Organ and Greene (1981): the formalization of organization processes is often negatively, not positively, associated with alienation. These research results suggest that the role clarity afforded by more tightly defined procedures outweighs the negative effects of formalization that are typically highlighted in the antibureaucratic discourse.

## STRUCTURE

Under cost pressure, an increasing number of firms are attempting to eliminate middle management layers. By the mid-1980s, the Bureau of Labor Statistics estimated that unemployment among managers and administrators was at its highest level since World War II. The Conference Board estimated that more than one million managers and staff professionals had lost their jobs since 1979. An executive search firm reported that more than one-third of middle-management positions were eliminated by the mid-1980s (Tomasko, 1987). Such structural changes could facilitate technological change by empowering lower-level participants and reducing the number of approval steps. The movement of contentious issues up and down the hierarchy can cripple the change project. Kurokawa (1988) has developed a model that explains the problem well. Imagine a business in which one subunit is developing a technology (a new product or a new manufacturing process) for use by another subunit. The two subunits each have $n$ levels of authority and there are a total of $m$ levels of management in the organization (including the $n$ levels in each of the two subunits).

The probability of one person concurring with his or her subordinate is $p$, and the probability of agreement between the players at the same level in the two subunits is $q$. Thus a formula for the probability of final agreement between the two subunits is $p^{m-1+n} q^n$. If $p$ is 80 percent and $q$ is 60 percent, $m$ is 6 and $n$ is 5, then the probability of success is virtually zero—0.83 percent. Increasing $p$ and $q$ is obviously useful, but so is decreasing $m$ and $n$—the number of layers in the organizational structure.

The implementation of new process technologies often seems to be more effective when associated with broader jobs and teamwork organizational structures. This, too, is clear from the MIT International Motor Vehicle Program research (MacDuffie and Krafcik, 1989): teamwork and job rotation are key elements of the lean production system.

In the broader area of participation in decision making, there appears to be something of a resurgence of interest in employee involvement in industry, particularly through quality circle (QC) programs and employee stock ownership plans (ESOP). The previous wave of interest in the 1970s was motivated by various symptoms of worker alienation—the "blue collar blues" that seemed to fuel worker insurgency and sabotage on many assembly lines. But the nature of the current wave of enthusiasm for employee involvement appears to have shifted, and the stories that circulate today are more often about how teams helped the company survive and compete against low-wage overseas competitors.

How far have such ideas penetrated? Freund and Epstein's (1984) survey of companies listed on the New York Stock Exchange found that 14 percent (and 22 percent of those based in manufacturing) had some form of quality circle program. But this may mean one circle that lasts only a few meetings in one plant. Levine and Strauss (1989) also caution that even where there are active programs, rarely do more than a quarter of the workers take part on QCs or similar programs. Gershenfeld (1987) concluded that fully operational employee involvement or Quality Work Life (QWL) schemes are found in only perhaps 10 to 15 percent of firms, but their number is growing.

Among these employee involvement activities, ESOPs have become more popular with changes in the tax code and declining industrial performance. In 1973, two years before the ESOP status defined in the Employee Retirement and Income Security Act (ERISA), Bloom (1985) found only 310 plans with ESOP features. The General Accounting Office (1986) estimated that in 1983 there were some 4,174 ESOPs. By 1987 the number had risen to 8,777

ESOPs covering 9 million employees (National Center for Employee Ownership, 1988). But ESOPs may or may not give workers any real increased involvement in decision making. The GAO (1986) estimated that in only 27 percent of the ESOPs they studied did managers report any increase in nonmanagerial decision-making power.

The interest in these various forms of employee involvement is growing, at least in part because the evidence is accumulating that they are good for business. In a recent review of the research on the relationship of ESOP structure and performance, Conte and Svejnar (1989) conclude that the productivity effects of ESOPs without increased worker participation are dubious. With worker participation, however, the evidence is unambiguous that productivity effects are substantial. Summarizing the effects of a broader range of worker participation in decision making on firm performance, Levine and Tyson (1989, p. 2) conclude that "there is usually a positive effect of participation on performance, sometimes a zero or statistically insignificant effect, and almost never a negative effect. . . . All other things equal, participation seems more likely to have a positive long-term effect on productivity when it involves decisions related to shop floor daily life, when it involves substantive decision-making rights rather than pure consultative arrangements, such as quality circles, and when it occurs in an industrial relations environment that creates employee commitment and the legitimacy of managerial authority." There are no data on whether these structural innovations are particularly common in more technologically dynamic firms nor whether their benefits are particularly great in such contexts.

Unions have in general been cautiously supportive of most of these structural changes—supportive because their members benefit either directly or through enhanced employment security, but cautious since such structural changes can sometimes raise thorny equity problems. In some cases unions have supported or even initiated these innovations, but they are resisted by a minority of the union movement. Katz (1988) outlines the various elements of this opposition. Linking compensation to company performance introduces an element of uncertainty into workers' pay that is almost never commensurate with the typically modest increase in workers' decision-making power. As such, performance-based pay is sometimes seen as a resurgent form of piecework. The critics also attack shop floor team structures as a subtle technique to achieve a speedup through increased peer pressure. They see direct involvement by workers in decision making as a way of undermining the union's representational role, fragmenting the work force within the plant, undermining worker solidarity, and projecting a false image of common interests between workers and managers. And the critics attack the broadening of job responsibilities as a way of speeding up work, and the abandonment of purely seniority-based promotion criteria as a legitimation of supervisor favoritism.

The power of these opposition arguments is not to be underestimated. Management sometimes provides indirect support for them by (1) using manifestly biased data as a pretext for change; (2) using automation to deskill work even when that is not the most profitable implementation approach; and (3) proposing unrealistically utopian visions of total commonality of interest in the "one happy family" of the firm.

Since they have so little of the institutionalized power held by workers in some of the social-democratic Western European countries, U.S. workers can hardly be expected to be enthusiastic about changes that, given the current balance of power, and given the declining strength of unions in the United States, can be expected to further reinforce management power.

## STRATEGY

One of the key reasons for poor performance in capitalizing on technology opportunities in manufacturing is simply that many firms have not seen manufacturing as a potentially important part of their competitive advantage. Marketing, sales, and finance have been more important elements in most corporate strategies. This is hardly surprising when so few chief executive officers come from a manufacturing background. The result has been underinvestment in manufacturing technology. The existing equipment has the almost irresistible advantage of having been already amortized: if investment strategy is allowed to become simply a matter of cost, no new investment project can ever compete with free equipment. The slow diffusion of numerically controlled machine tools and industrial robots seems to reflect this logic. Not surprisingly, U.S. manufacturing gets further and further behind the leading edge of international best practice.

Counteracting factors are emerging, however. Friar and Horwitch (1986) list four contributions to a growing awareness of technology as a competitive weapon: a loss of faith in other strategy doctrines, for example, those based exclusively on market share; the apparent success of small high-tech firms; the priority given to technology by very successful Japanese firms; and a growing awareness of the potential contribution of manufacturing strategy to competitiveness. One might also add that technology is bound to become a more important competitive variable if technological change is accelerating. Indeed, even a constant rate of technological change implies that from one period to the next, the absolute amount of change, and the corresponding technological and managerial challenge, increases exponentially. The result is an increasing number of firms attempting to manage technology strategically.

But strategic management of technology has a number of hurdles to surmount. First, technology strategy, like other forms of strategic planning, confronts the problem of the short time horizons of many corporate planners. The second hurdle to a more strategic approach to technology lies in the inevitable lags in management practice. Technology strategy as an organizational process presupposes a certain comfort level with the business strategy process. In most firms such a comfort level has been attained only recently if at all.

As firms surmount these hurdles, three trends have become visible. The strategy process is growing more sophisticated at both higher and lower levels of management, and the content of the new strategies ties technology choices more closely to human resource policies.

At the higher levels, the need to manage technology more strategically is leading more firms to created chief technology officer (CTO) positions (Adler and Ferdows, 1989; Rubenstein, 1989). A CTO can have a broad enough perspective to avoid pitfalls, to identify technological gaps, and, given sufficient organizational latitude, to be a catalyst in bringing together critical technological resources that might otherwise remain isolated in organizational fiefdoms.

The second trend in technology strategy is decentralization. As the rate of technological change accelerates, the strategy process must be decentralized because general management cannot deal alone with the growing information-processing burden. In a dynamic environment, technology and the associated strategy issues evolve too rapidly to maintain without excessive cost in the top-down hierarchical model. Functional managers must think and act more strategically, and general managers must lead a multifunctional and multilevel strategy dialogue.

The third trend is a closer linkage of technology and human resource strategies. The implementation of an organization's technology is very dependent on the organization's human resource strategy. Unfortunately, U.S. firms' human resource strategies too often treat labor as a variable cost. This leads to underinvestment in training. It also leads to workers' fear of displacement by automation, and therefore their resistance to new technology, as well as to fear that job-broadening initiatives will lead to the elimination of jobs, and thus a reluctance to share knowledge with incoming workers.

As a result, a growing number of firms are revising their human resource strategies. The previous section mentioned the growing interest in employee involvement strategies. We can also note that new technology clauses are now found in 25 percent of union contracts, up from 10 percent in 1961 (Bureau of National Affairs, 1986).

## CULTURE

In many ways, the most difficult challenges in adapting to the faster rate of emergence of new technology options are at the cultural level:

• When workers are asked to play a more active problem-identification and problem-solving role, the old authoritarian values that polarize "thinking" and "doing" and that separate workers from engineers and managers become obsolete.

• Innovation efforts are hobbled by the great status differences among different types of engineers, particularly by the gap that often separates product design engineers and manufacturing engineers.

• Innovation is constrained by status differences between lower and higher levels of managers—such differences impede the shift from the traditional autocratic, top-down strategy process to the more participative process that innovation requires.

Following Schein's (1984) suggestion, these cultural challenges can be analyzed at three levels of visibility: artifacts, values, and basic assumptions.

The repertoire of artifacts that divide workers from engineers and managers is well documented: white versus blue collars, reserved parking spaces, separate cafeterias. It is noteworthy that the firms that are seeking to communicate a greater commitment to worker participation often go to great lengths to change these outward signs of hierarchy. Managers at Saturn Corporation, for example, spent many months in joint meetings with workers to design the parking lots and their configuration with respect to the plant.

The artifacts that represent a status hierarchy between engineers are no less eloquent. One of the most visible expressions of the differentiation among engineers is in the fact that in many businesses design and manufacturing engineers are not only not at the same average pay levels but also not even on the same pay curves. In some companies with common curves, there is a lower maximum for manufacturing; in some others, manufacturing engineers are not included in profit sharing plans. Even where pay curves are similar across functions, a multiplicity of other symbols and prerequisites communicate the same message of inequality, such as the amount of office space and time to participate in professional activities.

Among managers, artifacts of corporate culture such as pay, bonuses, perks, and office location are often symptomatic of a hierarchy of influence that is characteristic of the "segmented" culture that Kanter (in this volume) has shown to be inimical to sustained innovation.

It is easy to ignore these artifacts as merely superficial symptoms. But consider the following case. A highly regarded, innovative company attempted to strengthen its technology development implementation capabilities by cultivating an ethos of teamwork between functions and layers. After several years, they found their efforts stalled by the compensation system. Compensation was managed the old way, with strong incentives for individual rather than group performance and strong differentiations between functions. While top management had supported the effort to change corporate values, it was not willing to incur the costs of the disruption that would ensue if the long-standing compensation system were changed.

Artifacts are part of a whole fabric of organizational routines. The degree of consistency of this fabric varies across organizations, but in organizations with "strong" cultures, each thread of the fabric reinforces the others. Cultural change efforts therefore cannot afford to ignore the obvious, the "merely artifactual." Efforts to make U.S. manufacturing more innovative will not succeed if they ignore the artifacts that embody the old ways.

Turning to the next, less visible, layer of culture—values—we find that the need for faster manufacturing introduction of new products, for more effective implementation of new process technologies, and for more aggressive improvement efforts appears to encourage the emergence of values of trust, cooperation, and respect. These values contrast with the values such as competitiveness and control that undergird the traditional power hierarchy between workers on the one hand and engineers and managers on the other.

The influence of these traditional values can be seen in traditional approaches to equipment design. Many engineers use an "idiot-proofing" approach in designing equipment, even though it limits the flexibility of the new systems. Some companies still install locks and antisabotage systems on their NC equipment. It is hard to imagine how they can compete effectively over the longer term against firms that by developing a culture based on greater mutual trust can benefit from shop floor programming.

Traditional values of competitiveness, hierarchy, and control also mark the relationship between manufacturing and design engineers, with a debilitating effect on many organizations' ability to introduce new products rapidly. The status hierarchy separating design and manufacturing is no longer a reflection of real differences in skill level and contribution, and this hierarchy therefore becomes increasingly dysfunctional.

Traditional status and power differentials within the management team are also being challenged. A new strategy is required to deal with the faster rate of technological change, and this strategy requires a shift in values. First, a more participatory process requires a reduction in the status differential that often separates functional from general managers. Second, when heightened competition and multifunctional technological opportunities require greater consistency of functional strategies, it becomes more difficult to justify the traditional hierarchy separating the functions. Finance and marketing have often dictated the overall direction of many organizations, while design engineering spelled out the desired new product line characteristics and manufacturing was left to "implement" the strategy that the other functions had articulated. In companies hoping to capitalize on the synergies between product and process technology opportunities, all the functions will need to enter the strategy formulation process as equals.

Value orientations typically reflect and reinforce an underlying set of implicit and usually unconscious assumptions. Some of the key assumptions shaping the values governing relations between workers and managers concern the unity or divergence of underlying interests. Assumptions play a key role in shaping behavior in these relations because firms face a real dilemma: given the unpredictability of a market economy, management needs workers who are both dependable and disposable (Hyman, 1987). It is easy for critics of values like cooperation and teamwork to scoff when management retains the right to dispose of "redundant" workers in business downturns (see, for example, Parker and Slaughter, 1988). How much of such trust can be expected to survive the trauma of layoffs?

This question, however, is not merely rhetorical. There is an accumulating number of case studies (reviewed by Greenhalgh and Rosenblatt, 1984) that suggest that management can indeed retain workers' trust even if they are forced to lay people off. The critical ingredient is whether management behaves in a way that warrants the workers' trust: if workers see the inescapable nature of the layoffs and if the process is managed with integrity, then even though the process is painful in the extreme, it does not have to destroy trust between workers and managers. Feelings of anger may well emerge, but they will be directed at the conditions that made the layoffs inevitable rather than at the "messenger bringing the bad news."

But this scenario depends critically on the assumptions that underlie managers' behavior and values. If managers see the firm as accountable only to themselves and the stockholders—if, in other words, they do not acknowledge the workers and the local community as legitimate stakeholders—then managers' behavior cannot but undermine any sense of trust that may have developed.

The assumptions held by unions are also important in this context. As Katz (1988) argues, union opposition to some of the current organizational redesign efforts reflects underlying assumptions regarding (1) the real extent of competitive pressures, (2) the nature of technological change, and (3) the underlying structural relationship between workers and managers. Opposition to these organizational innovations can be diversely motivated but often seems to be premised on three assumptions: (1) managers use the pretext of competitive pressure to squeeze workers when they could find other ways to compete, (2) the new process technologies are going to be used by managers to deskill work, and (3) the opposition between workers' and managers' interests is fundamental, and any effort to paper it over will, or should, fail.

U.S. industry must also contend with the broader cultural matrix in which it is embedded. The image of collaboration with which many Americans would spontaneously identify is that of baseball or American football, games with clearly defined, specialized roles based primarily on individual contributions. We rarely see ourselves as part of a basketball team engaged in spontaneous, reciprocal adaptation around a strategy defined only in its broad outline (Keidel, 1985). These individualistic assumptions are buttressed by the assumption that the most efficient principle of organization is competition rather than cooperation. The drawback of such a set of assumptions should be obvious, especially when compared with the team-oriented culture fostered by many Japanese companies.

These handicaps in artifacts, values, and assumptions are not beyond repair. They stem from and are exacerbated by the absence of a clear common external objective. In the absence of such an external objective, the goals of the organization's constituent groups turn inward, toward rivalry with each other. When senior management and union leaders, aided perhaps by real external challenges, can refocus the organization on a common external rival, competitive relationships can be turned into relations of cooperative complementarity.

The difference in the performance between externally focused, internally cooperative organizations and organizations that have turned inward and become absorbed by rivalry and hierarchical mechanisms of control will grow over time. A culture of hierarchy was perhaps efficient in more stable contexts; the increasingly dynamic character of product and process technology renders that culture obsolete. As the rate of technological change accelerates, hierarchical approaches will be progressively less effective than collaborative learning approaches.

## NEW TECHNOLOGY AND COMPETITIVE ADVANTAGE

The key problem framing this chapter was the relative undercapitalization of the technological potential by manufacturing industries. The previous sections have outlined the problems in six domains: the need for new technologies, for broader skills, for learning-oriented procedures, for organizational structures, for a more flexible strategy, and for a new cultural of collaboration.

These are not the only challenges facing industry, but they might provide us with a lens through which to view some of the others. Take for example the need for effective links to sources of information external to the firm: downstream links to customers; upstream links to materials and component suppliers, equipment vendors, and potentially relevant sources of scientific and technological knowledge; horizontal links through alliances, industry associations, and informal networking. In a more technologically dynamic environment, these linkages are precious elements in the firm's technological base, providing valuable knowledge that can leverage its internal technological capabilities.

Many observers have noted the growth of such linkages in recent years (Friar and Horwitch, 1986; Powell, 1987). Although an extensive analysis of this dimension is beyond the scope of this chapter, we should note that building and maintaining these external links require an appropriate set of internal organizational assets. Managing downstream linkages, for example, requires skills to interpret customers' comments, procedures to ensure the systematic collection and analysis of field information, organizational structures to ensure that results of this analysis flow to the appropriate people and that these people have some incentive to act on these results, a strategy that focuses attention on learning from users, and a cultural context that avoids the "not invented here" syndrome.

In concluding, I want to argue that augmenting U.S. industry's ability to capitalize on new technology will require a subtle change in the basic model that characterizes many organizations. In the traditional model, the organization was interpreted as a production system. Such a model is effective—it captures many of the key management challenges—when the rate of environmental change is slow. But in an environment of more dynamic technological and competitive change, the organization will need to be more flexible—it will need to be managed as a system with a dual objective of production and learning. As a result, policies in each domain will need to change:

• In the static model of the organization, it sufficed for the firm to pause every now and again to incorporate the equipment vendors' recent offerings. More dynamic approaches will demand that the organization be more proactive in creating its own technology development path.

• More dynamic learning-oriented policies in the skills domain will be needed to focus on problem-identification and problem-solving "know-why" rather than the operational "know-how" emphasized in traditional, static policy; training becomes development.

• In a more static environment, procedures were designed to buffer departments from each other, so that each department could better focus on its own distinct mission. But in a more dynamic context, missions change and response time becomes a critical competitive factor. Procedures, therefore, need to be seen as ways to consolidate ongoing learning—including learning how better to coordinate.

• In a static approach, structure was often allowed to degenerate into fiefdoms; in a dynamic approach, structures must be kept as flat as possible and flexible in their configuration of specialized, differentiated, and coordinated subunits.

• In the static model, strategy is elaborated by general management, and the role of functional managers is primarily to implement this strategy. The strategy is usually focused on attaining one-time improvements in market and financial outcomes. In the dynamic model on the other hand, strategy is collaboratively elaborated by all layers of the organization and defines both expected results and the path by which the requisite capabilities are to be developed.

• In the static model, culture is based on hierarchical authority. In the dynamic model, collaboration replaces rivalry, and culture is marked by encouragement to experiment and the right to fail.

Without this organizational redesign, the enormous potential of technology will be underexploited.

## REFERENCES

Adler, P. S. 1990a. Managing high-tech processes: The challenge of CAD/CAM. In Managing Complexity in High-Technology Industries, Systems and People, M. A. Von Glinow and S. A. Mohrman, eds. Oxford, England: Oxford University Press.

Adler, P. S. 1990b. NUMMI, Circa 1988. Department of Industrial Engineering and Engineering Management, Stanford University.

Adler, P., and K. Ferdows. 1989. The Chief Technology Officer. IEEM, Stanford University.

Allen, C. W. 1984. A case history of introducing CAD into a large aerospace company. In CADCAM in Education and Training, P. Arthur, ed. London: Kogan Page.

American Machinist. 1985. Manufacturing education. June:107.

Automation Technology Products. 1985. Sink or CIM? Campbell, Calif.: Automation Technology Products.

Aviation Week and Space Technology. April 11, 1988.

Bishop, J. 1989. Scientific Illiteracy: Causes, Costs and Cures. Cornell University Working Paper 89–12.

Bloom, S. M. 1985. Employee Ownership and Firm Performance. Ph.D. dissertation, Harvard University.

Brown, J. S., and S. E. Newman. 1985. Issues in Cognitive and Social

Ergonomics: From Our House to Bauhaus. Human-Computer Interaction 1:359–391.

Bureau of National Affairs, Inc. 1986. Collective Bargaining Negotiations and Contracts, Basic Patterns in Union Contracts. Vol. 2: Management and Union Rights. Washington, D.C.: BNA.

Collis, D. J. 1987. The machine tool industry and industrial policy, 1955–1982. Harvard University Graduate School of Business, Cambridge, Mass. February. Mimeo.

Commission on the Skills of the American Workforce. 1990. America's Choice: High Skills or Low Wages. Rochester, N.Y.: National Center on Education and the Economy.

Conte, M. A., and J. Svejnar. 1989. The performance effects of employee ownerships plans. Paper presented at the Brookings conference on Worker Compensation and Productivity, Washington, D.C., March.

Denison, E. F. 1985. Trends in American Economic Growth, 1929–1982. Washington, D.C.: Brookings Institution.

Dertouzos, M. L., R. K. Lester, R. M. Solow, and the MIT Commission on Industrial Productivity. 1989. Made in America: Regaining the Productive Edge. Cambridge, Mass.: MIT Press.

Flamm, K. 1986. International Differences in Industrial Robots. Washington, D.C.: Brookings Institution and World Bank.

Freund, W. C., and E. Epstein. 1984. People and Productivity. Homewood, Ill.: Irwin.

Friar, J., and M. Horwitch. 1986. The emergence of technology strategy: A new dimension of strategic management. Technology in Society 7, 2/3, M. Horwitch, ed.

General Accounting Office. 1986. Employee Stock Ownership Plans: Benefits and Costs of ESOP Tax Incentives for Broadening Stock Ownership. GAO/PEMD-87-8 (December 29). Washington, D.C.: Government Printing Office.

Gershenfeld, W. 1987. Employee participation in firm decisions. In Human Resources and Performance of the Firm, M. Kleiner, R. Block. M. Roomkin, S. Salsburg, eds. Madison, Wisc.: Industrial Relations Research Association.

Gouldner, A. 1954. Patterns of Industrial Bureaucracy. New York: Free Press.

Greenhalgh, L., and Z. Rosenblatt. 1984. Job insecurity: Toward conceptual clarity. Academy of Management Review 9(3):438–448.

Hodder, J. E., and H. E. Riggs. 1985. Pitfalls in evaluating risky projects. Harvard Business Review 63(1):128–135.

Hutchinson, R. 1984. Flexibility is the key to economic feasibility of automated small batch manufacturing. Industrial Engineering (June).

Hyman, R. 1987. Strategy or structure? Capital, labor and control. Work, Employment and Society 1,1(March):25–55.

Imai, M. 1986. Kaizen. New York: Random House.

Institute for Defense Analyses. 1988. The Role of Concurrent Engineer-

ing in Weapons Systems Acquisition, IDA Report R-338 (December).
Washington, D.C.: IDA.

International Association for the Evaluation of Educational Achievement.
1988. Science Achievements in Seventeen Countries: A Preliminary
Report. New York: Pergamon Press.

Jaikumar, R. 1986. Post-industrial manufacturing. Harvard Business
Review 64(6):69–76.

Jerahov, G. E. 1984. Training Requirements for an Interactive CAD/
CAM System. Autofact 6.

Kaplan, R. S. 1983. Measuring manufacturing performance: A new challenge for managerial accounting research. The Accounting Review
58(4):686–705.

Kaplan, R. S. 1986. Must CIM be justified by faith alone? Harvard
Business Review 64(2):87–95.

Katz, H. 1988. Policy debates over work reorganization in North American unions. In New Technology and Industrial Relations, R. Hyman
and W. Streeck, eds. Oxford: Basil Blackwell.

Keidel, R. 1985. Game Plans. New York: Dutton.

Kurokawa, K. 1988. Quality and innovation. IEEE Circuits and Devices
Magazine 4(4):3–80.

Levine, D., and G. Strauss. 1989. Participation at Work. University of
California, Berkeley.

Levine, D., and L. D. Tyson. 1989. Participation, Productivity and the
Firm's Environment. Paper presented at the Brookings conference on
Worker Compensation and Productivity, Washington, D.C., March.

MacDuffie, J. P., and J. F. Krafcik. 1989. Flexible Production System and Manufacturing Performance: The Role of Human Resources and Technology. Paper presented at the Academy of Management, August 16, 1989.

Majchrzak, A., T. Chang, W. Barfield, R. Eberts, and G. Salvenday. 1987.
Human Aspects of Computer-Aided Design. Philadelphia, Pa.: Fracis
and Taylor.

Marchisio, O., and G. Guiducci. 1983. Effect of the introduction of the
CAD system upon organizational systems and professional roles. In
Systems Design For, With, and By the Users, D. Ciborra and L. Schneider,
eds. Amsterdam: North Holland.

Monden, Y. 1983. Toyota Production System. Atlanta, Ga.: Institute of
Industrial Engineers.

National Center for Employee Ownership. 1988. The Employee Ownership Report, Vol. 8, No. 4 (September-October). Oakland, Calif.: National Center for Employee Ownership.

National Research Council. 1986. Human Resource Practices for Implementing Advanced Manufacturing Technology. Manufacturing Studies Board. Washington, D.C.: National Academy Press.

National Research Council. 1988. A Research Agenda for CIM. Washington, D.C.: National Academy Press.

National Science Board. 1987. Science and Engineering Indicators—
1987. Washington, D.C.: Government Printing Office.

Office of Technology Assessment, U.S. Congress. 1980. Technology and Steel Industry Competitiveness. Washington, D.C.: Government Printing Office.

Organ, D. W., and C. N. Greene. 1981. The effects of formalization on professional involvement: A compensatory process approach. Administrative Science Quarterly 26:237–252.

Parker, M., and J. Slaughter. 1988. Choosing Sides: Unions and the Team Concept. Boston, Mass.: South End Press.

Podsakoff, P. M., L. J. Williams, and W. D. Todor. 1986. Effects of organizational formalization on alienation among professionals and non-professionals. Academy of Management Journal 29(4):820–831.

Powell, W. W. 1987. Hybrid organizational arrangements: New form of transitional development? California Management Review (Fall): 67–87.

Rubenstein, A. H., 1989. Managing Technology in the Decentralized Firm. New York: Wiley.

Rumberger, R. W. 1981. Overeducation in the U.S. Labor Market. New York: Praeger.

Salzman, H. 1985. The New Merlins of Taylor's Automations?—The Impact of Computer Technology on Skills and Workplace Organizations. Department of Sociology, Brandeis University and Center for Applied Social Science, Boston University, Boston, Mass.

Schein, F. H. 1984. Coming to an awareness of organizational culture. Sloan Management Review (Winter):3–16.

Schonberger, R. J. 1982. Japanese Manufacturing Techniques: Nine Hidden Lessons in Simplicity, New York: Free Press.

Senker, P., and E. Arnold. 1984. Implications of CADCAM for training in the engineering industry. CADCAM in Education and Training, P. Arthur, ed. London: Kogan Page.

Singelmann, J., and M. Tienda. 1985. The process of occupational change in a service society: The case of the United States, 1960-1980. In New Approaches to Economic Life, B. Roberts, R. Finnegan, and D. Gallie, eds. Manchester University Press.

Spenner, K. I. 1988. Technological change, skill requirements and education: The case for uncertainty. In The Impact of Technological Change on Employment and Economic Growth, R. M. Cyert and D. C. Mowery, eds. Cambridge, Mass.: Ballinger.

Suzaki, K. 1987. The New Manufacturing Challenge. New York: Free Press.

Thurow, L. 1987. A weakness in process technology. Science 238(December):1659–1663.

Tomasko, R. M. 1987. Downsizing: Reshaping the Corporation for the Future. New York: American Management Association.

Traversa, L. L. 1984. High-touch Requirements for High-tech CAD/CAM. Autofact 6—Conference Proceedings. Dearborn, Mich.: Society of Manufacturing Engineers.

Tucker, W. W., and R. L. Clark. 1984. From Drafter to CAD Operator:

A Case Study in Adaptation to the Automated Workplace. SME technical paper. MM 84-629. Dearborn, Mich.: Society of Manufacturing Engineers.

U.S. Department of Labor. 1987. Apprenticeship: Past and present. Employment and Training Administration, Bureau of Apprenticeship and Training. Washington, D.C.: U.S. Department of Labor.

*Wall Street Journal.* 1989. October 19, p. B1.

Wingert, B., M. Rader, and U. Riehm. 1981. Changes in working skill in the fields of design caused by use of computers. In CAD in Medium Sized and Small Industries, J. Mermet, ed. Amsterdam: North Holland.

People and Technology in the Workplace. 1991.
Pp. 89–101. Washington, D.C:
National Academy Press.

# Design and Implementation of a Process for a Large-Scale System Change at Boeing

BRUCE GISSING

In 1988 the Boeing Company decided to construct a $235-million Sheet Metal Fabrication Center to replace an existing facility that employs 2,600 people. This case describes the initial stages—plans and organizational approaches—of Boeing's effort to involve employees and managers in the design of the physical plant and the production processes of the new facility. The effort, to be continued after the facility has opened, represents an experiment in creating a common commitment to continuous improvement in the efficiency and responsiveness of a large new production facility.

## COMPANY OVERVIEW

Boeing, together with its subsidiaries, is one of America's major aerospace firms, the largest manufacturer of transport aircraft in the Western World and the largest nonagricultural employer in the northwestern United States. Boeing was born in Seattle in 1916 (initially under the name Pacific Aero Products, Inc.) and continues to maintain its corporate headquarters there. Boeing's principal business is conducted through three major divisions, Boeing Commercial Airplane Group, Boeing Defense and Space, and Boeing Computer Services. Located throughout the world, the total employee population is nearly 155,000, approximately two-thirds of which is located in Seattle and surrounding areas of Puget Sound.

The Boeing Company is organized in a traditional work structure, with an established "pyramid" hierarchy. Many administrative functions are centralized, particularly in the support, or service, organizations responsible for policy development and implementation. A more decentralized structure exists in manufacturing and engineering disciplines. This has allowed for maximum flexibility and responsiveness to day-to-day production issues.

## A NEW FACILITY: DECISION AND DESIGN

The global market continues to shape the growth and development of the Boeing Company. World competition is on the rise. To remain a leader, the company must make the necessary changes to keep up with new technologies and to incorporate them into manufacturing strategies.

Technology has always been the major driver of change at Boeing. The Boeing Company's founder and namesake, William E. Boeing, once wrote, "Our task is to keep everlastingly at research and experiment, to adapt our laboratories to production as soon as practicable, to let no new improvement in flying and flying equipment pass us by." However, American industry today reveals a long and increasingly obvious record of less-than-optimum results in technological innovation and implementation, a record that overlooks the contributions of individuals. Today there is a clear need to design ways to develop successful relationships between automation, or advancements in technology, and people. As always, the challenge is to use most effectively the ideas, talents, and contributions of the work force to produce quality products at a reasonable and competitive price in a timely way while exploiting the latest developments in technology.

Today's work force is changing. Workers today

- have a stronger self-image;
- have greater self-respect and expect treatment as individuals;
- are less tolerant of authoritarianism and hierarchies;
- want to play participative role in their work;
- feel stronger entitlements;
- believe they will continue to improve;
- want to participate in decisions affecting their jobs, and moreover, believe they have a right to do so; and
- have increased concerns for leisure and family life.

These examples represent significant differences from what managers believed workers wanted just a few years ago. In short, the work ethic of employees is shifting. Today, more workers seek jobs that are interesting, meaningful, and challenging. Industry must listen, recognize the differences, and take the necessary steps to support these changes.

Within the context of global competition and a changing work force at Boeing, a specific element has provided an opportunity for organizational redesign. The Fabrication Division in Boeing Commercial Airplanes is an organization of approximately 15,000 employees located predominantly in a plant about 20 miles south of Seattle in Auburn, Washington. Many of these employees work many miles away from the home plant. The focus of this case study is a group of about 2,600 employees currently located in Seattle. This work force comprises both union-represented and non-union-represented employees. The hourly work force is covered by the International Association of Machinists and Aerospace Workers (IAM). In addition, the Seattle Professional Engineering Employees Association (SPEEA) represents technical nonexempt and engineering exempt staff. Together they make up approximately 72 percent of the existing sheet metal work force. The primary objective of this factory is to fabricate parts, where a need for in-house immediate-response capability is critical to meeting customers' requirements. Known as the sheet metal organization, its primary customers are the divisions responsible for assembly of Boeing Commercial Airplanes. The existing facility occupies one million square feet in four buildings in Seattle built between 1938 and 1949. It has 247 pieces of major equipment, mostly 20 to 30 years old. Material handling systems include fork lifts, tub skids, A-frame transportation dollies, and storage assembly boxes. The facility employs 2,600 factory and support personnel working on 101,000 active part numbers to produce 8.5 million parts per year. It receives on the average 1,000 new part numbers per week. Twenty-five percent of the workload is repetitive (i.e., production that is performed more than once and is within standard flow time); the remaining 75 percent is work requiring immediate response to unanticipated schedule changes (i.e., new customer introductions, new configurations, and short flow implementation). The flow process of a typical part is 40 days, during which it travels 1.5 miles from start to finish.

In July 1988, the corporation authorized a $235-million Sheet Metal Fabrication Center to be located with the parent plant facilities in Auburn. The three primary goals for the new center (in addition to the external issues already mentioned) are improvement in quality and increased efficiency; environmental efficiency; and support of emergent work (responsiveness to customer requirements).

The proposed 816,000-square-foot Sheet Metal Center is described as follows:

*Layout*
- Cell concept (streamlining work process flow); parts will travel 0.3 miles versus 1.5 miles.
- Automated material storage and retrieval system will be installed.
- 170 new pieces of major equipment; 272 existing rebuilt for new factory.

*Factory Systems Application*
- Shop floor control.
- Integration into existing related computer systems, e.g., Sheet Metal Analysis, Retrieval, and Tracking System, Computer-Aided Three-Dimensional Interactive Application, Order Location System.

*Work Force Administration*
- High employee commitment and involvement system; a Socio-Technical System (STS).
- Reduced job titles and broadened scope of responsibility.
- Business Production Unit, includes all functions responsible for product delivery along with related support functions.

With the introduction of the latest technology, not all 2,600 employees will be needed in the new factory. Although specific numbers are not yet available, Boeing's objective is to reduce the number of employees by about 45 percent. The majority of this decrease will come from the support functions. Affected employees will be afforded retraining opportunities for placement elsewhere in the company. Details of this redeployment are currently being developed. Boeing does not intend to lay off employees as a result of this new technology.

These comments are representative of a dynamic process that did not actually get under way until spring, 1989. Therefore, the company is in the preliminary stages, with a great deal more to learn and work through.

## SOCIO-TECHNICAL SYSTEM

Since Boeing had never before participated in such an enormous undertaking, the company sought the advice and guidance of a consultant with "hands on" experience in effecting organizational change. Richard Cherry of Consulting for Organizational Effectiveness, Inc., was hired as a consultant. He introduced the concept of a Socio-Technical System, or STS, to seek the best fit between the way people work and the work people do. It is comparable to the high-commitment, high-involvement, high-performance systems referred to above.

At the request of Dr. Cherry, a consultant from inside Boeing was identified to work closely with him. Specifically, Boeing sought someone who had a working knowledge of the existing factory, demonstrated open and progressive thinking, had established a high degree of integrity and credibility with all Sheet Metal employees, and had been involved in training, including quality improvement and group facilitation. In addition, this "first line" supervisor would be provided additional training at various seminars and workshops to gain specific tools to aid in this transition.

To work with Dr. Cherry, a group of managers was assembled. These men and women were included among the company's "stakeholders." Each represented a vested interest in the existing factory and would be an integral part of the new center. This was done specifically to ensure that these decision makers would actually have to "eat a piece of the cake they baked."

It is important to mention here that these stakeholders included representatives from each of the two labor unions that have employees from their bargaining units in the existing Sheet Metal factory.

This team adopted the name Socio-Technical Development Team, or STDT. They began preparing for their tasks through a series of team-building exercises. All team members visited at least one plant around the country where some form of STS had been implemented, and some attended conferences on this subject. The results of this exposure were shared with all members of the STDT. This in no way should be interpreted as an attempt at finding a blueprint to follow. The primary goal from the beginning was to design a system that would be tailored to the Boeing Company and the Sheet Metal Center, appreciating the uniqueness of that environment.

The initial learning process of these stakeholders took about three months. Also included during this time was the development of a structure that would support the work to be done. It consisted of a steering committee, the Socio-Technical Development Team, a diagonal slice (or cross section, of Sheet Metal employees), focus groups, integrators, and implementation groups.

At the same time, the following mission statement for STDT was developed:

> *Development and recommendation of a plan that "best fits" employee needs with systems and processes, while providing an environment in which people can be innovative in the production of hardware to the quality, cost, and schedule objectives of our customer.*

The group saw itself as the primary design or "sanction" group. Given its charter, the STDT then created mission statements for each of the groups in the support structure. The following charter was developed for the new Sheet Metal Center:

> *The Sheet Metal Center is responsible to provide detail components, minor subassemblies fit for use on a high-quality, least-cost, schedule-responsive basis that fully meets the needs of its customers. The Sheet Metal Center organization is an autonomous manufacturing business unit within the Fabrication Division, and as such is responsible for operational and financial performance within the boundaries of this charter.*
>
> *The Sheet Metal Center acts as Boeing Commercial Airplane's (BCA) primary sheet metal manufacturing capability for fabrication of designated product line hardware and unique fabrication capabilities.*
>
> *Support to Boeing organizations other than BCA is limited to developmental programs requiring unique capabilities or emergent support not available elsewhere.*

### Design Principles

Obviously, the STDT needed a shared vision and support for the Socio-Technical System and its application to the Sheet Metal Center. Introduced by Dr. Cherry and after much discussion, the following design principles were endorsed:

• *People support what they help create.* Effective organizations are more likely to be developed when the individual employees who make the organization work are involved in the design of the organization. They are closer to the work that gets done, their ideas are necessary and valuable to effective design, and if they have been involved they will work hard to make their ideas work.

• *A balance and symmetry between all stakeholders must be maintained.* All groups that have a stake in the performance of an organization ought to be involved in the design of that organization. No one group should have all the say or get everything it wants, but all must be listened to and have their ideas and points of view explored. For example, SPEEA, IAM, management, employees, the Fabrication Division, and the Boeing Company are major stakeholders. The company's customers are also major stakeholders and ought to be listened to closely.

• *Control (the ability to make certain things happen or not happen) is widely dispersed through an organization.* All employees in an organization have some degree of control over what happens or does not happen within the organization. This principle relates directly to the next.

• *Authority should be consistent with control.* In designing effective organizations, it is critically important to provide employees with control and appropriate authority to exercise that control. To continue to put control only at the supervisor level or above is inconsistent with where the authority is needed. For this reason, in many newer organizations, employees at all levels are given greater authority to control or manage their operations.

• *Management is the responsibility of all employees—not just managers.* With appropriate authority, employees today are planning, solving problems, making decisions, and monitoring the performance of their operations. Planning, decision making, and controlling are functions carried out by all employees—labor as well as management—in any organization.

After the STDT embraced these principles as its own, Dr. Cherry introduced the structure around which the team would apply its beliefs. This model is referred to as the Bull's-eye, a set of 12 statements reflecting the managing plant organization's beliefs about people and work and the relationship between these beliefs and the objectives for the plant organization. The Bull's-eye concept includes the following features:

*Primary Features*

1. *Technology*:   The manufacturing process(es) to transform raw materials into finished products.

2. *Jobs and People*:   How work is arranged to accomplish the responsibilities of the job.

3. *Layout*:   The physical allocation and design of equipment and facilities within the plant.

4. *Information Systems*:   The flow of communications within the unit.

*Second-Level Features*

5. *Structure*:   The formal reporting relationships, typically represented by a physical drawing or chart.

6. *Supervisor/Management*:   The definition of duties and re-

sponsibilities expected of individuals occupying particular posi-
tion(s) of leadership within the unit.

7. *Union/Management*:  The relationship between the two in
achieving agreed-upon objectives.

8. *Rewards*:  Mechanisms and processes developed within the
unit for recognizing differences in performance and learning.

*Third-Level Features*

9. *Recruitment/Selection*: Mechanisms and procedures employed
in developing an applicant pool, and the screening of potential
employees from within this pool.

10. *Orientation/Training*:  Providing employees with the information and skills necessary to operate effectively in the organization and to perform their work.

11. *Personnel Policies/Practices*:  Corporate, divisional, and local unit policies regarding the treatment and roles of employees
within the plant.

12. *Symbols*:  Those characteristics of the unit which serve to
distinguish or differentiate one class of employees from another.

As a point of reference, using the elements of the Bull's-eye and
the endorsed design principles, the STDT put together its own set
of beliefs, one for each one of the 12 features.  This was done to
solidify a common vision as well as to further the notion of taking ownership of our own beliefs collectively in support of the
Bull's-eye.


*Early Implementation*

Having achieved a common appreciation and understanding of
work design, the STDT then began to put its ideas into action.  In
an unprecedented event, the STDT received approval to conduct a
three-day, off-site working meeting to bring, for the first time
thus far in the process, a representative group of current Sheet
Metal employees together.  Existing management was consulted
on the number of employees they felt should attend.  The decision resulted in about 8 percent, or 250 employees, being made
available.  The group of 250 represented a cross section, or "diagonal slice," of personnel in the Sheet Metal factory.  All paycodes,
including management,  were included, based on the current per-
centages each represented, by payroll.  A video explaining the process was shown to all 2,600 Sheet Metal employees, who were
asked to volunteer and to send in their "application."  About 800
employees responded, and the STDT made the final selection.

Both internal and external assistance was called upon to design the three-day session. In addition, because of Boeing's three-shift operation, attention was given to include appropriate representation from each shift. Age, sex, and Equal Employment Opportunity codes were considered as the choices were made.

The meetings were held at the Seattle-based IAM Local 751 (hourly employees) Union Hall. On the first day of this three-day working session, participants listened to various Boeing executives and labor leaders talk about the reasons for change in relation to both external and internal pressures. In addition, the company's commitment was reinforced, as well as the unions' support for the process.

Participants were given a general overview of what they could expect over the next three days. Particular emphasis was placed on explaining that employees would play an important part in making recommendations about how the new factory would operate. Presentations were made describing the current status of design and development of the new Sheet Metal Center, and the parameters within which participants would focus their attention were identified based on the assumptions and decisions that had already been made. On the second day, the participants were introduced to the specific design principles, philosophy, goals, and mission of the Sheet Metal Center. Groups were organized representative of a work crew. All groups were given instructions for participating in a simulation of a traditional factory. This is referred to as the Flying Frisbee Factory exercise. It had all the roles of a traditional factory; there was a supervisor, cutters, painters, quality control inspectors, material handlers, etc., and customers who either accepted or rejected "frisbees" based on their expectations.

After following the predetermined time for this exercise, the participants discussed the results of their work. Collectively, they determined that their quantity was relatively high, but their quality was not. Participants were then given an opportunity to discuss what they would do differently to improve quality. Their ideas were put into action when they were given yet another opportunity to build "frisbees." The results this time produced less quantity, but greatly improved quality. At this point, participants began to embrace with a heightened sense of awareness the reality of their task.

On the last day of the session, participants were asked to write down their ideas on "Post-it" notes and place them on a large piece of paper that supported each element of the Bull's-eye. Later, each participant was given 12 red dots (strong support) and 12 yellow dots (no support). At intervals controlled by the facilitators and logistics personnel, participants placed the dots on the same large sheets of paper until they had gone through all of the 12 Bull's-eye features. This process, which is designed to capture information in a structured way, is commonly referred to as synergy.

Compiling these recommendations was no small task; it resulted in more than 3,000 different ideas, both pro and con. These results were made available to each participant along with the information exchanged over the three-day session.

Following each day's work, the participants were asked to evaluate their feelings about what had gone on. The STDT and the three-day design group joined in the review. An agenda for the next day also was reviewed, and concerns or issues were included for the purpose of clearing up misconceptions.

At this point, it is important to note that the employees were organized into a "structured" event because the fact that Boeing operates in a traditional environment could not be ignored. Although participants were afforded the greatest possible degree of creativity, realistic parameters and boundaries were set to support and guide their work. This is a most delicate process and requires careful balancing to be effective. Also, it is true that you get out what you put in. Every effort to achieve a most successful Sheet Metal Center was, and will continue to be, applied.

As noted earlier, on the third day of the meeting, participants were given instructions concerning the next step. They learned that there would be focus groups consisting of six people for each of the 12 elements of the Bull's-eye. Then the participants would again be Sheet Metal employees asked to volunteer from the original group of 250 and would have to state in 25 words or less why they wanted to be involved in this next step.

The STDT selected a committee to act as interviewers. It included one STDT management representative and one STDT union leader from each bargaining unit. After about a month, this group of three had selected 72 participants to make up the focus groups.

The STDT decided that the focus groups would be given maximum freedom to explore and understand the issues that came out of the synergism exercise. This meant establishing, in addition to their responsibilities, their own budget to use for plant visits and time spent on the project, estimated to be eight hours (on first shift) per week for a period of six months.

This time frame was established based on the STDT's knowledge of deadlines that would have to be met by April 1989. The steering committee expects a set of objectives for the 1993 period. They have been assigned the task of defining both the what and the why of these objectives, *not* at start-up, but five years hence from 1988 when they began; in other words, what they want the organization to be like in the new center by 1993. Included in the model, along with the design principles and Bull's-eye, is the realization that focusing only on start-up expectations gives the people involved nothing to work toward.

### Labor and Management Cooperation

Because the Boeing Company has been structured largely on a traditional hierarchical structure, its labor and management roles have been adversarial from time to time. Although some work had already been done in breaking down those walls to progress, the planning process for the Sheet Metal Center has provided a unique setting for more effective communication and mutually beneficial negotiations.

From the start, the Boeing Company has not avoided the reality of bargaining agreements; instead it has recognized the absolute necessity of reaching acceptable agreements that support the objectives of both labor and management.

As late as 1986, Boeing introduced into the IAM agreement an article that allowed for pilot projects and, more important, opportunities for exploring new ways of doing business. This direction provides a new opportunity for agreeing on the future success of the aerospace and aircraft industry. Although Boeing is not breaking new ground in American industry, it recognizes the benefits of such a cooperative relationship.

The IAM bargaining agreement, as well as SPEEA's, is up for renewal in fourth quarter of 1989. That adds a unique feature to the negotiation process for the Sheet Metal Center.

There are numerous labor issues that will be addressed in upcoming months. Until the steering committee receives recommendations from the focus groups, it is impractical to elaborate on what these will be. In any event, a joint labor-management committee under the steering committee and the STDT will review the recommendations further for possible future adoption.

### LESSONS

The following lessons embody the essence of work to date:

- Get the unions involved early.

• Identify the management who are "stakeholders" and empower them to be responsive and responsible for the "deliverables."
• The employees directly involved will test the system.
• Allow more budget and time for all teams to do their jobs.
• Be more relaxed (especially executives) regarding the deliverables.
• Break through indifference and resistance.
• Do hire a consultant if in-house capability does not exist.
• Recognize that a consultant does not have all the answers.
• Do assign in-house personnel to work with the consultant.
• Do not be talked off your course of action once the commitment is made.
• Include *all* stakeholders.
• Communicate frequently with all employees involved, especially  first- and second-level management.
• "Walk the way you talk," or demonstrate your understanding of, and belief in, the STS through your daily activities.
• Plan to do it right the first time; that is, plan, check, and act to ensure a successful outcome.
• Maintain a record of process development, design, and implementation for future reference.
• "Trust the process," or stay on course with the objectives.

## NEXT STEPS

Boeing does not expect to have all the issues and recommendations in place when the new factory opens. Implementation groups will be formed, bringing together representatives from the unions and a diagonal slice of all employees, including management. Their task will be to determine how to accomplish those recommendations that have been endorsed for application in the new facility. Their role will be to ensure congruence and systemic compatibility, that is, building in an interdependence between all functions and supporting procedures throughout the organization.

The steering committee is expected to develop the "roadmap" for achieving the changes agreed upon. Further, all involved employees, unions, and functional management will have to pay particular attention to integration of their efforts into the transition plans to provide for a smooth phasing-in and phasing-out process. For example, issues that must be considered include the attrition rate of existing employees, matching workers' abilities with the phasing schedule for movement of equipment and the training and retraining required, as well as an increased rate of airplane production in support of Boeing's customers. This is no small task!

In summary, the large-scale organizational redesign that Boeing is undertaking is not only precedent-setting but necessary as the company moves into the next century. This experience offers the opportunity to learn not only a new way of doing business but also a new way of involving employees in achieving continuous improvements in both the quality of the product and the quality of their working lives.

People and Technology in the Workplace. 1991.
Pp. 102–118. Washington, D.C:
National Academy Press.

# A Case History of Organizational Change: People and New Technology

JAMES R. HETTENHAUS

International Bio-Synthetics (IBIS, Inc.) is a shareholder-originated joint venture between the Shell Group and Royal Gist-brocades to commercialize the results of research and development. Formed in 1987, IBIS produces fine organic chemicals, biopolymers, pharmaceutical intermediates, and enzymes. This case study describes the process by which IBIS increased its productivity by more than 30 percent and reduced its costs of operation through organizational change and the concurrent introduction of centralized process control technology.

The company has three manufacturing locations—Kingstree, South Carolina; Halebank, United Kingdom; and Brugges, Belgium. Products in Kingstree are primarily industrial enzymes used by the starch, detergent, and textile industries. The Kingstree plant was built in 1960 and expanded in 1962 and 1966. Extensive modifications to plant processes were made in 1978, and expansion occurred in 1983.

Manufacturing operations are mostly large-scale fermentation. Fermentors include batch, fed batch, and solid substrate types of varying size, exceeding 100 cubic meters. Recovery of products is by aqueous or solvent processing. Unit operations include filtration, evaporation, ultrafiltration, drying, and blending.

## TRADITIONAL APPROACH

For the first 24 years, the plant was organized by function (Figure 1). Six levels existed between the operator and the president or managing director. Departments worked independently, relying on the hierarchy to coordinate activities. Shift supervisors were assisted by lead men in various processing areas to direct operator activities. Decision making was necessarily autocratic, since information relating to cost, customer requirements, and technical and administrative facts was available only to management. Other people were not trained to use it. Operator training was limited to specific processes, resulting in little flexibility for assignment. Production tracking was referred to as the "paper mill" and required time and clerical assistance. Production results were often delayed because of detailed documentation of the batch process that occurred as part of production tracking.

Cyclical swings in business resulted in temporary layoffs. The work force reduction was determined by seniority. Performance appraisals were not made for production operators. As new work assignments were made to fill in behind the vacancies, a decline in performance was inevitable. The shift supervisor received the brunt of the blame associated with the disruption and, paradoxically, had more work in directing people in the new assignments.

Overall plant performance was considered satisfactory. Regular investments were made to keep the plant technically current. In 1983, as part of the solvent-recovery process, a distributed process

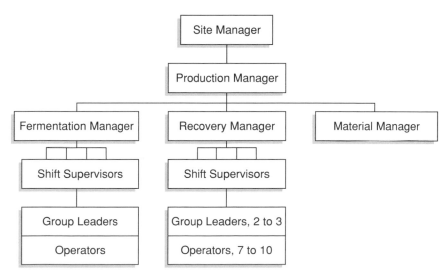

FIGURE 1  Organization of the Kingstree plant, by function, before 1984.

control system was installed along with programmable logic controllers (PLCs) for operation of new membrane filtration and ultrafiltration equipment. In 1982 Quality Circles were established. About 20 percent of the employees volunteered to work on projects that would improve quality. A facilitator met with five groups, provided some basic training, and completed one cycle—one project per group. The activities were outside of normal work requirements, and participation was limited to less than 20 percent of employees. Training for first-level supervisors was also initiated. A traditional text was used to introduce basic supervisory concepts. As an outgrowth of Quality Circle exposure and supervisory concepts, the first-level supervisors undertook a project to develop an operator performance appraisal system in 1984.

## A CONCURRENT APPROACH TO SYSTEM CHANGE

In 1984 a plant evaluation team was formed to determine the potential for improvements. An assessment of both the organizational and technical system capabilities yielded recommendations for moving toward a more participatory work environment. At the same time, enabling technologies were installed to consolidate data for analysis and better disseminate the information. The job redesign that resulted from the assessment employed a sociotechnical approach.

Autonomous self-regulating teams would be formed for material handling, maintenance, laboratory administration, and production, with initial emphasis on production. The organization would be pushed to make effective use of material requirements planning (MRP), manufacturing resource planning (MRP II), decision support systems, and centralized control of the process operations.

In addition, first-level supervisors would move to a supportive resource role, providing direction and support to the team as needed. As supervisory technical resources (STRs), they ensure that the level of operations is maintained and improved congruent with the team concept. Essentially everyone in the plant would have a new and expanded role.

In 1985 plant implementation began when the new site manager, a member of the evaluation team, held a series of plantwide meetings to communicate to all employees the future work environment. He enlisted their participation in developing and implementing the plan to achieve the new environment.

## ORGANIZATIONAL RENEWAL

The Quality Circle training and supervisor training, begun in 1984, were good reference points for the plantwide effort in 1985. The Quality Circles provided an introduction to problem-solving skills and interpersonal skills essential for the emerging teams. The basic management knowledge gained by the supervisors helped them begin the transition from direct control of workers to becoming a "resource" with multiple roles.

In 1985 the department shift supervisors were replaced by one plant superintendent who rotated with the shifts to be available as a "resource." This permitted the work groups to evolve into teams while freeing former shift supervisors to carry out their new assignment as team resources. In 1986 the role of plant superintendents was discontinued on the shift, and they also moved to a new, more focused role as team resources.

### A New Shift Schedule

The production team rotation was changed to permit five crews to rotate through a five-week schedule. Developed with the assistance of a physiological psychologist, the schedule was designed to accommodate five crews so that training could be accomplished without overtime.

In determining the new schedule, a representative from each shift was selected by the members of that shift. The representative was to participate in evaluating other schedules. Initially, the representatives assumed their role would be simply to rubber stamp a predetermined scenario. The consultant who was directing the effort was quite explicit that there was no predetermined schedule, that it was up to them as representatives to evaluate alternatives, take the evaluation back to their fellow shift members, and discuss the pros and cons. After several iterations, the teams should have an understanding on disagreements and agreements and approach a consensus for the new work schedule. This first experience was an important precursor to getting participation in other activities. During the early stages of implementation it became clear that many of the participants needed to improve interpersonal and meeting skills.

### Individual Performance Appraisals

In 1984 pro forma appraisals were given as a trial. Feedback was used to adjust for actual appraisals, to begin in 1985. As planned, the following year the performance appraisals for all individuals, including operators, were implemented.  This permitted a move from work force curtailment by seniority to work force curtailment based on performance.  Although layoffs are certainly undesirable and can generally be attributed to poor management, the cyclical nature of the business in 1985 required a temporary work force reduction.  Without performance appraisals, some of the most capable operators would have been lost and the new organizational efforts would have been jeopardized.

### Process Performance Measurement

In 1985 a personal computer (PC) network was installed to link the laboratory with the production and accounting departments to improve process performance measurement.  The lab results, coupled with production information, permitted fast determination of material balances around each unit operation: fermentation, harvest, treatment, filtration, concentration, and blending. The rapid feedback of these results to the operating teams allowed them to measure their performance and make adjustments as required.

Clipboards, manual calculators, and paper shuffling were eliminated. More time was available to analyze and solve problems.  By year end, process performance had improved 40 percent from the baseline established in 1984. The improvement was primarily attributed to rapid feedback of results to better trained operators. The operators were using their new autonomy to work smarter. When a variance from production targets was identified, it would be identified earlier, and action would be more rapid and more correct.

In addition, the results of the innovation, or corrective action, were easily communicated over the PC network.  The network's common data base included all operating amendments, the reasons for changing the process, and shift logs.

### Training

The training program was established using the reassigned shift supervisors as instructors.  Two former supervisors attended a special course to provide them the necessary training skills.  The new five-week rotation provided four days for training without overtime.  Two days were initially used for group training; the other two for individual training.  The first training focus was on job skills—why we do what we do. New mistakes were taken as a learning experience. A pass-or-continue policy was emphasized to reduce the fear of failure and to help people gain some self-improvement. When a mistake in processing occurred, it was termed an "unusual incident." Team meetings were held to analyze the problem. Problem-solving skills were developed simultaneously. Alternatives were evaluated and corrective action taken. In some cases discipline was recommended, especially as the team matured.

The second phase of team training focused on skills and knowledge required for administrative responsibilities. These tasks were previously performed by the supervisor. They included production coordination, safety, maintenance direction, quality, people administration, good manufacturing practice (GMP), and sanitation. The third training phase focused on interpersonal skills: communication, conflict resolution, and group process. As the teams develop, the administrative and interpersonal skills and knowledge are as important as the core job skills and knowledge of the process.

### Sunshine Concept

The administrative roles evolved into the Sunshine Concept (Figure 2). This concept was introduced in 1986 when a group composed of managers, STRs, and team members attended a team

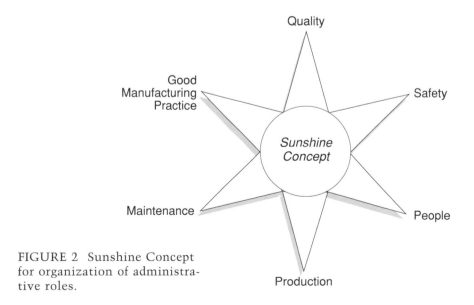

FIGURE 2 Sunshine Concept for organization of administrative roles.

leader course offered by Ketchum Associates. Attending one week per month over five months permitted assimilation and emergence of the Kingstree Team Concept. The course has evolved and improved, using feedback from the original attendees, and other internal and external influences. In 1988 a second group completed the improved training.

Responsibilities and tasks for each ray in the Sunshine Concept (as shown in Figure 2) are defined between the ray and the resource persons designated among the STRs. Each team member has two assignments: one as the team "ray" for a designated area; the other is a secondary, or backup, for another area. The dual role ensures that the team is always represented and broadens the individual perspective.

The rays provide the measure of self-regulation needed for team performance. For example, the GMP ray is not responsible for cleaning but ensures that everyone on the team carries out sanitation and GMP as an integral part of the job. The ray serves on the plantwide GMP Steering Committee and meets regularly with GMP rays from other teams along with resources. They track and review overall plant performance and adjust the work plan as required to meet plant objectives and goals.

The people ray especially distinguishes the Sunshine Concept from unsupervised work groups or teams under the direction of a team leader. The people ray carries out routine administrative responsibilities such as coordinating vacation, overtime, training schedules, and time sheets. The people ray also provides the measure of self-regulation of team and individual performance and, with the team's participation, identifies training needs for the team members. The people ray also represents the team in determining the pace of organizational development and overall personnel needs.

The Sunshine Concept requires many meetings to exchange information, plan, critique performance, and adjust activities. Daily meetings are held with other team members. Monthly meetings are held with rays from other teams to review results and adjust work plans for each area: quality, safety, GMP, people, maintenance, and production. In addition, each team ray can meet as needed with STRs and others.

### Self-Evaluation

In 1988 the organizational development of the teams continued as teams and resources met for self-evaluation in a series of workshops off-site. Internal team performance, performance between teams, and the relationship between the resources and teams were evaluated. The workshop also addressed the overall goal toward which IBIS is working. A statement describing this goal was used to draft a specific related, supportive statement pertinent to the team. A series of action points was developed. A reevaluation followed in six months. This continuous self-evaluation establishes an improved level of performance as the team concept matures, achieving more complete self-regulation.

### Inside/Outside Concept

For more than 20 years, large petrochemical and refinery installations have operated integrated processes from central control rooms. An inside operator directs activities of field workers. The control center often serves as a meeting place. It may also house the process control lab and meeting rooms.

Although the Kingstree processes are not continuous, the same control philosophy was adapted to the batch and semicontinuous operation. The installation of a centralized process system was planned in 1987. A job skills training program was initiated in 1986 to broaden the knowledge of team members. Each team is composed of both inside and outside operators. Rotation is based on individual capabilities, work requirements, and available time for training and rotation to keep skills current. Figure 3 shows

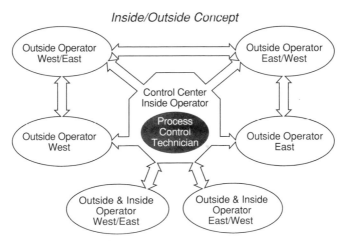

FIGURE 3 Inside/Outside Concept for the movement of operators between the control center and the east and west plants.

the movement of outside operators between the control center and the east and west plants. Regular rotation of assignments is important to maintain a plant organization, empathy for other positions, and an understanding of both outside and inside work. Just as there are primary and secondary ray roles for each team member, there is a minimum of two per team for each assignment for the Inside/Outside Concept.

The inside operator is designated as the quarterback. The new PC network and Process Control Center allow the quarterback to manage the process by exception, identifying variances. Although quarterbacks set priorities and call the plays, they are not supervisors, but equal team members. Because of the position in the control center, the quarterback has access to the information necessary for overall work coordination of the shift.

The rotation sequence helps ensure that an egalitarian atmosphere prevails. If the team has just two qualified quarterbacks, they rotate between the inside and outside assignment. When a team has more than two qualified operators, the rotation is extended from outside only; outside, relief for inside; and then inside.

The outside operator is not a set of arms and legs but a knowledge worker applying a high level of training to a multitude of situations. Guidelines for the outside operator apportion work times equally among three functions: regular routine; process batch cycle; and breaks, exceptions, and time to think.

The regular routine includes equipment checks in the field according to a schedule established by the resource and production ray members. Outside operators check the water level in cooling towers and the oil temperature of compressors and monitor other field instruments and activities that are not included on the inside operator's console. Process batch cycles result in a varying work load. For each batch there are solutions to prepare, samples to take, and equipment to assemble, dismantle, sterilize, or clean, along with numerous other activities. Although some flexibility exists, work planning is essential to smooth out busy periods when available resources may be exceeded. The outside operator also requires time for breaks and dealing with exceptions. Most important, time is required to plan the work with fellow team members and to think. The control center is designed to be the meeting place so that the team can regularly see each other and interact personally, apart from their routine radio and telephone communications.

Team performance has continued to improve. In 1984 the shift operators functioned independently, receiving direction from their shift supervisors. In 1985 they began to work as an unsupervised group. In 1988 the group became a largely self-regulating team.

The team's work skills and knowledge have continued to improve. Productivity has improved by more than 30 percent while following the 1/3, 1/3, 1/3 guidelines. The team determines the shift staffing level following the guidelines. Current production teams consist of six members, with some overtime required.

## Production Team Staffing

| Year: | 1985 | 1986 | 1987 | 1988 | 1989 |
|---|---|---|---|---|---|
| Team size: | 10 | 8 | 7-8 | 6-7 | 6 |

In 1988 a production team quarterback and an STR made a presentation to the Manufacturing Automation Users Council in Phoenix, Arizona (Dennis and Rogers, 1988). In their presentation, both stressed that the system continues to evolve, ensuring continuous improvement of the process.

### Learning

Nearly all of the operators' learning was new learning, which extended their understanding of why things occurred the way they do. Most operators welcomed the organizational changes. About 15 percent, however, found it too difficult to accept the responsibility or work without direct supervision and chose to go elsewhere. It was regrettable that approximately half were excellent performers with the old system but were unable to adjust to the changes.

The role transition is perceived as a more difficult adjustment for first-level supervisors, since they need to unlearn the way they have been working for more than 15 or 20 years. Moreover, there was no role model for a "resource" in 1984.

Indeed, the concept of autonomous teams met with skepticism when it was presented to the supervisors. They perceived the safest assignment would be as plant superintendent, working with the rotating shifts. At the end of 1986, no shift supervision was required and, in contrast to the expectations of many, progress was accelerated as former first-level supervisors assumed resource roles that evolved into STRs.

To assist the former supervisors in making the paradigm change, new learning was emphasized. A manager of change was named immediately in January 1985 to ensure that IBIS moved away from bureaucratic procedures toward more innovation. However, too much change could result in confusion, excessive mistakes, and lack of coordination. IBIS recognized the need for procedures and controls and continued with some parts of the hierarchy such that both the teams and the resources could request support as well as give direction. There is also interdependence within levels to promote interpersonal relationships between the functional roles.

The IBIS organizational structure is redrawn in Figure 4 to represent the team concept. Information and resource sharing, along with mutual support, are emphasized. The teams connect with the core process, supported by resources and managers. However, the boundaries for much of what IBIS does are not as clear as Figure 4 indicates. As skills and knowledge develop, all boundaries shift and become broader.

A third organizational type—an adhocracy—illustrates an organization's readiness to accept boundary adjustments to facilitate innovation and change. The effort goes into implementing change and not dealing with organizational resistance to overcome inertia.

A fourth organizational type recognizes the need for individual

FIGURE 4 Current organization of the Kingstree plant, by teams.

contribution, clear goals, and direction. In contrast to most firms, IBIS perceives each individual as the *center* of the network, connected with information technology and capable of continuous organization transformation.

Organization always lags what is required today because it was organized to accomplish yesterday's tasks. The shorter the time lag, the more effective the business. To achieve high performance, organizations have continuous self-destruction and reconstruction. IBIS must also master the paradox of dealing with conflicting organizational types: hierarchy and adhocracy, teams and individuals. These concepts are more fully developed by Davis (1987) and Quinn (1988).

If teams are overemphasized, a country club atmosphere can prevail. However, a lack of information sharing by individuals results in duplication of costly learning experiences. It also deprives the team of essential information. On the other hand, individual performance and contribution are important and are recognized by the significant work and administrative responsibilities each team member has as both a lay and a key decision maker in the manufacturing process.

As the role of the supervisory technical resources evolved, they were initially reluctant to intervene, feeling much more comfortable with coordinating, observing, coaching, facilitating, and training. Managing the paradox, between intervention and resumption of what could be perceived as role reversion to the old paradigm, was a delicate balance. IBIS's success is attributed to positive results being achieved as we moved toward self-regulation, which more than offset the unusual incidents. IBIS abided by the basic precept of Lyman Ketchum: "Teams learn self-regulation by self-regulating."

## Outside Resources

Most of the outside resources employed for IBIS organizational development and assistance in making the paradigm shift dealt with people rather than technology. Early in 1985 a Dale Carnegie course was offered to everyone in the plant. Eighty percent of the people completed the six weeks of training offered outside of regular work hours. The level of self-confidence of all participants improved, and communication abilities were enhanced. IBIS was off to an excellent start. About 10 percent of the people were also enrolled in the full 12-week course off-site. Concurrently, Rational Problem Solving courses were provided to all employees. About

20 percent of the managers and resources attended Kepner-Tregoe week-long courses off-site.

Recognizing that rapid change contributes to stress, IBIS established a stress-management and wellness program. The physiological psychologist who assisted in the schedule resolution was retained for the first three years. During the psychologist's week-long visits, generally once every four or five months, small group sessions were scheduled for everyone in the plant. The causes of stress were discussed, along with stress management techniques, exercise, and proper nutrition. Time was made available for individual counseling.

A survey at the end of three years showed that one-third of the plant community made some adjustments as a result of the program. Another third said they made a significant change in their life-styles. The remaining third stated they were better informed but had made no change. All believed the program results were mutually beneficial in accelerating the change process, recognizing that stress was present, and providing the tools to manage it.

Another practice that had to be encouraged was asking for help. In the past, asking questions was often viewed as an inability to comprehend "what everybody else already knows." It was especially awkward when a subordinate questioned a person in authority. Because it is essential for IBIS's success that everyone be comfortable in asking for help, Interaction, a course offered by Development Dimensions, Inc. (DDI), was provided to everyone. An individual was trained off-site by DDI to become a facilitator and six in-house facilitators were selected and trained. Next, plantwide courses were scheduled using a combination of videotapes, exercises, and open discussion over a three-month period. The videotapes and other materials were unusual in the way they avoided reference to the traditional relationship between supervisors and subordinates.

In addition to encouraging people to ask for help, the training reinforced two other principles: having respect for others and having empathy for the person in the other position. The program also helped to establish a common language. The timing was important. The need for this course was well recognized and appreciated as another tool in facilitating the organizational change.

## TECHNOLOGY

The 1984 baseline study identified potential advantages of installing a PC network to improve information flow and using manufacturing resource planning (MRP II) to reduce working capital requirements and improve equipment use and productivity. The study also recommended a centralized control station for better integration of plant operations. The PC network was installed in 1985 and has been continuously expanded. The MRP II system was selected in 1985, brought up later that year, and fully implemented in 1986. The centralized control was designed in 1986 and implemented in 1987. All plans have met or exceeded expectations (Horton, 1988; Jansen, 1987; Nisenfeld, 1988; Weber and Nisenfeld, 1987).

## PC Network

Design and implementation of the PC network was accomplished using computer science students from the local university. An elementary approach allowed rapid results. After several iterations with the users on the plant floor and in the control room, laboratory, and other areas throughout the plant, current operating results were available. The performance measurements facilitated the communication that was essential for cost improvements. More than 50 PCs are now used on applications ranging from simple document retrieval to expert systems that support operator decision making.

## MRP II

In 1985 a cross-functional team was charged with selecting generic software to replace the "paper mill" used for production tracking. At the same time, the team was to identify opportunities to redesign the work to enable people to better use the technology. Members included representatives from customer service, order entry, accounting, accounts payable, accounts receivable, purchasing, warehouse, production planning, project engineering, and maintenance. After a cursory screening, two vendors provided software for a week-long evaluation by the potential users. A selection was made, and the next nine months were required for more complete training, configurations, and start-up. The results met or exceeded all objectives. More than 10,000 square feet of warehouse space was opened up by better resource planning. The maintenance stock reduction was greater than the software cost, and a large reduction in raw materials was achieved.

## Centralized Control

In 1984 local control areas existed around the plant, along with much field instrumentation.  An automation plan was designed for integration by stages to match IBIS's capital budgets and resources, and Combustion Engineering Corporation proposed a shared-risk/shared-benefit venture (Blickley, 1987).  After a detailed engineering study of costs and savings, a distributed process control system, MOD 300®, was installed.  IBIS and Combustion Engineering share in the benefits in proportion to their investments for five years or until the system is paid off.  A former first-level supervisor was given the title manufacturing representative (MR) and assigned to ensure that the project met the production operators' needs.  In this new role, the MR was responsible for training of operators, speaking for production, providing information to engineering and others necessary for the design, and communicating project status to everyone in the production organization.

The design of the operator interface display was a cooperative effort between the control engineer and the operators.  Tag numbers were used and extensive training was provided.  Operators became knowledgeable about every component in the instrument loop:  sensor, transmitter, controller, and final control element.  They reviewed the algorithm development.  Process piping and instrumentation drawings were put on AUTOCAD®, a computer-aided design system, so that revisions could be readily accommodated and always available to anyone.  Most important, all operators interpret and troubleshoot malfunctions and variances as they occur.  This minimizes start-up problems and maintenance calls.

In mid-1987 the first fermentation controlled from the new system saved $6,000.  Since then the remainder of the fermentors and the recovery operations have been consolidated into the control center.  Again, all results have met or exceeded expectations.

## Systems Integration

Currently the PC network, MRP II, and distributed control system are independent islands of information.  An integration project is in process to establish a common platform for the enterprise.

A manager of enabling technologies has been named.  This position combines management information systems with process control systems.  The information systems team serves as a resource to accounting, sales and marketing, finance, manufacturing and engineering, and others.

Combustion Engineering has offered to extend the contract to include many of these additional capabilities under the shared-risk/shared-benefit concept. This commitment of continued vendor support provides IBIS a significant extension of resources to help ensure project success. In addition, organizational flexibility, continuous training, and commitment to continuous improvement ensure that the gains will be realized.

## CONCLUSION

In the old paradigm, change is implemented as chapters in a book, with each department or function completing a chapter. There is little interaction and even less iteration through various stages of implementation. The results of this approach are periodically brought into focus when airline pilots and flight controllers threaten to "go by the book." In nearly any location, when one goes strictly by the book, using the old paradigm, effectiveness and productivity suffer. Innovation is restricted if not eliminated.

In the new paradigm, change is implemented using a plan that can also be compared to a book. But the development occurs in a more participatory sense: the outline provided first, and people responsible for the implementation participating in the design, development, start-up, and all other phases. Iterations are expected and promoted. In this way innovation continues to occur, and an atmosphere for continuing change is created.

With the new paradigm, capabilities of many are used on a broader scale. The "big picture" or "helicopter view" is available to everyone. People are permitted, indeed encouraged, to close the gap between what they are doing and what they are capable of doing.

## REFERENCES

Davis, S. M. 1987. Future Perfect. New York: Addison-Wesley.

Dennis, R. E., and R. A. Rogers. 1988. Training education and incentive systems socio-technical design: The plant floor view. The Yankee Conveyor (April):18–21.

Blickley, G. J. 1987. Process control users can be tough customers. Control Engineering (October).

Horton, M. 1988. The Technical, Economic, and Social Issues and the

Results of an Automation Retrofit to a Biotechnical Plant. AIChE Spring Convention, New Orleans, March 7, 1988.

Jansen, R. 1987. An Energy Enhancement Project: One Step on the Road to CIM. Thirteenth Annual Advanced Control Conference, Purdue University, September 28–30.

Nisenfeld, E. 1988. Plant automation: A five-year plan that worked. Control (October):93–102.

Quinn, R. 1988. Beyond Rational Management. San Francisco: Jossey-Bass.

Weber, M. G., and E. Nisenfeld. 1987. Operator Decision Support System as Part of CIM. Thirteenth Annual Advanced Control Conference, Purdue University, September 28–30.

People and Technology in the Workplace. 1991.
Pp. 119–130. Washington, D.C:
National Academy Press.

# Achieving Excellence Through People, Technology, and Teamwork

JOSEPH C. HIGH

Consolidated Diesel Company began in 1978 as a joint venture between Case IH and Cummins Engine Company for the design, development, and manufacture of two new series of diesel engines in the 48- to 250-horsepower range. Consolidated Diesel Company (CDC) was formed in October 1980, the fifth largest industrial investment made in the state of North Carolina at that time. The company's mission is to be a world-class producer of diesel engines, kits, and components of the highest quality and the lowest cost delivered on time to meet all customers' expectations.

## THE ENVIRONMENT, THE FACILITY, AND THE OBJECTIVES

The CDC facility is located in Whitakers, North Carolina, a small rural community about 10 miles north of Rocky Mount, 60 miles east of Raleigh, and 130 miles south of Richmond, Virginia. The entire region east of Raleigh is in transition from an agricultural to an industrial economy. The physical structure encompasses 1.1 million square feet and is located on 250 acres. The building was designed to reinforce many of the operating concepts that are important to the functioning of the facility. A local newspaper story described the building as "a conflict of cultures."

Upon entering the front door, one is immediately connected with the operating technology. Skylights are strategically placed in areas where there is a high concentration of people activity to

*119*

connect employees with the outside elements. Complementing the skylights are vertical light-walls that diffuse the sunlight as well as provide acoustical protection. Color is used throughout the facility not only to brighten the work environment but also to play a functional role. Major operating areas are identified by a unique color coding.

Extending through the center of the building is a main support corridor, which houses facilities necessary for the effective functioning of the company. Housed within the main corridor are a hospitality room for customer and other VIP visits and an elaborately equipped quality laboratory containing one of the few scanning electron microscopes in an industrial lab. The lab has the capability to perform metallurgical testing, fine measurements, gauge calibration, and chemical analysis. A cafeteria, medical center, computer room, and mechanical room complete the main support corridor facilities. Partitions and the absence of doors between office cubicles throughout the facility promote an open atmosphere.

In the production areas, the extensive use of glass continues the theme of accessibility and connection with the product and the technology. The support corridor also serves to separate the two operating environments—machining and assembly/test—to maintain clean assembly conditions.

The entire assembly section of the new building is fully air-conditioned. A new concept in task cooling and lighting of areas with high concentrations of people activity in the machining portion of the building serves to reduce both the capital costs and the operating costs of maintaining a comfortable working environment for all employees.

All engines manufactured at CDC are shipped to Case IH or Cummins Engine Company. Case is the second largest construction equipment manufacturer and the third largest agricultural tractor manufacturer in North America. Engines produced at CDC are used in such machinery as new Magnum tractors, agricultural loaders, cable-layers, crawler loaders and dozers, compaction equipment, forklifts, horizontal boring units, hydraulic excavators, industrial cranes, loaders/backhoes, logging equipment, mining and quarry equipment, skid steer loaders, trenchers, and wheel loaders.

Cummins sells the engines to a broad range of customers for a variety of uses, including the U.S. military 5-ton tactical truck. The engines are also used in recreational vehicles, school buses, fire pumps, generator sets, industrial and construction applications, and both light- and medium-duty trucks such as the step van. The 1989 Chrysler Dodge Ram pickup is the first pickup truck with a turbocharged, full-sized diesel engine designed by Cummins with technical support from CDC and Chrysler employees. Most recently, marine applications have been added to this list.

The principal market, however, for Cummins engines still remains the U.S. on-highway truck industry, with every major truck manufacturer offering Cummins engines. Cummins' average share of the heavy-duty truck market is more than 60 percent.

With a detailed partnership arrangement, and an agreement that Cummins would be the managing partner, Consolidated Diesel produced its first engine in July 1983. Originally planned to achieve an ultimate capacity of 150,000 assembled engines and 80,000 kits of blocks, heads, and rods per year, CDC is beginning to realize its projected potential. In 1987 there were nearly 600 employees manufacturing 200 engines per day. In 1988 CDC approached 900 employees producing nearly 400 engines per day. The company employed slightly more than 1,000 people to produce more than 500 engines per day in 1989 and operated at more than 600 per day in 1990 with approximately 1,100 employees.

With parents who are giants in their markets, CDC was born with a tremendous challenge: to be a world-class manufacturer. With capabilities to produce engines and major components at a rate of more than 600 per day, CDC expects to

- offer significant cost/price reduction over the competition
- produce a quality product correct the first time
- offer a reliable and durable product
- make on-time delivery with minimum inventory
- create an environment that generates continuous improvement

## ELEMENTS OF A STRATEGY TO BECOME WORLD CLASS

The question that had to be answered was, "How can CDC develop and accomplish these objectives better than the competition?" Three principles emerged from the strategy to become world class. CDC would accomplish these objectives through reliance on the best proven technology, the most motivated and best-skilled people it could find and develop, and the best-integrated system of technology, people, and teamwork it could design.

## Technology

The critical element of the strategy was the development of a philosophy and culture that used automated technologies in a way that promoted flexibility, teamwork, continuous learning and human development, mutual respect, self-accountability, and responsibility. The technological design of the facility includes the following elements:

- modern high-speed transfer lines
- automated assembly and test
- worldwide sourcing capability
- world-class quality systems and gauging
- a motivated and capable work force
- internally machined cylinder blocks, heads, and connecting rods and external sourcing of other components
- assembly, testing, painting, customizing, and shipment of completed engines
- installing capacity for expected requirements at the production rate of 600 per day (engines and components)
- installing the latest applicable technology from proven manufacturing sources
- providing space for future opportunities (additional components, customer application, and optional parts)

CDC's machining areas are designed to operate three shifts at maturity, including scheduled preventive maintenance. All six machining lines are highly automated and have the following characteristics:

- automatic conveyance between machines and automated loading and unloading
- low labor content
- automatic in-process gauging

Assembly and test is one function that encompasses two assembly lines: (1) testing, painting, and customizing and (2) shipping. This area, although highly automated in material handling and inventory, is one of the most labor intensive of all the activities. Eight fully automated production test cells are in place and supported by additional engineering test capability. The area contains an electrostatic paint system.

The first assembly line is called the shortblock line, where all the internal components of the engine are installed. The second line is called the trim line, where all components external to the engine are added. On the assembly lines, a waist-high, nonsynchronous conveyor moves the engines through a series of manual and automatic workstations.

At each station, a video terminal that is part of the assembly information management system displays a "bill of materials" to the assembly operator and virtually eliminates paper on the shop floor. This display tells the operator the serial number of the engine coming through and necessary parts to be assembled on the engine. It also tracks inventory, production, and proliferated parts options. The assembly, testing, and painting process is designed to operate two shifts at maturity, including preventive maintenance.

CDC's purchasing department was critical to the company's cost-reduction objective, since material is a major cost element of the engine. CDC integrated purchasing into the strategy with concentrated attention in the following areas:

- minimizing the number of suppliers
- sourcing from anywhere in the world
- creating a partnership between CDC and supplier
- expecting delivery on time, 100 percent to specification
- involving supplier top management and using their technical support and cost-reduction ideas
- using supplier quality engineering

CDC is committed to a "total quality" approach in everything it does, and automation is the single greatest factor allowing CDC to move into levels of quality to compete worldwide. CDC's quality control uses a modified version of statistical process control with emphasis on prevention. The approach is built on automatic in-process gauging, work with Dr. Val Feigenbaum of General Systems Company, Inc., on total quality methods, statistical process control on critical characteristics, error proofing, and equipment capability and process control.

CDC manufactures three basic components: cylinder blocks, cylinder heads, and connecting rods for both four-cylinder and six-cylinder diesel engines with 32 basic configurations. These components are machined and assembled into engines that are then tested, painted, and fitted with accessories. Component machining is performed on state-of-the-art high-speed, automated transfer lines. In-process gauging, automatic tool compensation, industrial robots, and computerized machine maintenance monitors are featured in the machinery.

A state-of-the-art material-handling system based on an electrified overhead monorail is used throughout the facility to transport components from machining to assembly, as well as to convey engines within the assembly and test process. This system eliminates a significant amount of fork truck activity. Once castings are loaded onto the block and head lines, they are not handled again until they are loaded onto a shipping skid as part of a finished engine.

An automatic, computer-controlled test system tests the performance of each engine. This testing can determine the probable cause and suggested repair for any performance deficiency. After paint application, finished engines are discharged onto automatic sort lines for appropriate sequencing before being placed on skids for shipping preparation.

## People

If a company is to compete successfully, it must generally look at three areas to improve its competitive edge—the product, the technology, and the people. CDC has explored two of those areas. Cummins, the managing partner, already had a product that was respected in the market, and the facility was built around proven technology. So when CDC considered what would give the company a competitive edge, it had to concentrate on its people. What the company found was a southern agrarian and light manufacturing community that had never seen anything similar to CDC's manufacturing equipment or managing style. That concentration on people became a dilemma: "How does a highly technical diesel engine operation in an agrarian community with little or no technical skills and knowledge of heavy manufacturing become world-class?"

CDC had to pay particular attention to how it recruited, organized, trained, and developed people to assume responsibility. The company needed people who not only had the technical skills needed to perform specific functions, but would also participate in leading the organization toward fulfilling its mission. CDC made a conscious decision early on for selective recruiting and training of its work force. As a result, 25 percent of CDC employees during that period had four-year college degrees.

The company sought to create an environment in which employees are stakeholders and have an opportunity to approach self-actualization through a high degree of participation in the decision-making processes.

The CDC work system was based on high standards and commitment to a technician-driven work environment consisting of dedicated people who would be constantly focused on improving their capabilities. The company's human resources strategy was designed to

- place heavy emphasis on the selection process for capability and skills
- center around significant investment in in-house and developmental training
- deemphasize organizational structure and titles
- emphasize communication
- allow people in the decision-making process, including pay and disciplinary action
- create flexibility in employees' willingness and ability to handle different tasks
- be contingent upon working in teams
- hold individuals and teams accountable
- be structurally flat
- recognize and capitalize on the benefits of a culturally diverse work force
- get everyone involved in developing approaches to work
- emphasize that all work and all people are valuable to the company
- provide similar benefits for all employees

As part of the strategy it was decided that all nonexempt employees would be called technicians and would be salaried. They would work in teams and be supported by individuals called resources, who are highly skilled in their areas of expertise. The role of the resource, in theory, was to provide and transfer both managerial and technical skills to members of the team. They would act as facilitators for the group and as liaisons between teams. CDC was interested in an organization strong in participatory management using teams and management as resources and facilitators. The strategy was to pass on technical skills so that at some point, technicians would perform all technical and management functions. Although the basic framework remains, the social and technical systems continue to undergo evolutionary changes in response to changes in the diesel engine business and the nationwide crisis in work force preparedness and local and social economic issues.

CDC's first direct action to deal with the low skills of the available labor force is in recruiting. Because the skills are lacking, the company concentrates on identifying people who demonstrate a willingness to learn and take on responsibility. It looks for people who are assertive and display leadership qualities or potential and for people who are cooperative yet inquisitive.

The organization CDC envisions and the technologies it employs not only require more technical and team participation skills than the local work force is accustomed to or prepared for, but also require critical thinking skills. CDC's approach to work requires that the work force have problem-solving capabilities. Workers are expected to apply statistical process control methods, communicate effectively, and adapt to change. In essence, the company looks for people who exhibit flexibility and an ability to reason and can develop work habits around team methods.

The application is structured with subjective questions to convey how the applicants think and feel about work in general and about themselves. It is designed to reflect whether the person seeks continuous improvement in skill, personal, and career development.

The interview exercise is structured to give an idea of how candidates handle confrontation and conflict. Deductions are made based on the qualities CDC wants its employees to possess. Interviews are done by teams, and the selection of an applicant is derived from a consensus of the members. There is no standard or programmed testing to measure aptitude or specific skills.

CDC has had to recruit outside the local community and out of state to fill such critical positions as those of electricians, toolmakers, cutter grinders, machine operators, and engineers in all disciplines. Consequently, the company has had to reconsider its recruiting technique and incentives; for example, it now offers relocation assistance and temporary housing for the candidates recruited from out of town for the highly skilled positions. It also offers monetary incentives to employees who identify skilled candidates who are successful in the selection process.

Within 30 days of employment and placement, new hires, rehires, and transfers must complete a work plan/performance review. During a four-month assimilation period, all new hires are evaluated by their managers or manager designees, with additional comment from a peer and a customer. A customer is defined as any person, team, or company that receives some benefit from work performed by the employee. Decisions are made at this time about continued employment or eligibility for pay increases.

The construction of a training facility was necessary in the early stages because CDC's labor force had little or no experience in heavy manufacturing. From 1982 to 1987, groups of employees received more than 28 weeks of training, encompassing such di-

verse topics as company philosophy, group dynamics, conflict resolution, blueprint reading, economic theory, diesel technology, and
sophisticated machining skills. Again, although the basic framework remains, the company has had to reevaluate many elements
of how it assimilates employees into the work environment and
has had to modify its approach.

CDC found itself in a change crisis. The one-style "vanilla" engine design that was anticipated turned into 10 and now 32 designs with unlimited options as the product is customized to meet
specialized applications. Production demands rose dramatically
from 150 engines a day to 385 per day at the end of 1988 and more
than 500 per day by the end of 1989. Production demands rose to
more than 600 per day in 1990. Clearly, the company had to do
some things differently.

It became clear that the importance of the highly skilled "resource" people in the company organization would not diminish
over time. As a matter of fact, the organizational structure was
redesigned to include team managers who would provide managerial support to teams. As part of the organizational development
process, these new managers are placed in a 12-month on-the-job
management development program. This group of people is the
primary communication link for the organization.

Because production demands increased at a rate CDC was not
prepared to address, the company had to discontinue its focus on
rapid rotation in the technician work force and placed more emphasis on depth rather than breadth of skills. Whereas technicians once rotated through training modules acquiring proficiency
to perform all the tasks in their functional areas, it became necessary to station employees to acquire specialized proficiency. An
internal posting system was put in place to accommodate the
transfer of employees between business and functional areas.
Intrabusiness rotation is managed by the team in that area, and
posting is not required. The company had to restructure its training program to support a work force in which about 50 percent
had less than one year of company service.

Even though CDC is a large metalworking operation, it has no
need for an exaggerated number of true machinists. However, the
company did need high-quality machining technicians and maintenance employees and therefore designed an 18-month program
to prepare machining technicians. CDC established an apprenticeship program that is broad based enough to produce skilled
technicians and narrow enough in focus to produce CDC certified
maintenance personnel.

*Teamwork*

CDC's mission is to be a world-class producer of engines, kits, and components of the highest quality and the lowest cost, delivered on time, to meet customers' expectations. CDC will fulfill that mission through the teamwork of the company's stakeholders—customers, employees, suppliers, partners, and the community—working together to achieve excellence.

CDC's customers are the reason the company is in business. To serve them with excellence means meeting their expectations better than the competition. The customers define their needs, and the company serves those needs through dedication to continuous improvement in quality, technology, delivery, and cost. There is continuous communication between Cummins, Case, and CDC to improve cost, quality, and delivery.

CDC's employees are the company's greatest asset. Their individual and collective contributions are keys to CDC's success. CDC values the growth in both maturity and competency of people who view the company as a career choice. With ongoing training, CDC will develop a productive and flexible work force that shares in the rewards for CDC's success through an incentive program called Variable Pay. The company values diversity—the individual differences each person brings to the organization. All employees are expected to show respect for one another; racism, sexism, and classicism are not tolerated. It is this mutual respect and people development that have supported much of the growth in production that CDC has experienced. The company is a leader across the region in the team concept approach and participative management.

CDC's managers must enable the organization to meet objectives by empowering teams to perform work, by promoting teamwork, by allowing people to develop, and providing the tools to complete work in a safe and efficient manner. They must create a positive employee relations environment that values human dignity and is free of harassment. The company's overall management approach must be preventive and proactive.

Suppliers are CDC's business partners. Their primary goal is to support the company in achieving its mission, and CDC expects this commitment from each supplier. Each supplier, like CDC itself, must be dedicated to continuous improvement in quality, technology, delivery, and cost. Suppliers and customers participate in problem-solving sessions at CDC.

As owners of Consolidated Diesel Company, the partners expect and will receive a fair return on their investment. The company's success relies on the support and strong working relationships between and among both partners.

The community in which CDC works and lives must offer the high quality of life necessary to attract and retain an excellent work force. CDC plays a socially responsible and active role in the social and educational development of the community to achieve this goal. The company's work in the community is guided by the principle that social problem solving must be good business as well as good citizenship.

CDC delivers a strong and consistent message on the need for equality and human dignity in the community as well as inside CDC. Because its employees are involved in key activities throughout the community, CDC contributes to the future direction of issues critical to quality of life. This notion of continuous improvement drives the company's community action plans such that issues of poverty, education, recreational opportunities, and issues affecting women and children, among others, receive attention as CDC strives for excellence. The company backs its human involvement with financial support and is considered a leader in efforts to help improve the educational, social, and economic conditions in the community.

## CONCLUSION

All of the elements of CDC's strategy for excellence form a synchronized integrated system. There is physical linkage by means of hardware and information linkage by means of computers and people. All value-added and support functions, both direct and indirect relationships necessary for manufacturing the product are included. The relationship between these attributes is organized in such a way as to achieve a predetermined objective—to manufacture 600 engines a day better than the competition; to become world class.

Consolidated Diesel faced many challenges during its evolution:

• partners with complementary but significantly different managerial styles
• the original intent of building a "vanilla" engine quickly changing because of the demand for many different engines
• major increases in production volumes
• a labor force with little or no experience in heavy manufacturing and unaccustomed to participatory management

- a rural southern community in an economic and social transition
- maintaining consistency in training while faced with constant production changes

Any one of these challenges might be considered a formidable intrusion on even a mature organization. For a young organization, any one of these could limit or even prevent the company from attaining its goals.

CDC has been able to adapt creatively to its partners' methods of operation without adversely affecting its own style. Flexibility and managing customers' needs and specifications have allowed the company to maintain its progressive position in the marketplace. The company deliberately engaged with the community through key positions in organizations that could support CDC's internal operational needs in both the short and the long term. CDC believes it is appropriately adjusting its processes to meet the requirements of a high-volume facility without shifting significantly from its original concepts. Has the company successfully integrated people, technology, and teamwork? The evidence suggests that it has. CDC believes it is headed in the direction it envisioned.

# 2

## *Medical Technologies*

People and Technology in the Workplace. 1991.
Pp. 133–158. Washington, D.C:
National Academy Press.

# The Process of Adopting Innovations in Organizations: Three Cases of Hospital Innovations

ANDREW H. VAN DE VEN

It is increasingly being recognized that the process of adopting innovations in and by organizations is far more complex than it is by individuals. The former entails all the social, political, and bureaucratic complexities of large organizations, while the latter is largely a marketing effort that informs and persuades individual consumers of a desirable new product or procedure. Yet, the basic model that most management scholars and practitioners appear to use in organizing their thoughts and actions about adopting innovations in organizations is based on a model of individual innovation adoption. It is not surprising, therefore, that most innovation adoption efforts by organizations fail.

Fortunately, some succeed, as exemplified in this book in the three case studies on the adoption of hospital innovations: the evolution of new technologies and administrative arrangements in the ambulatory care unit of Pennsylvania Hospital described by Robert Cathcart; the introduction of a new technology (ECMO—extracorporeal membrane oxygenation) in a neonatal intensive care unit of Columbia Presbyterian Hospital described by John Driscoll; and experimentation and implementation of alternative working schedules for nurses in Rochester Methodist Hospital of the Mayo Clinic described by Thomas Choi, Helen Jameson, and Milo Brekke. The three cases represent highly selective examples of successful innovation adoption. They are stimulating to read, and provide rich descriptions of the process of innovation adoption in hospitals. But if our knowledge of innovation adoption is to go beyond description and on to explanation, we need to ask, *"Why were these hospitals successful in adopting their innovations?"* Moreover, we need to ask, *What can we learn from these cases to improve our understanding of the innovation adoption process in organizations?*

Valid answers to these questions are not possible from these cases alone, because generalizations from three cases are difficult to substantiate, particularly when they include no instances of failure. To address these questions we will expand our sample by leaning on other published studies as well as research currently under way by the Minnesota Innovation Research Program, which since 1983 has been tracking a wide variety of technological, product, and process innovations as they develop from concept to reality in their natural field settings (see Van de Ven, Angle, and Poole, 1989). The three cases presented here will be treated as examples to illustrate key research findings that are relevant to our questions.

Our point of departure will be a brief review of Everett Rogers's basic model, which is perhaps the most widely shared view of the process of innovation adoption and diffusion. Although this model is robust in explaining innovation adoption by individuals, it does not adequately incorporate many complexities often observed in other studies and exemplified in our three cases when the organization is the locus of adoption. Innovation researchers are currently examining these complexities, which is leading to revisions in Rogers's basic model that explains the process of innovation adoption by organizations. Such a revised model, when empirically verified, can make a major contribution by providing practical suggestions for maneuvering the innovation adoption journey in organizations.

## ROGERS'S BASIC INNOVATION ADOPTION AND DIFFUSION MODEL

Everett Rogers (in Rogers, 1962, 1983; Rogers and Schoemaker, 1971) has set forth perhaps the most widely accepted view of the innovation process as a result of his own research (encompassing more than a quarter of a century) and a synthesis of more than 3,100 publications on innovation diffusion. Innovation scholars and practitioners would do well to study this model carefully, for it captures much of what we know implicitly or take for granted about innovation adoption. This model, shown in Figure 1, views the process of innovation as a simple linear sequence of three basic stages: (1) the invention of an idea (which comes from recognition of needs or problems and basic or applied research); (2) its development, production, and testing as a concrete device or program; and (3) its diffusion to and adoption by users. Depending on the innovations being examined, various authors have expanded or modified activities in these three basic stages.

Indeed, specialized fields of study and research have emerged over the years to focus on each stage. In the idea invention stage, psychologists have developed an extensive literature on individual and group creativity (e.g., Amabile, 1983; Angle, 1989; Cummings, 1965); and economists, on "technology push" versus "demand pull" (e.g., Rosenberg, 1982; Thirtle and Ruttan, 1987). Although less extensively studied than the other stages, the process of innovation development is gaining more research attention by management scholars (e.g., Kanter, 1983; Tushman and Romanelli, 1985; Van de Ven, Angle, and Poole, 1989). Finally, Rogers (1983) notes that perhaps no other topic in the social sciences has received as much study as innovation diffusion and adoption.

Whereas most of this research has focused on *diffusion*, which is largely concerned with the marketing, dissemination, and transfer of an innovation to individual end users, far less has dealt with *adoption*, or the process by which recipient users select and implement an innovation. Of this smaller subset of adoption studies, most have focused on statistically examining relationships between various "input" factors (characteristic of users, organizations, and the innovation) and "output" (rates of innovation adoption)—leaving the adoption *process* itself least understood. Yet it is well established that functionally similar organizations respond and perform differently when adopting similar innovations (Barley, 1986; Kimberly and Evanisko, 1981). In other words, the process by which organizations adopt innovations makes a difference on subsequent performance.

As Figure 1 shows, Rogers's basic model focuses on and elaborates five substages in the process of innovation diffusion and adoption. First, the diffusion agency starts by marketing and creating awareness of its innovation through a variety of communication channels, such as journals, advertisements, and leaflets, often followed by personal contacts and informal influence of opinion leaders. Once there is an awareness of an alternative, the next subphase is the arousal of interest by a potential user of the innovation. This arousal of interest is influenced by various preconditions, such as felt need and organizational innovativeness, norms, resources, and communication behavior. The model assumes that

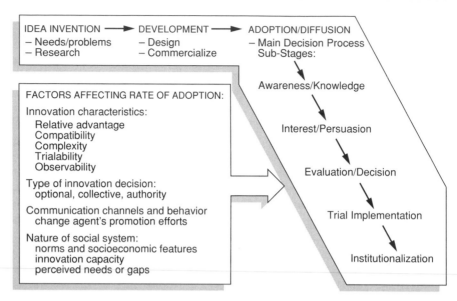

FIGURE 1   Rogers's basic model of the process stages in innovation invention, development, and diffusion and adoption. This figure combines Rogers's basic stages of the innovation process with factors that predict the rate of innovation adoption. SOURCE: Adapted from Rogers (1983, pp. 165, 233).

the potential adopter engages in a mental evaluation of the innovation and that likelihood of adoption increases when the innovation: (1) promises to have a strong advantage over alternatives, (2) is highly compatible with existing practices, (3) is not too complex, and (4) when it can be tried out and the results can be observed. An adoption decision typically leads to an actual trial implementation of the innovation. Positive outcomes from the trial will lead to continued use and institutionalization of the innovation by the adopting organization; negative outcomes will lead to rejection.

Although extensive empirical support for this adoption process model has been established for individual adopters (such as farmers adopting best practices promoted by the Extension Service of the U.S. Department of Agriculture), mixed results have been obtained when the organization is the locus of innovation adoption. Organizations (particularly hospitals) are complex political systems consisting of many functional specialties and administrative hierarchies (e.g., different medical and administrative staffs) that often compete for influence and resources in the adoption and implementation of project priorities. As a consequence, innovation adoption decisions tend to be used for partisan purposes— usually heralded by some, attacked and sabotaged by some, and apathetically ignored by the majority of others who are preoccupied with other organizational priorities (Dahl and Lindblom, 1976).

For example, Clark (1987) reports on a study of a hospital-design team initially consisting of the senior administrative staff and a small group of professional nurses working with the British Department of Health and Social Security. They decided to adopt a standard design package that had been devised and developed in the department for producing cost-effective decisions by placing all treatment activities in a central location. During the early stages of design, the medical staff of the design team made no serious interventions or contributions, even though the proposed designs had considerable implications for the medical hierarchy and for the allocation of space and resources. Then at a very late stage, when it became apparent to them that the new hospital, if built as designed, would involve considerable change in their working conditions and in their professional control of activities, they became much more active, thereby necessitating structural alterations during the commissioning of the new hospital.

## REVISIONS NEEDED IN MODEL FOR INNOVATION ADOPTION BY ORGANIZATIONS

As this example suggests, innovation adoption by organizations is far more complex than by individuals. In particular, we will focus on six specific process complexities that are evident in the three cases of hospital innovation adoption in this volume and which are not adequately explained by the basic model in Figure 1.

1. The three cases exist in organizational contexts that motivated and enabled successful adoption of innovation. Moreover, the stage for adopting the innovations was set over a period of several years and involving many organizational participants.

2. In each of the three examples of successful hospital innovation adoption, the innovators experienced "shocks" (not merely persuasion) as a result of direct personal confrontations with needs or problems. These shocks were sufficient to trigger their attention and action for innovation. When people become dissatisfied enough with existing conditions, they initiate action to resolve their dissatisfaction.

3. Once adoption activities begin, the process does not unfold in a simple linear sequence of stages and substages; instead, it proliferates into complex bundles of innovation ideas and divergent paths of activities by different organizational units. In the three cases of successful adoption, the innovation process was kept relatively simple in the face of these inexorable pressures for proliferation.

4. Setbacks and mistakes are frequently encountered during the innovation process, either because plans go awry or because unanticipated environmental events significantly alter the assumptions of the innovation. These setbacks signal either rejection of the innovation or opportunities for learning through reinvention. Learning fails when events are caused, and consequences are felt, by different people. Through reinvention, participants in the three cases of successful innovation adoption learned by reconnecting the causes and consequences of innovation invention, development, and adoption activities.

5. In the three successful cases, reinvention of the innovation developed elsewhere was facilitated by modifying the innovations to fit the local organizational situation, having top management extensively involved and committed to the innovation, and using various techniques to maintain task completion and momentum throughout the adoption process.

6. The adoption processes varied to fit the specific contingencies of the innovations being adopted by the three hospitals.

Many of these six process complexities, which occurred in our three cases of successful adoption, would be viewed as characteristics leading to failure by the adoption model shown in Figure 1. These empirical observations are inconsistent with our conceptual model. We will now discuss how revisions in the basic model might be made to deal with each of the six observed processes. Doing so may not only explain why the three hospitals were successful in adopting their innovations but also propose a revised conceptual model to understand the process of innovation adoption by organizations.

### Temporal and Contextual Preconditions for Innovation Adoption

Innovations are not initiated on the spur of the moment, nor are they initiated by a single dramatic incident or a single entrepreneur. As observed in all the innovations considered in a recent study (Van de Ven, Angle, and Poole, 1989), each of the three hospital innovation adoption cases in this volume shows that there was an extended gestation period, often lasting three or more years, in which medical, professional, or nursing staffs in the hospital engaged in a variety of activities that set the stage for innovation. Many initial events during this period were not intentionally directed toward adopting an innovation. As we will discuss in the next section, some events triggered recognition of the need for innovation (e.g., infant deaths or a shortage of nursing staff), while others generated awareness of the technological feasibility of an innovation (e.g., microscopic surgical procedures, extracorporeal membrane oxygenation, or alternative work schedules). Technology-push and demand-pull events such as these often launched intrepreneurs (Pinchot, 1985) on courses of action that, by chance, intersected with independent actions of others. These intersections provided occasions for people to recognize and access new opportunities and potential resources. Where these occasions were exploited, people modified and adapted their independent courses of action into interdependent collective actions to undertake concerted efforts to initiate an innovation.

Although the basic model in Figure 1 posits that an innovation adoption decision is a relatively straightforward result of knowledge and persuasion, these observations emphasize that *chance plays a significant role in affecting the decision and subsequent course of innovation adoption*. The sheer volume of initiatives undertaken by a large number of interacting people increases the probability of stimulating innovation. The findings also reinforce the bias-for-action principle of Peters and Waterman (1982). Perhaps Louis Pasteur's adage that *Chance favors the prepared mind* best captures the process that sets the stage for innovation.

The important practical question then becomes, "What can organizations do to increase their preparedness to capitalize on the chance of innovation?" Angle (1989) provides a core suggestion for dealing with this question: *Design and develop the organization's conditions to enable and motivate innovative behavior*. These conditions include the legitimacy, resources, structure, and culture of the encompassing organization that innovation groups draw upon to enable and constrain their innovative behaviors. Amabile (1988), Angle (1989), and Kanter (1988) summarize an extensive body of research indicating that innovation is facilitated in organizations that provide both enabling and motivating conditions for innovation; it does not occur where either enabling or motivating conditions are absent.

The three cases of successful adoptions of innovations in hospitals exemplify many of the organizational conditions that enable and motivate innovative behavior. Each of the hospitals housing the innovations is a highly respected, long-established, and a very successful institution located at the hub of its industry and community networks. During their respective periods of innovation adoption, the hospitals were reported to have moderately low personnel turnover rates, long-run strategic time horizons that connected diverse organizational activities to core institutional missions (providing quality care to meet changing patient needs), and a high degree of commitment of top management and medical staffs to their respective innovations; in addition, the hospitals were reported to be making significant investments both in new technologies and in their professional staffs. Although the relative influence of any one of these conditions on innovation is difficult to assess, when combined they exemplify the ingredients of an organizational setting that enables innovation. Moreover, in each case, recognition of the need for innovation was triggered by many (not one or a few) events over an extended period of time (often several years) and involved many different people both within and outside the hospitals.

In the short term there is little that managers can do directly to change organizational culture, legitimacy, and prestige, because they are the historical by-products of all previous activities and interactions of an organization with its environment. Thus, it is erroneous to expect that these innovation-enabling characteristics can be changed quickly. However, long-term macroconsequences are produced by the accumulation of many microactions that preoccupy the short-term attention of organizational participants.

The immediate setting for most innovations is the organization itself, and much can be done to modify the immediate operating conditions of an organization. Organizations are complex social systems that provide templates for playing out many distinctive roles important to an innovation. Organizational attributes, such as structure, systems, and practices influence the likelihood that innovation ideas will be surfaced, and once surfaced that they will be developed and nurtured toward realization. Furthermore, the organization is the most direct source of material, financial, and other resources needed to support innovation efforts.

With respect to structure, there are several features that will affect the gestation of innovative activities. The more complex and differentiated the organization, and the easier it is to cross boundaries, the greater the potential number of sources from which innovative ideas can spring. However, with increasing organizational size and complexity comes segmentation (Kanter, 1983) and bureaucratic procedures; these often constrain innovation unless special systems are put in place to motivate and enable innovative behavior. Key motivating factors include providing a balance of intrinsic and extrinsic rewards for innovative behaviors (Amabile, 1983). Pay, in itself, seems to be a relatively weak motivator for innovation; it more often serves as a proxy for recognition. Individualized rewards tend to increase idea generation and radical innovations, whereas group rewards tend to increase incremental innovations and their implementation (Angle, 1989).

However, the presence of motivating factors, by themselves, will not ensure innovative behavior. Enabling conditions are equally necessary. Examples of such enabling conditions include the following:

- Resources for innovation
- Frequent communication across departmental lines, among people with dissimilar viewpoints
- Moderate environmental uncertainty and mechanisms for focusing attention on changing conditions
- Cohesive work groups with open conflict resolution mechanisms that integrate creative personalities into the mainstream
- Structures that provide access to innovation role models and mentors
- Moderately low personnel turnover
- Psychological contracts that legitimate and solicit spontaneous innovative behavior

In short, normal people have the capability and potential to be creative and innovative. The actualization of this potential turns on whether management can create an organizational context that not only motivates but also enables individuals to innovate.

### "Shocks" That Trigger Innovation

Although a conducive organizational climate appears to set the stage for innovation, concrete actions to undertake specific innovations are triggered by "shocks" from sources either internal or external to the organization. In the three hospital cases, these shocks included the introduction of the Diagnostic Related Group payment reimbursement system, increasing competitiveness of the hospital industry, infant deaths in the neonatal intensive care unit, as well as results of an employee survey.

The reason why shocks are needed to trigger innovation is based on a simple model of decision making that is embedded in Rogers's basic model: when people reach a threshold of dissatisfaction with existing conditions, they initiate action to resolve their dissatisfaction. Thus, we have no problem with Rogers's basic model since it recognizes that necessity, opportunity, or threat is the mother of invention. Instead, *the problem lies in not appreciating the physiological limitations of human beings and the conditions that trigger their thresholds for action.*

Human beings are unconsciously highly adaptable. Small and gradual changes over time provide insufficient stimulation to reach people's recognition thresholds for action (Helson, 1964). People adapt to gradually changing conditions and often fail to notice that conditions have signaled the appropriateness (through opportunity or threat) of a change. As a consequence, unless the stimulus exceeds their action thresholds, i.e., a shock, people do not move into action to correct their situation, which over time may become deplorable. Opportunities for innovation are either not recognized or not accepted as important enough to motivate innovative action.

With regard to perception, organizations establish structures and standard operating procedures to run efficiently and reliably. But these structures also have the effect of programming people into cognitive routines or habits, which desensitize them to novel events. Ironically, this habit-bound perception is particularly prevalent where the people are most competent. As argued elsewhere (Van de Ven, 1986, p. 595), "what people do most is often what they think about least."

People's reluctance to accept change is equally relevant. Change is often threatening, because it offers the possibility that coping mechanisms that were at least adequate under the old situation may no longer suffice. People who were "winners" may now be lucky to break even. Adding to the relatively passive blinders that people wear, because of habit or inattention, are the active blinders related to such defense mechanisms as denial. So for a variety of reasons, it may be difficult for people to notice change of the sort that should by all rights stimulate them to innovate. The management of attention is a central problem in managing the innovation journey (Van de Ven, 1986).

What can organizations do to solve the problem? Although there is no panacea, Angle (1989) suggests that mechanisms can be put into place for redirecting and jostling the attention of organizational members, so that subtle changes and needs will be noticed. For example, Normann (1985) observed that well-managed companies are not only close to their customers, as Peters and Waterman (1982) suggest, they also search out and focus on their most demanding customers. Empirically, von Hippel (1981) has shown that ideas for most new product innovations in an industry come from customers. Utterback (1971) also found that about 75 percent of the ideas used to develop product innovations came from outside of the organization.

In each of the three hospital innovation adoption cases in this volume, nurses and physicians often came face to face with demanding patient needs, people at the cutting edge of technology, hospital nursing staffs, and consultants. These personal exposures increased the likelihood of triggering actions to pay attention to changing technological, patient, and community needs. In general, *direct personal confrontation with sources of problems and opportunities is needed to reach the threshold of concern and appreciation required to motivate most people to act* (Van de Ven, 1980b).

### Adoption Activities Become Complex, Divergent Progressions

As Schroeder et al. (1986) found across a wide variety of innovations, the three hospital cases in this volume show that shortly after the adoption decision was made, the process became increasingly complex to manage, as the initially simple innovation process proliferated into diverse pathways. More specifically, after the onset of a simple stream of activity to develop or adopt an innovative idea, the process quickly diverged into multiple and parallel paths of activities. Some of the proliferation is produced by dividing the labor among functions and organizational units (e.g., nurses, doctors, administrators) necessary in developing different conceptions of the innovation. Some of the proliferation is produced because a given innovation typically entails a bundle of related innovations (e.g., a new technological procedure requires adopting new administrative procedures, new occupational roles, and new conceptions of patient care). Each path represents a different development and adoption process. Finally, other organizational activities may appear unrelated to the innovation but often compete for scarce resources and thwart the innovation adoption process (e.g., the introduction of new computerized reporting procedures during the nursing schedule experiment). As a consequence, after a short initial period of simple unitary activities, the management of innovation soon proliferates into an effort to direct controlled chaos (Quinn, 1980).

This proliferation of activities over time appears to be a pervasive but little-understood characteristic of the innovation adoption process. The basic model in Figure 1 assumes that the innovation in concept and scope remains intact as it is adopted. These observations suggest a need to revise the model to address the continuous redefinitions or enactments (Weick, 1979) of the innovation that are made by organizational participants into terms that they can understand and are compatible with their cultures. Moreover, they show that it is not correct to depict the user as adopting only a single innovation; many users are simultaneously choosing from diverse sets of innovations in many different areas, such as equipment, organizational structures, and new work practices (Clark, 1987).

So what might be done to cope with this proliferating complexity? Like Peters and Waterman (1982), we recommend *Kiss (Keep It Simple, Stupid!).* We believe that much of this complexity is the result of striving to achieve too much too soon and thereby becoming embroiled in many activities that are not necessary or essential to adopting an innovation. For example, in the ECMO case, one way of decreasing complexity of the innovation was to focus on adopting it in the neonatal intensive care unit before efforts were made to introduce it for regional use with other hospitals in the metropolitan area.

In our studies of innovation, we observed organizational adopters to exhibit an impatient quest to leapfrog into a large program or technology without evaluating the merits of the core innovation (Van de Ven, Venkataraman, Polley, and Garud, 1989). Ironically, this tendency often delays adoption of core innovations because organizational participants become preoccupied with efforts peripheral to the immediate tasks needed to develop the basic idea. Instead, much effort is devoted to preengineering systems that may be needed to adopt families or generations of the innovation. In the process of doing so, basic problems inherent in the core idea are often masked and go unquestioned until setbacks arise (as discussed below).

Administrative reviews are periodically conducted to evaluate innovation adoption progress. However, administrative reviews tend to be poor substitutes for the acid test of the market. Restricting and simplifying adoption activities to the core innovation idea decreases implementation cost and time. Moreover, it tends to decrease the costly mistakes of investments in innovations that do not meet the market test. Small mistakes are more tolerable and correctable than large costly mistakes.

## Setbacks Provide Learning Opportunities

All three hospital cases show that mistakes and setbacks were frequently encountered during the process, either because initial plans go awry or because unanticipated environmental events significantly alter the ground assumptions and context of the innovation. Although detailed analyses of these setbacks was not reported in the three hospital cases, other studies can provide insights into the anatomy of setbacks and the opportunities they provide for learning and reinvention during the innovation adoption process.

In recent innovation studies in Minnesota (Van de Ven, Angle, and Poole, 1989) the typical initial response to setbacks was to adjust resources and schedules, which provided a grace period for innovation development. But with time, many of the problems snowballed because additional resources or slack time only masked more fundamental problems; namely, difficulties in detecting, correcting, and learning from mistakes. Many of these setbacks and errors went uncorrected for the following reasons: (1) it was difficult to discriminate substantive issues from "noise" in systems overloaded with mixed signals about performance; (2) innovation champions escalated their commitments to a course of action by ignoring naysayers and proceeding full speed ahead; (3) some innovation participants became hypervigilant, calling prematurely for changes in a course of action when minor or correctable problems were encountered; and (4) in-process criteria of innovation success often shifted over time as the initial euphoria with an innovation waned and new, more exciting alternatives became apparent to organizational participants. Thus, although extensive errors were detected in the Minnesota innovation studies, very few were corrected, and they snowballed to crisis proportions before they were addressed. Many learning experiences could not be acted on because of the time lag required in changing a course of action.

In their classic study, Pressman and Wildavsky (1973) examined the efforts of the federal Economic Development Administration to implement a new program that appeared to be destined for success in providing jobs for Blacks in Oakland through public works grants and loans to local enterprises. But more than six years later, public works construction had not been finished and there were few new jobs for unemployed Blacks. Initial agreements among federal, regional, and local officials slowly dissolved into a host of disagreements over the details of implementation. These details included changing actors, diverse perspectives, and multiple negotiations and clearances among decision makers, all leading to a geometric growth of interdependencies and delays. Delays came from (1) unplanned accidental occurrences, (2) blocking efforts by participants who wanted to stop the program, (3) alternative time priorities, and (4) delays caused by delay itself— with every delay momentum declines in the commitment to seeing the program through to completion.

An immediate recommendation that emerges from these findings is to structure opportunities and resources to detect and correct mistakes when they occur and before they become vicious cycles, as suggested in the chapters by Driscoll and by Choi et al. However, it is not clear that additional slack time, alone, will result in adaptive learning. We have found no empirical evidence in the literature that additional resources and slack time will facilitate trial-and-error learning in highly ambiguous situations.

Trial-and-error learning may be far more difficult than has been assumed. With highly novel undertakings, one can seldom rely on past routines or plans to guide behavior. Moreover, the highly ambiguous information that participants typically receive and the idiosyncratic experiences they encounter greatly circumscribe rational learning processes (March and Olsen, 1976). Instead, these conditions spawn "superstitious learning" (Levitt and March, 1988). Because information is often unreliable, ambiguous, or late, and because most innovation participants have not experienced other innovations from which to develop inferences, it becomes difficult to identify cause-and-effect relationships. As a consequence, there is a blurring between "success" and "failure" as results are interpreted in relation to differing personal perspectives and frames of reference (Dornblaser et al., 1989).

Perhaps the root problem for why little learning is observed as setbacks arise exists in the basic adoption process model itself, which many organizations have come to use to guide their action. *The linear sequence of invention, development, and adoption stages in Figure 1 minimizes opportunities for learning.* As Pressman and Wildavsky (1973) emphasize, "Learning fails because events are caused and consequences are felt by different organizations. Just as "planners should not be separated from doers" (p. 135), and "implementation should not be divorced from policy" (p. 143), neither should innovation adoption be separated from innovation invention and development. In other words, as Rogers recognizes (Rice and Rogers, 1980), *reinvention facilitates adoption.*

Reinvention is fundamentally a learning process that is triggered by the inevitable setbacks and mistakes people encounter as they attempt to implement innovation. Learning is a trial-and-error process, and its essential steps include idea invention, development, implementation, evaluation, and adjustment. When invention and development activities are divorced from implementation and adoption, the learning process is short-circuited because different people experience these activities. As Pressman and Wildavsky (1973) conclude, implementation and adoption must not be conceived of as processes that take place after innovation invention and development. Learning requires that these activities become fused in the innovation process, and that interaction occurs among the people principally concerned with invention, development, and implementation. This happens more easily when innovations are "home grown" than when they are developed elsewhere.

In the organizations where innovations are "home grown," Schroeder et al. (1986) found that implementation and adoption activities often occur throughout the development period, by linking and integrating the new with the old, as opposed to substituting, transforming, or replacing the existing organizational arrangements with the new innovation. The implication of this observation is that, because of limited organizational resources, innovations cannot often be mere additions to existing organizational programs. Neither is it practical for many innovations simply to replace existing organizational programs because of the history of investments and commitments made to make these programs (yesterday's innovations) work. However, such a possibility is often perceived by organizational participants not involved in the development of the innovation. Therefore, new innovations often represent a threat to the established order. Instead, if they are to be implemented and become institutionalized, the new innovations must overlap with and become integrated into existing organizational arrangements.

Concentrated efforts to link the new with the old throughout the development period provide not only more time but also more opportunities to address problems and modify the developing innovations to applied situations than is possible for organizations that adopt innovations developed elsewhere. Therefore, we expect "home-grown" innovations normally to require less time to implement and institutionalize than externally induced innovations (Van de Ven, 1980a).

### Reinventing Innovations Developed Elsewhere

As was done in the three hospital cases, organizations can take a number of steps to facilitate reinvention and learning as they adopt innovations initially developed elsewhere. These steps include (1) modifying and adapting the innovation to the organization's local situation, (2) active involvement of top management, and (3) applying techniques that facilitate coordination among diverse and distracted groups of people to meet key deadlines and maintain momentum for innovation adoption.

First, conventional wisdom suggests that successfully implemented innovations start small and spread incrementally with success (Greiner, 1970). Although this approach provides one way to deal with proliferating complexity (others will be suggested below), this may often not be a wise strategy to deal with organizational political life. Lindquist and Mauriel (1989) compared two common alternative strategies for adopting and implementing innovations: a *breadth* strategy in which the innovation is implemented across all organizational units simultaneously, and a *depth* strategy in which the innovation is implemented and debugged in a demonstration site before it is generalized to other organizational units. They found that the breadth strategy was more successful than the depth strategy in adopting and institutionalizing site based management in two public school districts. Several explanations were provided for this surprising finding:

• Once the depth strategy is introduced and heralded by top management, the demonstration project loses visible attention, as their agendas become preoccupied with other pressing management problems.

• With a breadth strategy, top management stays in control of the innovation implementation process—thereby increasing (rather than decreasing) its power. Moreover, slack resources within the control of top management can ensure success better than limited budgets for innovation to a demonstration site.

• There is a trade-off between implementing a few components of an innovation in breadth versus implementing all components in depth in a particular demonstration site. Less resistance to change is encountered when a few (and presumably the easy) components of an innovation are implemented across the board to a few (and presumably supportive) stakeholders than when all (both easy and hard) components of a program are implemented in depth with all partisan stakeholders involved.

• With a depth strategy, it is easier for opposing forces in other parts of the organization to mobilize efforts to sabotage a "favored" demonstration site than it is to produce evidence of the merits and generalizability of an innovation.

Experimenting with alternative forms of an innovation introduces several variations of the depth strategy in an organization. For example, Choi, Jameson, and Brekke describe their efforts to conduct an experiment of three different hospitals in Rochester Methodist Hospital. Rigorous methods of scientific experimentation (such as making random assignment, minimizing contamination between groups, standardizing observations, and replicating procedures) were used to determine which schedule was most appropriate. Although it might be argued that these scientific methods enhanced the validity of findings from the experiment, they had the trade-off effects of creating animosity among the staff because experimental procedures permitted no choice or participation in their design or in the work schedules to which nurses were randomly assigned. Furthermore, as is common to any depth innovation adoption strategy, nurses in each experimental schedule were isolated from those working on other schedules. Such isolation restricts communication between groups and may explain the decrease in perceived teamwork among nursing staff. When compounded with other setbacks or "glitches" that inevitably occur during the process, the experiment significantly jeopardized the successful adoption of the innovation. Indeed, only the staunch support of the nursing department managers prevented the staff from rejecting the innovation.

As it turned out, the experiment found that nurse staffing, not scheduling, influenced the cost of care. Further, the experiment findings had little affect in determining the work schedules that the nurses actually adopted. Most nursing units chose the select-a-plan, which permits each unit the greatest flexibility to design and adopt its own work schedule. This is predictable and again underscores a consistent research finding: *performance, satisfaction, and motivation of individuals are higher when they implement their own plans than when they carry out someone else's plan* (Bass, 1971; Bennis et al., 1962; Delbecq et al., 1975).

From this experience, Choi, Jameson, and Brekke conclude that "good management does not necessarily allow for good science." Over the years, Argyris has argued a different conclusion: "Good science calls for good management." Precisely because of the kinds of unintended consequences of rigorous research illustrated in this case, Argyris (1968, p. 194) has called for adopting good management principles to improve the quality of scientific studies:

> *In our experience the more subjects are involved directly (or through representatives) in planning and designing the research,*

*the more we learn about the best ways to ask questions, the
critical questions from the employees' views, the kinds of resistance each research method would generate, and the best way
to gain genuine and long-range commitment to the research.*

In another study, Bryson and Roering (1989) examined the introduction of an administrative innovation (the adoption of new
planning systems) in six local governmental agencies. They found
that each attempt to adopt the innovation was prone to disinte-
gration because:

- external events and crises frequently occurred, distracting participants' attention and taking away any slack resources available
to adopt the innovation;
- the adoption process itself was partially cumulative—what
occurred before was remembered and had to be accounted for; and
- participants became bogged down with information overload,
conflicting priorities, and divergent issues that were outside their
jurisdictions.

Bryson and Roering developed several useful recommendations
for enhancing innovation adoption efforts. First, *not only have a
powerful innovation sponsor but also an effective process facilitator* who is committed to continuing with the adoption process,
particularly when difficulties and setbacks occur. Second, since
disruptions and setbacks cause delays, and interest wanes with
time, *structure the process into key junctures*—deadlines, conferences, and peak events. These structured junctures in the adoption process establish key deadlines to perform planned intermediate tasks, force things to come together, and facilitate unplanned
intersections of key ideas, people, transactions, and outcomes.
Finally, *adopt a willingness to be flexible* not only about what
constitutes acceptable innovation adoption, but also in construct-
ing arguments geared to many different evaluation criteria. In
short, innovation-adoption success more often represents a socially constructed reality than an objective reality (Dornblaser et
al., 1989).

Finally, because organizations are complex hierarchical systems,
contradictory part-whole relations are often produced when sys-
tem-wide innovations are introduced. The invention and development of an innovation at one organizational unit or level often
represents an externally imposed mandate that other (often lower-
level) organizational units also adopt the innovation. Thus, we
have often observed a top management or policy unit express
euphoria about the innovation it developed for the entire organi-

zation, while frustrations and opposition to that same innovation are expressed by affected organizational units. Such a situation often presents itself when a systemwide innovation is attempted by mandating that all organizational units adopt the innovation.

Such a situation was reported by Marcus and Weber (1989) who studied actions taken by 28 American nuclear power companies in response to a new set of nuclear safety procedures mandated by the U.S. Nuclear Regulatory Commission and the implications of those actions for organizational effectiveness. They found that the nuclear power plants with relatively poor safety records tended to respond in a rule-bound manner that perpetuated their poor safety performance. On the other hand, those plants whose safety records were relatively strong tended to retain their autonomy by adapting the standards to their local situations, a response that reinforced their strong safety performance. Ironically, those least ready or willing to adopt the innovation may be those that need it the most.

The Marcus and Weber study provides an important and generalizable inference for the management of externally imposed innovations: *Be forewarned of the possible consequences of passive acceptance of external dictates by those who strictly follow the letter of the law; they may do so in "bad faith" that may not achieve the results intended.* Some autonomy is needed for an adopting unit to identify with and internalize an innovation; mere formal compliance is insufficient. The disposition of innovation adopters is likely to be negatively affected if they are not granted a sufficient level of autonomy; and it is their disposition that is often critical in assuring successful adoption. The "not invented here" syndrome is well known in all sorts of organizations. Adopting agencies or organizations that have not developed any sense of commitment to those innovations may well behave bureaucratically and simply do what the letter of the law requires.

## Contingencies in the Innovation Adoption Process

We may never find one best way to innovate. As the three cases of hospital innovation adoption in this volume suggest, a sophisticated manager of innovation will try instead to identify those contingent factors that influence what works and what does not. In particular, we believe that many of the key innovation processes described in the previous section are more pronounced for innovations of greater novelty, size, and duration.

*Radical Versus Incremental Innovations*

Some innovations change the entire order of things, obsoleting the old ways and perhaps sending entire businesses the way of the slide rule or the buggy whip. Others simply build on what is already there, requiring only modest modification of one's old world view. We expect that innovations of different levels of novelty need to be managed differently. Indeed, some organizations may be well suited to one type of innovation but not another. For example, an organization that values and rewards individuals may have the advantage in radical innovation, while a more collectivist system may do better at incremental innovation (Angle, 1989). Empirically, we found that statistical relationships between perceived effectiveness and various measures of innovation ideas, people, transactions, and context were weaker for highly novel than for less radical innovations (Van de Ven and Chu, 1989). Pelz (1985) found that the stages of the innovating process were more disorderly for technically complex innovations than for technically simple innovations.

*Innovation Stage and Temporal Duration*

Transitions from innovation invention to development to adoption activities often entail shifts from radical to incremental and from divergent to convergent thinking. As innovations approach the culminating institutionalization step, they become more highly structured and stabilized in their patterns and less differentiated from other organizational arrangements (Zaltman et al., 1973; Lindquist and Mauriel, 1989).

The developmental pattern and eventual success of an innovation are also influenced by its temporal duration. The initial commitments and investments in launching an innovation represent an initial stock of assets that provide an innovation unit a "honeymoon" period to perform its work (Fichman and Levinthal, 1988). These assets reduce the risk of terminating the innovation during its honeymoon period in case setbacks arise or if initial outcomes are judged unfavorable. The likelihood of replenishing these assets depends on how long it takes to complete the adoption process. Interest and commitment wane with time. Thus, after the honeymoon, innovations terminate at disproportionately higher rates in proportion to the time needed for their adoption. As Pressman and Wildavsky (1973, p. 130) state, "The advantages of being new are exactly that: being new. They dissipate quickly over time. The organization ages rapidly. Little by little the regulations that apply to everyone else also apply to it."

*Size and Scope of the Innovation*

It may be that small organizations have the advantage in starting up an innovation but that larger organizations with more slack resources have the advantage in keeping an innovation alive until it is completed. We found that venture capital was more risky and more difficult to obtain than was internal corporate venture funding (Van de Ven et al., 1989). Larger organizations offer a more fertile ground for sustaining and nurturing spin-off innovations. Also, there may be more places to "hide" something in a larger organization, until an innovation can stand on its own. Yet, large organizations seem to need bureaucratic systems in order to survive, and this is not particularly conducive to innovation. The message to managers is to keep finding ways to remain flexible, to permit sufficient power to concentrate on innovation, to build access to technical competence, and to listen attentively to the views of those directly responsible for implementation—factors that Nord and Tucker (1987) found were critical to successful adoption of innovations in large organizations.

## CONCLUSION

This chapter has attempted to explain why the three hospital cases presented in this book were successful in adopting their innovations and what can be learned from these cases to understand organizational innovation adoption. To address these issues, we relied on an extensive and growing body of research literature on innovation adoption, and used the cases to illustrate some of the key findings in this literature. Our starting point was a review of Rogers's basic model, which is perhaps the most widely shared view of the process of innovation adoption and diffusion. Although this model is robust in explaining the adoption of innovations by individuals, it must be revised to incorporate the complexities exemplified in our three hospital cases and often observed when the organization is the locus of adoption.

The key points raised by the case studies in this volume are as follows:

1. The cases of hospital innovation adoption took place in organizational contexts that motivated and enabled successful adop-

tion. Moreover, the stage for adopting the innovations was set over a period of several years and involved many organizational participants.

2. In each of the three examples of successful hospital adoption of innovation, the innovators experienced "shocks" (not mere persuasion) as a result of direct personal confrontation with needs or problems. These shocks were sufficient to get their attention and trigger action for innovation. When people experience sufficient dissatisfaction with existing conditions, they initiate corrective action.

3. Once adoption activities begin, the process does not unfold in a simple linear sequence of stages and substages; instead, it proliferates into complex bundles of innovation ideas and divergent paths of activities by organizational units. The three cases of successful adoption demonstrated ways to keep the innovation process relatively simple in the face of these inexorable pressures for proliferation.

4. Setbacks and mistakes are frequently encountered during the innovation process, either because plans go awry or because unanticipated environmental events significantly alter the assumptions of the innovation. These setbacks signal either rejection of the innovation or opportunities for learning through reinvention. Participants in the three cases of successful innovation adoption learned through reinvention by reconnecting the causes and consequences of innovation invention, development, and adoption activities.

5. In the three successful cases, reinvention of the innovations developed elsewhere was facilitated by modifying the innovations to fit the local organizational situations. Moreover, top management was extensively involved and committed to the innovation, and various techniques were used to maintain momentum throughout the adoption process.

6. The adoption processes varied to fit the specific contingencies of the innovation being adopted by the three hospitals.

No doubt, other explanations can be offered to answer why the three hospital cases were successful in adopting their innovations. However, this chapter focused on six explanations because they suggest the revisions needed in Rogers's basic model to explain more accurately the process of innovation adoption by organizations. These revisions have important implications for the practice of organizational innovation adoption. Some of these implications were presented as normative guidelines for maneuvering the innovation adoption journey in organizations. When verified in subsequent research, we believe they can substantially improve the odds of successful innovation adoption.

It should be emphasized that the applied principles offered here will not ensure success in adoption of an innovation. The reason for this caveat rests with a concluding lesson that we believe underlies all the key processes along the innovation journey: *management cannot control innovation success; only its odds* (Angle and Van de Ven, 1989). This lesson implies that a fundamental change is needed in the control philosophy of conventional management practice.

Professor William McKelvey at the University of California, Los Angeles, tells a story of the 1976 Winter Olympics, where Franz Klammer won the men's downhill skiing competition. When interviewed after the event and asked how he managed to turn in such an incredible performance, Klammer said that he had chosen to "ski out of control." He knew that there were many other top-level skiers entered against him, several of whom might outpace him on any given day, if he were to ski his normal speed—that is, under control. He chose, instead, to ski so fast that he abandoned any sense of control over the course. Although this was obviously not a sufficient condition for victory, he saw it as a necessary condition. Staying in control would virtually ensure a loss, whereas skiing out of control would make it at least possible to win.

Innovation managers may have an important lesson to learn from this vignette. By definition, an innovation is a leap into the unknown. In order that innovations have a chance to succeed, traditional notions of managerial control may need to be relaxed.

A number of practical consequences follow if innovation success is recognized to be a probabilistic process. First, innovation success or failure would more often be attributed to factors beyond the control of innovators. This, in turn, will decrease the likelihood that the careers of innovation managers will be stigmatized if their innovation fails, and increase the likelihood that they will be given another chance to manage future innovations. After all, one cannot become a master or professional at anything if only one trial is permitted. As we reported, relatively little trial-and-error learning occurred once the journey was begun for a given innovation. Repeated trials over many innovations are essential for learning to occur, and for applying these learning experiences to subsequent innovations. It is largely through repeated trials and the accumulation of learning experiences across these trials that an organization can build an inventory of competence, and thereby progressively increase its odds of innovation success.

## ACKNOWLEDGMENTS

I appreciate comments from Bright Dornblaser (University of Minnesota) and Rosabeth Kanter (Harvard University) on an earlier draft of this chapter.

## REFERENCES

Amabile, T. M. 1983. The Social Psychology of Creativity. New York: Springer-Verlag.

Amabile, T. M. 1988. A model of creativity and innovation in organizations. In Research in Organizational Behavior, Vol. 10, B. M. Staw and L. L. Cummings, eds. Greenwich, Conn.: JAI Press.

Angle, H. A. 1989. Psychology and organizational innovation. Chapter 5 in Research on the Management of Innovation: The Minnesota Studies, A. Van de Ven, H. Angle, and M. S. Poole, eds. New York: Ballinger/Harper & Row.

Angle, H. A., and A. H. Van de Ven. 1989. Suggestions for managing the innovation journey. Chapter 21 in Research on the Management of Innovation: The Minnesota Studies, A. Van de Ven, H. Angle, and M. S. Poole, eds. New York: Ballinger/Harper & Row.

Argyris, C. 1968. Some unintended consequences of rigorous research. Psychological Bulletin 70(3):185–197.

Barley, S. 1986. Technology as an occasion for structuring: Evidence from observations of CT scanners and the social order of radiology departments. Administrative Science Quarterly 31:78–108.

Bass, B. 1971. When planning for others. Journal of Applied Behavior Science 6:151–172.

Bennis, W. G., K. D. Benne, and R. Chin. 1962. The Planning of Change. New York: Holt, Rhinehart and Winston.

Bryson, J., and W. Roering. 1989. Mobilizing innovation efforts: The case of government strategic planning. Chapter 18 in Research on the Management of Innovation: The Minnesota Studies, A. Van de Ven, H. Angle, and M. S. Poole, eds. New York: Ballinger/Harper & Row.

Clark, P. 1987. Anglo-American Innovation. Berlin: Walter de Gruyter.

Cummings, L. L. 1965. Organizational climates for creativity. Academy of Management Journal 8:220–227.

Dahl, R. A., and C. E. Lindblom. 1976. Politics, Economics, and Welfare. Chicago: University of Chicago Press.

Delbecq, A. L., A. H. Van de Ven, and D. H. Gustafson. 1975. Group Techniques for Program Planning. Glenview, Ill.: Scott-Foresman.

Dornblaser, B. M., T. Lin, and A. H. Van de Ven. 1989. Innovation outcomes, learning, and action loops. Chapter 7 in Research on the Management of Innovation: The Minnesota Studies, A. Van de Ven, H. Angle, and M. S. Poole, eds. New York: Ballinger/Harper & Row.

Fichman, M., and D. A. Levinthal. 1988. Honeymoons and the Liability of Adolescence: A New Perspective on Duration Dependence in Social and Organizational Relationships. Pittsburgh, Pa.: Graduate School of Industrial Administration, Carnegie Mellon University. Unpublished paper.

Greiner, L. E. 1970. Patterns of organizational change. In Organizational Change and Development, G. Dalton, P. R. Lawrence, and L. E. Greiner, eds. Homewood, Ill.: Irwin-Dorsey Press.

Helson, H. 1964. Current trends and issues in adaptation-level theory. American Psychologist 19:23–68.

Kanter, R. M. 1983. The Change Masters. New York: Simon and Schuster.

Kanter, R. M. 1988. When a thousand flowers bloom: Structural, collective and social conditions for innovation in organizations. In Research in Organizational Behavior, Vol. 10, B. M. Staw and L. L. Cummings, eds. Greenwich, Conn.: JAI Press.

Kimberly, J., and M. Evanisko. 1981. Organizational innovation: The influence of individual, organizational, and contextual factors on hospital adoption of technology and administrative innovations. Academy of Management Journal 24:689–713.

Levitt, B., and J. G. March. 1988. Organizational Learning. Annual Review of Sociology, 14. Greenwich, Conn.: JAI Press.

Lindquist, K., and J. Mauriel. 1989. Depth and breadth in innovation implementation: The case of school-based management. Chapter 17 in Research on the Management of Innovation: The Minnesota Studies, A. Van de Ven, H. Angle, and M. S. Poole, eds. New York: Ballinger/ Harper & Row.

March, J. G., and J. P. Olsen. 1976. Ambiguity and Choice in Organizations. Bergen: Universitetsforlaget.

Marcus, A., and M. Weber. 1989. Externally induced innovation. Chapter 16 in Research on the Management of Innovation: The Minnesota Studies, A. Van de Ven, H. Angle, and M. S. Poole, eds. New York: Ballinger/Harper & Row.

Nord, W. R., and S. Tucker. 1987. Implementing Routine and Radical Innovations. Lexington, Mass.: D. C. Heath.

Normann, R. 1985. Towards an action theory of strategic management. In Strategic Decision Making in Complex Organizations, J. Pennings, ed. San Francisco: Jossey-Bass.

Pelz, D. C. 1985. Innovation complexity and the sequence of innovating stages. Knowledge Creation, Diffusion, Utilization 6(3):261–291.

Peters, T. J., and R. H. Waterman, Jr. 1982. In Search of Excellence: Lessons from America's Best Known Companies. New York: Harper & Row.

Pinchot, G. III. 1985. Intrapreneuring. New York: Harper & Row.

Pressman, J. L., and A. B. Wildavsky. 1973. Implementation. Berkeley: University of California Press.

Quinn, J. B. 1980. Strategies for Change: Logical Incrementalism. Homewood, Ill.: Irwin.

Rice, R., and E. Rogers. 1980. Reinvention in the innovation process. Knowledge: Creation, Diffusion, Utilization 1(4):499–514.

Rogers, E. 1962. Diffusion of Innovation. First Edition. New York: Free Press.

Rogers, E. 1983. Diffusion of Innovations. Third Edition. New York: Free Press.

Rogers, E., and F. Schoemaker. 1971. Communication of Innovation: A Cross-Cultural Perspective. New York: Free Press.

Rosenberg, N. 1982. Inside the Black Box: Techonology and Economics. Cambridge: Cambridge University Press.

Schroeder, R. G., A. H. Van de Ven, G. D. Scudder, and D. Polley. 1986. Managing innovation and change processes: Findings from the Minnesota innovation research program. Agribusiness Management 2(4): 501–523.

Thirtle, C. G., and V. W. Ruttan. 1987. The Role of Demand and Supply in the Generation and Diffusion of Technical Change. New York: Harwood Academic Publishers.

Tushman, M., and E. Romanelli. 1985. Organizational evolution: A metamorphosis model of convergence and reorientation. Pp. 171–222 in Research in Organization Behavior, Vol. 7, B. M. Staw and L. L. Cummings, eds. Greenwich, Conn.: JAI Press.

Utterback, J. 1971. The process of technological innovation within the firm. Academy of Management Journal 14:75–88.

Van de Ven, A. H. 1980a. Problem solving, planning, and innovation. Part I. Test of the program planning model. Human Relations 33(10): 711–740.

Van de Ven, A. H. 1980b. Problem solving, planning, and innovation. Part II. Speculations for theory and practice. Human Relations 33(11): 757–779.

Van de Ven, A. H. 1986. Central problems in the management of innovations. Management Science 32(5):590–607.

Van de Ven, A. H., and Y. Chu. 1989. A psychometric assessment of the Minnesota innovation survey. Chapter 3 in Research on the Management of Innovation: The Minnesota Studies, A. Van de Ven, H. Angle, and M. S. Poole, eds. New York: Ballinger/Harper & Row.

Van de Ven, A. H., H. Angle, and M. S. Poole, eds. 1989. Research on the Management of Innovation: The Minnesota Studies. New York: Ballinger/Harper & Row.

Van de Ven, A., S. Venkataraman, D. Polley, and R. Garud. 1989. Processes of new business creation in different organizational settings. Chapter 8 in Research on the Management of Innovation: The Minnesota Studies, A. Van de Ven, H. Angle, and M. S. Poole, eds. New York: Ballinger/Harper & Row.

von Hippel, E. 1981. Users as innovators. In Corporate Strategy and Product Innovation, R. R. Rothberg, ed. New York: Free Press.

Weick, K. 1979. The Social Psychology of Organizing. Reading: Addison-Wesley.

Zaltman, G., R. Duncan, and J. Holbek. 1973. Innovations and Organizations. New York: Wiley.

People and Technology in the Workplace. 1991.
Pp. 159–170. Washington, D.C:
National Academy Press.

# Managing the Ambulatory Care Unit

H. ROBERT CATHCART

The development of insurance for hospitalization and surgery began in the 1930s, just over 50 years ago. Now the payment system for health care is a major national issue. The efforts to control health care costs, led by the purchasers of health care—insurers, consumers, and employers who pay for health insurance—have resulted in revolutionary changes in the way physicians and hospitals use technology to perform their work more cost-effectively. This case presentation uses Pennsylvania Hospital as an example to illustrate how technology has facilitated these changes in response to financial demands.

## A REDEFINITION OF HEALTH CARE COST PAYMENTS

In the early 1980s, the payment system for Medicare, the federal health insurance system for 31 million elderly and disabled, and Medicaid, which covers 24 million low-income Americans, was redefined by the federal government. Instead of reimbursing hospitals for their costs on a per diem basis, the government set fixed prices for about 500 different illnesses and treatments, known as diagnostic related groups (DRGs). As a result, a hospital is paid a predetermined amount for a specific case no matter what services are rendered or how long the patient stays in the hospital. In other words, hospitals are rewarded financially if they discharge patients sooner and perform fewer procedures.

Ten years ago, a physician's decision to perform surgery or ad-mit a patient to the hospital for tests was rarely challenged. Now, the review of such decisions is an essential task for hospitals— most have a staff of professionals who scrutinize admissions and medical records to analyze the appropriateness of procedures, surgery, and general medical care. Some hospitals and insurers hire independent consultants who review and assess efficiency of health care providers.

The commercial insurers, including those employer-sponsored plans that cover 160 million Americans, have followed the lead of the federal government. Any inpatient admission or procedure must be called in to the insurance company by the physician for clearance and approval before payment will be authorized. Emergencies are an exception to this rule, but procedures must be carefully monitored to ensure that the hospital will be reimbursed. For example, if a person comes in to the emergency room with symptoms of a heart attack and is treated for that but then is found to have indigestion instead, the hospital is reimbursed only for treatment of indigestion. Once again, the onus is on the hospital to ensure accuracy of diagnosis and appropriateness of treatment.

Consumers are also more conscious of prices for health care because, depending on their insurance plan, they are held responsible for higher premiums, deductibles, and sometimes copayments. Employers are acutely aware of cost control—the single largest expense for General Motors in manufacturing a car is paying for the employees' health benefits.

Second opinions on surgery are often required by insurance companies, and consumers also are more likely to seek professional confirmation of a diagnosis before they follow a doctor's advice. As a result, physicians have modified their practice routines to accommodate second opinions.

These external financial pressures mean that hospitals have to continually reexamine how they are doing business. Changes in technology have been one answer—to develop methods to permit more work to be done outside the inpatient hospital setting.

## TECHNOLOGY'S CONTRIBUTION

Technology has played an important part in the adaptation of hospitals to changes in payment systems, especially in surgical procedures. When Medicare stopped paying for surgery to be done in the inpatient operating rooms if it could be done in an ambulatory care setting, physicians, researchers, and engineers worked together to develop new techniques and instruments to advance outpatient surgery. Procedures that had previously been cause for automatic admission to the hospital are being routinely performed on an outpatient basis, at great cost savings. And many minor procedures have been removed from the operating room environment altogether and are now performed in physicians' offices. Hospitals built operating rooms and larger facilities dedicated to ambulatory surgery.

In many cases, technology was already paving the way to make it easier for surgeons to perform procedures with less invasive methods under local anesthesia, so the patient could walk into the operating room and go home again in just a few hours. In turn, instruments and surgical techniques have been refined so that operations can be done in less time with less pain for the patient, resulting in shorter healing time and less risk of complications.

A good example of this kind of technological change is the role of the arthroscope in knee surgery. The arthroscope was developed in the 1960s as a diagnostic tool. The physician would make an incision in the knee joint, insert the arthroscope with a magnifying lens and light, and examine the interior of the knee in order to access injury and plan for more extensive surgery. The ensuing surgery involved opening up the knee while the patient was under anesthesia and then using normal surgical instruments to remove foreign bodies or repair damaged ligaments.

Early arthroscopic techniques were limited because the materials used to make the scope were stiff. The scope had a large diameter, so the incision had to be large enough to accommodate it. In addition, surgical instruments were large, making surgery in the small confines of the joint extremely difficult. With new materials, the more flexible fiber-optic scope can now probe into the joint without breaking, and the refinement of scopes and cameras allows the surgeon broader capabilities in the procedure. Now arthroscopy includes surgery as well as visualization; the site is magnified and projected on a television screen, which the surgeon watches as he or she operates. A typical arthroscopic knee procedure takes less than an hour to perform.

In the past decade, technology has developed to the point that the arthroscope and the surgical instruments now fit into a 4-5 millimeter incision. The surgeons work with tools that are smaller than a pencil and sutures that are finer than a human hair. Orthopedic surgeons who perform arthroscopic joint operations can now do procedures that were impossible before, such as actually mending damaged ligaments. This work is extending to other joints, such as shoulders, wrists, and ankles, that were previously considered too small for outpatient surgery. Many arthroscopies are performed under local anesthesia, thus facilitating same-day surgery.

## ESTABLISHING THE SHORT PROCEDURE UNIT

In 1985 Pennsylvania Hospital applied for a certificate of need to increase the number of operating rooms because of the large volume of surgical cases. Between 1980 and 1985, total surgical cases at Pennsylvania Hospital increased 24 percent, from 9,540 to 11,810, representing an average annual increase of 4.4 percent. Total surgical hours increased 42 percent, from 18,035 in fiscal 1980 to 25,524 in fiscal 1985. In fiscal 1984 the operating rooms were in use a total of 299 days, including 45 Saturdays. The average annual change in hours of surgery was 7.2 percent, nearly two-thirds greater than that of the growth in cases. This meant that patients scheduled for minor surgery might wait for many hours. It was apparent that what was needed was a facility that accommodated less complex procedures that did not require long periods of time in the surgical suite. Thus, whereas two rooms in the inpatient operating room suite had been designated exclusively for outpatient procedures, in 1983 the movement toward creating an outpatient operating room facility separate from the inpatient operating rooms had begun.

By 1985 the use of the inpatient operating facilities exceeded guidelines. Surgery was scheduled every weekday in three of the rooms from 8 a.m. to 8:30 p.m., or 12 1/2 hours. Scheduled surgical procedures were regularly being performed throughout the evening hours in those rooms, with cases beginning as late as 10:30 p.m. and sometimes continuing into the early morning hours. Urgent surgical cases that had not been scheduled, such as wound debridements and removal of ectopic pregnancies, occurred frequently and exacerbated the problem of extended hours. As a result, in 1985 the hospital opened a free-standing suite of two fully equipped rooms designed under the same specifications as the inpatient operating rooms. These outpatient rooms had all the equipment necessary for surgery, including anesthesia and radiological equipment, and a staff of perioperative nurses, scrub technicians, unit assistants, and clerical staff.

By establishing this Short Procedure Unit (SPU), the hospital was able to use all 12 rooms in one building for inpatient surgical cases and to centralize the entire outpatient program in an adjacent building. This configuration also enabled the hospital to establish more reasonable schedules for both areas and achieve a more appropriate level of utilization in conjunction with state standards.

Soon two additional outpatient rooms were added to the SPU; then in 1987 another two rooms were added for a total of six. As these developments took place, outpatient procedures grew from 30 percent to 45 percent of the surgeries performed at Pennsylvania Hospital each year, and the sophistication of those operations increased correspondingly. In 1988, 5,800 of the 12,500 total surgical procedures were performed in the SPU, from cataract removal to in vitro fertilization, and most of those patients went home on the day of surgery to recover. In 1987 three services— obstetrics and gynecology, ophthalmology, and oral surgery—did 80 percent or more of their surgical procedures in the outpatient setting.

## Effect on Quality of Care

What have these changes meant for patients? There are both obvious and subtle answers to that question. One obvious result is that smaller incisions and finer tools allow for less invasive procedures, so the body can heal more quickly. In addition, patients recover faster because anesthesia has been refined—in many cases, only local anesthesia is used, and in others, new drugs that dissipate more quickly have been developed. The more subtle implications for patients lie in their own changing role. Rather than entering the hospital days before an operation and relying on a nurse to monitor their care, the patients are responsible while at home for following the physician's instructions for preparing for surgery. For example, patients have to pay attention to what medications they take and the food they eat in the days before the operation, and often may be required to take nothing by mouth the night before.

After the surgery, they must be aware of their own healing processes, paying attention to their incision scars and reactions to any medication, as well as keeping up with any postoperative exercises or precautions delineated by the physician. Surgeons and perioperative nurses alike comment on the effect this has on patient recovery: as they become more involved in the process, they take more responsibility and are more aware of their own physical changes. As a result, patients often assume independence sooner and may help the physician by being more attuned to changes in their own system. In addition, the elderly in particular often do better when they convalesce in the familiar environment of their own home.

What do these shifts to outpatient procedures mean for surgeons? First, here is an explanation of how surgery commonly takes place. The operating suite is very busy, with many procedures going on simultaneously. Nurses, technicians, and resident physicians are involved from the start of an operation, setting up the room and the instruments and preparing the patient. A surgeon uses time efficiently to complete a number of operations in as few hours as possible. Since the SPU at Pennsylvania Hospital is in a separate building from the inpatient operating rooms, surgeons cannot always perform both types of procedures in the same morning. In response to that situation, they now schedule full or half days in the SPU, organizing surgeries to take place on specific days of the week. This makes scheduling more efficient for the nurses, who can plan the setups for orthopedics, otorhinolaryngology, or urology, for example, because they know for the most part which surgeons are on the roster each day of the week.

Rather than fragmenting their time between the inpatient and outpatient surgical areas, anesthesiologists work full days in the SPU. In addition, when patients come into the hospital for preadmission testing several days before the surgery, they are interviewed by a member of the anesthesiology staff. At that time, the appropriate course is planned and patients are given instructions regarding their preoperative preparation.

The role of the perioperative nurses who work in the SPU has also changed. In contrast to the circulating nurses in the inpatient operating room, who talk to the patients and reassure them just before they are anesthetized, the nurses in the SPU greet them while they are still in their street clothes, discuss their preoperative preparation, and walk with them after they have changed to help them onto the operating table. The nurses in the SPU have an important educational role with the patients and their families, answering questions and clarifying issues for them. After the requisite recovery period, the nurses ensure that the patients leave the SPU safely. Nurses telephone patients the day after surgery to see how they are doing and to follow up on instructions for medications or any other questions the patient may have.

The first scheduled surgery in the SPU is at 7:30 a.m., and the last at 4 p.m. The unit averages 25 surgical procedures each day, Monday through Friday.

## Common Procedures

One of the most common procedures performed on an outpatient basis throughout the country is cataract removal; nationally, it accounts for 66 percent of Medicare ambulatory surgery expenses. At Pennsylvania Hospital, 94 percent of the cataract surgery is done on an outpatient basis. A cataract is a clouding of the lens of the eye, which blocks the passage of light to the retina and impairs vision. A cataract is usually the result of natural aging, though sometimes it results from trauma. To correct this condition, the ophthalmologist removes the cloudy lens and replaces it with a plastic intraocular lens. This procedure is particularly significant as the population ages. Physicians comment that since the aging population is more active, their expectations for good vision are higher, and this results in higher demand for cataract surgery.

As with knee surgery, cataract surgery was revolutionized by the introduction of microscopes that allowed the use of very small instruments. A needle is inserted in the 4-5 millimeter incision, and the cloudy lens is pulverized by ultrasound. In recent years a technique has been developed that enables the lens capsule to be left in the eye, cleaned thoroughly, then used to hold the plastic implant in place. This results in less disturbance to the eye, less pain, and fewer adverse reactions. The very fine sutures make it possible to have smaller, safer wound closures, and that leads to a much quicker healing process. As in arthroscopic knee surgery, a video camera is attached to the scope so assistants, nurses, and observers can view the work on a television screen. In ophthalmologic surgery, however, the surgeon looks through a microscope, which permits depth perception not possible in television.

Technology permitted making just a small incision, but the diameter of the hard plastic lens was wider than the incision needed to be for the surgery. Ophthalmologists are now beginning to use a softer lens made of silicone that can be folded in half to fit into a smaller incision.

Other instruments used in the procedure, such as those for irrigation and aspiration, have also been improved greatly in recent years. These tools let the surgeon draw the cataract material out while flushing the eye at the same time. These functions formerly were determined by how high the surgeon held the bottle of fluid and how quickly the assistant pulled on a syringe. Now the surgical team uses foot-pedal controls and computer-guided, mechanized suction to manipulate the flow, achieving much greater accuracy.

## TECHNOLOGY IN OBSTETRICS AND GYNECOLOGY

In obstetrics and gynecology, physicians use magnifying laparoscopes to view women's reproductive organs and perform a variety of procedures with very small instruments similar to those used for orthopedics and ophthalmology. Pennsylvania Hospital gynecologists tried many new techniques when they were first proposed by researchers. For example, laparoscopic tubal ligations were first performed in the late 1960s. This is a permanent sterilization method for women, now one of the most common procedures done in ambulatory surgery settings. As a result, hundreds of women each year undergo the procedure and recuperate at home, often returning to work just a few days later. Once again, the small incision, in contrast to the longer ones previously required, means there is less trauma and easier and quicker healing.

Percutaneous umbilical blood sampling (PUBS) is a significant new tool used to determine the health of a fetus in high-risk pregnancy. The test involves the use of ultrasound to guide a needle directly into the mother's abdomen through the uterine wall to the umbilical cord where a blood sample is taken from the fetal umbilical blood vessel. Using PUBS, doctors can administer medication, monitor medication levels that reach the fetus, and perform fetal blood transfusions. The procedure is performed on an outpatient basis with local anesthesia and little or no maternal-fetal sedation. It provides the physician with much more information about the development and genetic makeup of the fetus, thereby allowing better and earlier treatment of the unborn baby.

Technology also aids couples who are infertile. In vitro fertilization/gamete intrafallopian transfer (IVF/GIFT) procedures involve fertilizing an egg in the laboratory and implanting the embryo into the uterus. With the help of ultrasound and small instruments, there is just one small incision in the abdomen, and the operation is done under local anesthesia. The patients can watch the procedure on a television screen and even make a videotape for themselves.

## LASERS IN OUTPATIENT SURGERY

The past 10 years have seen a dramatic increase in the use of lasers in surgery. Because the laser produces light of uniform wavelength in a focused, powerfully intense beam, it is useful to surgeons working on a small area of tissue. The energy of the laser beam is absorbed by the tissue, causing a localized temperature increase, resulting in vaporization and tissue removal. The laser makes a clean, precise cut and instantly cauterizes the wound, so that little or no bleeding occurs.

The laser minimizes the formation of scar tissue and is self-sterilizing, so the risk of postoperative infection is much less than that associated with conventional surgery. Swelling is minimal, and healing is rapid.

When lasers were first being manufactured for surgical uses, Pennsylvania Hospital's chief of urology encouraged vendors to provide him with equipment that he could use to find clinical applications in urology. The doctor was able quickly to refine procedures and increase the number of ways in which lasers could be used. For example, lasers have made removal of cancerous tumors in the bladder much safer because the beam can be so precisely controlled that there is no longer risk of damaging the bladder wall, which was a serious complication when the old method of electrocautery was used.

In gynecologic oncology many patients with preinvasive cancer of the cervix are treated with lasers. In the recent past, these women would have had surgery under general anesthesia and a hospital stay of one to three days. The costs would have been high, and because a large part of the cervix had to be removed, the procedure could result in infertility. Today gynecologists vaporize specific layers of cells from the surface of the cervix instead of excising a section of it. These treatments can be done without anesthesia in the physician's office. The cost is considerably less, as is the discomfort, and healing is much more rapid. With laser surgery, there is less damage to normal structure because the physician can meticulously limit the area of destruction. There also is less blood loss and less scarring. For gynecologic patients, this helps to preserve childbearing capacity.

In addition to surgery, other medical uses for lasers have also been developed. Since 1982 a pulmonary disease specialist at Pennsylvania Hospital has been using lasers successfully to open the airway passages of people suffering from lung cancer and other bronchial obstructions. In 1987 he and the chief of radiation oncology began to follow the clearing of the obstructions with the temporary implantation of a wire laden with radioactive material. This procedure, known as pulmonary brachytherapy, allows the radiation to be delivered in close proximity to the tumor over a shorter period of time—approximately 12 hours instead of the two-week course of normal radiation treatments. Again, the result is decreased damage to healthy tissue as well as a shorter hospital stay. Because of their extensive experience in the development of the uses of lasers, Pennsylvania Hospital physicians are also active in educating other doctors in the use of lasers.

## DIAGNOSTIC TECHNOLOGY IN RADIOLOGY AND PATHOLOGY

Magnetic resonance imaging (MRI), a radiologic technique that provides a multidimensional picture of the entire body or of a specific area in question, aids the surgeon in determining the plan for an operation because it can view parts of the body that would not have been accessible until surgery. This visualization minimizes invasiveness and saves time on the operating table. The application of this important diagnostic tool illustrates the use of new technology in the patient care setting. Although research-oriented institutions developed the technique, other hospitals, like Pennsylvania Hospital, adapted its use to enhance patient care and increase efficiency.

Pathologists also play an important role in determining the appropriateness of treatment and surgery. When a tumor is correctly and accurately classified, a patient can receive the optimal therapy. New technologies for analyzing tissues on the cellular level have contributed to the efficiency of patient care.

For example, diagnosis of tumors of the breast can now be done on an outpatient basis because of fine needle aspiration and the technology to study very small biopsies. Surgeons can take the biopsies under local anesthesia in the Short Procedure Unit, and the women often avoid inpatient surgery altogether if laboratory examination shows that the tumor is benign. Before this technique was developed, a much larger specimen was surgically removed from a women's breast, resulting in more trauma and scarring for the same diagnostic result.

Pathologists also are able now to make diagnoses with smaller amounts of tissue. Immunocytochemistry uses specific antibodies to identify cells in small biopsies. These methods are more precise than conventional methods and can be used with much smaller samples of tissue. With electron microscopy, cells are magnified up to 100,000 times, in contrast to the normal microscope magnification of 1,000 times.

Flow cytometry is a technique that uses antibodies to diagnose tumors or disease in blood samples. In this technique, antibodies are stained with a fluorescent dye, mixed with the blood cells, and then analyzed with a flow cytometer, which measures fluorescence emission from each cell that passes through it. It shows the relationship between the blood sample cells and the tagged antibodies as they flow through it in a fluid stream. The presence of the antibodies is then plotted on a graph by a profile analyzer as the stream runs through the cytometer, giving the lab immediate illustration of the antibody count. Once again, the results enable better diagnosis of the pathology of the cells and help to determine the most appropriate care for the patient.

## WHERE TECHNOLOGY WILL LEAD

In the 237-year history of Pennsylvania Hospital, technological change has been fostered and encouraged because of the hospital's fundamental mission of providing the best possible patient care. Pennsylvania Hospital is not a research institution, but one dedicated to providing the most advanced clinical care. Many of the physicians are innovators in the application of research results in the clinical setting.

In the first years of the nineteenth century, the hospital's ability to perform its mission was advanced dramatically with its building of a surgical amphitheater unique in the Western Hemisphere. At a time when most cities did not yet have hospitals, Pennsylvania Hospital surgeons were removing gall stones, improving amputation methods, and educating a new generation of physicians who watched from the rows of benches encircling the operating theater. This positive attitude toward technological advancements and medical education continues today.

The past 10 years have seen revolutionary changes in the health care system coming about because of the redefinition of medical insurance and payment systems. This has forced researchers to develop new technology to treat patients in a less costly manner. The results have been seen in more outpatient surgery, more efficient inpatient surgery, and more effective methods of diagnosis and treatment of disease. One of the practical effects of this change is that more patients in the hospital are more acutely ill. Whereas a nurse previously took care of a mix of patients—some preoperatively, some after minor surgery, and others more seriously ill—now virtually all hospitalized patients need close attention.

As new technology has led to reduced lengths of stay and more outpatient procedures, it has not reduced the inflationary cost of health care.  After all, new technology is expensive.  Pacemakers, for example, have been refined greatly in the past 10 years and are now smaller and more efficient.  The cost of the research and development affects the price of the pacemaker but also results in better prognosis for the patient.  It is highly likely that as health care costs continue to rise, even more new technologies will develop, and the rate of change will continue through the 1990s.

People and Technology in the Workplace. 1991.
Pp. 171–188. Washington, D.C:
National Academy Press.

# Technology and Intervention in the Neonatal Intensive Care Unit

JOHN M. DRISCOLL, JR., AND CHARLES J. H. STOLAR

Over the past 15 years the Neonatal Intensive Care Unit at Columbia Presbyterian Medical Center has developed a system of medical care, transportation for sick mothers and infants, professional staff education, and performance evaluation for a regional network of New York area hospitals. During the past eight years, they have successfully introduced a new technology, extracorporeal membrane oxygenation (ECMO), to save the lives of a group of infants with very high mortality rates.

This case study describes the process of implementing the new technology, identifying factors facilitating success as well as limitations, and continuing unresolved problems. Implementation was aided by the basic effectiveness of the technology to save lives, which was not known beforehand, as well as by the dedication and skill of two pediatric surgeons. The process was hindered by continuing staff resistance related to lack of control over the technology and physical isolation from the work unit. Expanding the program as a regional resource continues to be limited by the unanticipated costs of the program coupled with a shortage of nursing staff, increased demand for other health services, and general budget constraints.

## ORGANIZATION

The Neonatal Intensive Care Unit (NICU) at Babies Hospital Columbia Presbyterian Medical Center (CPMC) is a super tertiary care unit that serves a network of hospitals on the west side of Manhattan and several suburban hospitals in New Jersey, Connecticut, and north of New York City. A super tertiary unit provides a total range of medical services to infants and virtually never transfers an infant to another unit for a medical service. On the west side of Manhattan, there are other neonatal units that can provide certain intensive medical services, but require transfer for selected surgical and medical problems. In the suburban hospitals, sharply limited services are available and transfer to the NICU is therefore more frequent. The network involves provision of medical care, transportation of sick mothers and infants, education of professional staffs, and evaluation of performance.

The Neonatal Intensive Care Unit is the central component of the network and contains several units that provide care to infants currently in the hospital, as well as to new patients recently born either in the center or at a network hospital. Inherent in the network design is the guarantee of bed availability and transportation 24 hours per day. In addition to the requests for transfer from the network hospitals, there are requests from other hospitals for a specific service unique to the tertiary care unit, for example, pediatric cardiology or pediatric surgery.

Regionalization of care is essential to meet the needs of any area. In most large metropolitan areas requests for beds far exceed the capabilities of any one unit. In New York City there are six other medical schools, with units to help meet regional requirements. To establish realistic expectations with regard to regional needs, physicians identified hospitals that contacted their NICU regularly as a primary referral hospital. These hospitals form the base of the network, with approximately 25,000 births and with an additional 5,000 births at CPMC annually. Until the recent past, regional requirements have been met within the current distribution of 53 beds.

As a tertiary, university hospital, there is also an educational arm to the clinical service. Education includes medical, nursing, and paraprofessional, as well as graduate and postgraduate components. The education of house staff and postgraduate fellows in various subspecialties specifically requires the availability of a wide range of patients. As accreditation bodies have selectively reduced training programs, the survival of remaining residency programs is critically dependent on patient availability. This educational need creates yet another demand on the unit, that is, "open" admission for infants outside network hospitals with specific problems, such as pediatric cardiology. A hospital can have the best available program in a given subspecialty, but if the NICU continually rejects admissions because of a shortage of beds or staff the adverse impact is obvious. So, as a tertiary unit both hospital and regional needs must be met for newborn care as well as the specific needs of the different subspecialty services and their educational component.

The organization of the NICU rests in the hands of its director who is responsible to the chief of the Pediatric Service (education, policy) and to the president of the hospital (patient care, administration, and regionalization). The director establishes policies jointly with nursing colleagues that direct the provision of patient care, guarantee a standard of care, ensure effective flow of patients through the system, and meet educational goals of the university as well as regional needs. Thus, changes that affect the level of care at the bedside, subspecialty training, or standards at the network hospital flow through this combined medical/nursing hierarchy. The current team of neonatologists has been together for 15 or more years, which provides a continuity not available in other units.

The nursing staff is highly organized, very experienced, skilled, and demanding of itself and its medical colleagues. They form the backbone of the unit and are the primary implementers and guarantors of care. Their inclusion in the process, whether it be evaluation or change is essential to the success of the clinical service. The realized philosophy of joint professional responsibilities for administration of the unit is in large part responsible for a high retention rate of nurses (more than 60 percent with more than 5 years of service) and successful realization of established goals.

CPMC is a world renowned institution that has been totally supportive of the development of the NICU and the changes that have ensued over the past 20 years. They have placed the unit in the enviable position of being able to deliver superior tertiary care by providing the finances required to have the most sophisticated equipment and the manpower to operate the technology. In the new age of Diagnostic Related Groups in New York State, the financial burden for the hospital has increased geometrically, however, and fiscal constraints are being enforced.

In summary, the NICU is a critical part of a large metropolitan hospital as well as a regional network, with a busy clinical service that has a large obstetric service with approximately 5,000 deliveries annually, and pediatric subspecialties that jointly produce more than 700 annual admissions. It has a large medical staff with total subspecialty support and a nursing staff second to none. The unit also plays an important regional leadership role in the innovation and evaluation of care.

## MOTIVATION FOR CHANGE

The area of our 53-bed operation that was most directly affected by the introduction of new technology was direct patient care in the 9-bed intensive care unit. The technology to be introduced was extracorporeal membrane oxygenation (ECMO). Introduction of the new technology occurred late in the historical evolution of the intensive care unit and late in the history of the current medical/nursing leadership. Fifteen to 20 years ago, significant technological and organizational changes related to the modernization of newborn intensive care had occurred. In the interval, changes were limited to modification of the technology and minor changes at the organization level related to the introduction of the regional concept of neonatal care. Introduction of ECMO was the first major change in patient care in at least 15 years.

### The Problem

The motivation for change was pure and simple. There was a group of infants, born after full pregnancy, who progressed to the point of respiratory failure and died. There was no successful treatment and these infants were the leading contributors to neonatal mortality among full-term infants. The two medical conditions that contributed most frequently to this mortality were infants born with a congenital absence of the diaphragm, so-called congenital diaphragmatic hernia, and infants born with a lung condition known as meconium aspiration, that progressed over the first 24 to 48 hours of life to the state of respiratory failure. In addition, a third condition, called primary pulmonary hypertension of the newborn, also resulted in respiratory failure and had a high mortality rate.

Historically, the pediatric surgeons were particularly frustrated by the postoperative course of the infant with a diaphragmatic hernia who initially did well, a "honeymoon period," only to die 24 to 48 hours later. They began to investigate alternative forms of therapy for such infants. Neonatologists had unsuccessfully tried different ways of ventilating infants and had tried pharmacologic manipulations in an attempt to reverse the relentless respiratory failure of infants with all three conditions. The mortality rate with maximal conventional therapy was in excess of 90 percent. Five years ago all respiratory therapy was unsuccessful in saving this group of infants and professionals were continually frustrated by their inability to treat term infants in respiratory failure with these three conditions. Therefore, the motivation for change was related to the need to lower mortality and the availability of a new technology for which preliminary data suggested improved mortality and limited longitudinal morbidity.

## Technology

Transitional circulatory difficulties are not new. In 1748 Catagon had observed, "The infant requires some intermediate time of abstinence and rest to compose and recover from the struggle of birth in the change of circulation." Newborn infants with intractable respiratory failure are unable to make the transition from the fetal to the newborn circulatory-respiratory system. ECMO is an aggressive life-support system that employs partial heart and lung bypass for long periods. It essentially enables a period of lung rest by providing an alternative source of gas exchange and oxygen delivery for an extended period of time during which the pathologic processes causing respiratory failure resolve of their own accord.

The concept of prolonged extracorporeal support is not new. Its modern history began 35 years ago with the description of mechanical oxygenation and perfusion by Gibbons. Subsequently, there have been modifications in the initial technology leading to today's current state of the art. In the mid-1960s the work of a number of investigators culminated in a National Heart, Lung, and Blood Institute study of the efficacy of extracorporeal membrane oxygenation for adult respiratory distress syndrome. This study failed to prove any advantage of ECMO over conventional ventilator management for adults afflicted with this disorder. However, in the interval, initially White (White et al., 1971) and subsequently Bartlett (Bartlett et al., 1977) began treating newborn infants with respiratory distress syndrome with ECMO. In 1976, Bartlett and his colleagues described the first series of ECMO-treated infants that had a significant number of survivors.

As previously mentioned, ECMO is a form of partial heart and lung bypass. The usual means of perfusion is by inserting a catheter to drain the venous blood from the right atrium and returning it through another catheter to the ascending aorta. This is accomplished by a extrathoracic cannulation performed in the neonatal intensive care unit. Once the appropriate catheters are in place the infant then receives partial cardiopulmonary bypass with the membrane oxygenator assuming the function of the damaged lung and the infant's prior respiratory support gradually decreased to minimal levels. Just before initiation of ECMO, patients are treated with maximal conventional ventilator and pharmacologic support and believed to have an expected mortality rate between 85 and 95 percent. Once the infant has been stabilized on ECMO, this support is no longer necessary. The ventilator is generally turned to minimal settings that are sufficient to inhibit development of small areas of collapse in the lung and to maintain pulmonary toilet while the infant is on ECMO.

As a consequence, the management of the infant undergoing ECMO is considerably more straightforward than one might expect. In fact the condition of most acutely ill infants in the nursery quickly becomes stable. All intravenous lines are removed, leaving only an umbilical artery catheter for monitoring and sampling. All medications and intravenous nutrition are given into the extracorporeal circuit. Drug doses are appropriately increased and fluid and electrolytes provided by standard requirements. The infants remain on ECMO for variable periods of time. As the lung injury is repaired, the flow of oxygen required to maintain the infant decreases and the oxygen level in the blood increases. Once the infant has begun to improve and is stabilized, the bypass is weaned and terminated. The perfusion catheters are removed after a mean ECMO duration of approximately 90 hours.

### Staff Concern

Introduction of ECMO involved a great deal of risk. There was considerable concern about the potential harm of ECMO before its introduction into the unit. It was a major break from previous therapy. There was potentially a significant compromise of blood flow to the brain, and the data available at that time about long-term outcomes were scant. There were no other units in the metropolitan area with ECMO; the nearest units were in Ann Arbor and Pittsburgh. This was only the third unit in the world to introduce ECMO and the only role model for the application of ECMO was Dr. Bartlett's program at the University of Michigan.

In addition, mastery of the technology rested in the hands of the pediatric surgeons. For the first time in the recent history of the neonatal unit, both the neonatologist and the nursing staff were placed in the position of not having direct control over the technology that would be applied to their patient. However, the unit had a background in risk taking in the recent past with the development and application of respiratory technology to the premature infant with birth weights of less than two pounds. The application of technology in this instance involved risk taking in treating these very small infants with a previously high mortality rate and once again an unknown morbidity rate. The positive prior experience with the application of respiratory technology was an important factor in the ultimate acceptance of this more recent technology into the armamentarium of the unit.

Before the introduction of ECMO, the obvious supporters of the technique were the pediatric surgeons who had perfected it in the animal laboratory, with cautious support from the leadership of neonatology. The anesthesiologist assigned to the unit was also supportive of ECMO as a logical extension of the respiratory care developed under his leadership. There were marked reservations from the junior attending staff and the nursing staff was appropriately cautious about the introduction of a new technology, but both were willing to be risk takers in the controlled environment of the ICU.

## Related Factors

The decision process also included a review of the fiscal aspects of the new program. There were insufficient funds within the hospital, and grant support from NIH was not available. Therefore, the initial support for the program came from the pediatric surgical service, which provided not only the pediatric surgeons but also the technical support and the funds necessary to initiate the program. Without the financial, human, and technical support of the Division of Pediatric Surgery, the new technology would never have been introduced.

A major factor outside of the organization that played a facilitative role in the acceptance of the technique was the positive experience being reported by Bartlett and his colleagues at the University of Michigan. Their reputation as careful investigators and outstanding clinicians provided substantial support for the adoption of this technique. Outside businesses played little role in the introduction of the new technology since the membrane oxygenator was already available. There was no pressure being applied to the unit from industry for adoption of the new technique.

A major driving force in the eventual adoption of ECMO was a perceived need to assume leadership in exploring the application of this technique to the care of newborn infants. Staff members recognized that the likelihood of other units using this technique was high and that it was better to assume a leadership position early in the process. If the technique was found to be either lacking or helpful, they would have accumulated first-hand experience. It was also absolutely clear that there was no alternative therapy for these infants; without an alternative therapy, the death of a certain group of infants would continue.

## PROCESS AND CONSIDERATION

After discussion among the professionals involved that lasted over six months, a decision was made to implement the technology. At that point the need to develop appropriate administrative channels and a process for admitting infants and treating them efficiently and effectively was developed at the medical and nursing levels with the active participation and leadership of surgical colleagues.

Once the decision had been made at the administrative level, then both the nursing and the medical staffs were jointly involved in the development of the policies and procedures that would govern both nursing and medical practices. The nursing and medical staffs were also involved in the development of the "ECMO Room" and there was an active attempt to develop a team concept. This was an attempt to develop the necessary collegial relationship essential for the success of an ongoing program.

The development of these policies and procedures, however, intentionally did not involve the neonatology and the nursing staffs in learning hands-on application of the technology. This was entrusted to the surgical team who assumed total responsibility for the application and maintenance of the technology. This decision was made to ensure the highest standard of care, alleviate anxiety, and facilitate interaction among professionals who previously did not work together on a daily basis.

To notify colleagues in other neonatal intensive care units and practicing pediatricians about the availability of the new technique, letters were sent to the directors of other neonatal programs in the tristate area. Following this mailing a young pediatric surgeon who had directed the program in the laboratory and who was responsible for its clinical application, began visiting neonatal intensive care units in the tristate area to discuss ECMO in general and the development of the program in our newborn intensive care unit. Extensive correspondence and lectures provided colleagues in the area with an information base on which they could make decisions about their infants with respiratory failure. Based on both the internal and external discussions, a number of planning considerations emerged before implementation.

## Planning

1. For infants with congenital diaphragmatic hernia, should surgeons at outside institutions refer those infants before correction of the defect in the diaphragm to facilitate their care postoperatively if they should require ECMO? Or should the infants have the initial repair and then be transferred if they became candidates for ECMO? In units where university hospitals had training programs that mandated certain experiences for trainees, an automatic transfer of such infants created a serious training shortfall. In smaller units without pediatric surgical training programs, the same sort of educational consideration did not prohibit the transfer of those infants before surgical repair of the lesion. As the program has evolved, referring units have adopted different approaches to the resolution of this issue, ranging from transfer of all patients before surgery to transfer of no patients before surgery.

2. Medical colleagues in referring hospitals were also confronted with a decision about the timing of transfer that would allow a sufficient interval for the infant to be moved from one institution to another while he or she is critically ill and still allow time for introduction of ECMO upon arrival in our unit. In this particular situation, it is important to note that 50 percent of the infants transferred for ECMO never receive the treatment either because of mortality, a contraindication for the application of the technique, or because they improve with the application of the standard ventilatory therapy in our unit. In such a process, communication between units is essential to the continued success of this operation and the timing of each case had to be handled individually.

3. Internally there was a decision about how many infants could be treated at one time. It was decided before the introduction of the technique that resources allowed acceptance of only one ECMO candidate at a time. It was also agreed that there would not be "back-up candidates" in the unit until it was quite clear that an infant on ECMO was going to be successfully weaned from the

machine. The interrelationship between the ECMO centers in the Northeast also made it easier for patients who could not be accepted for therapy to be referred to other units that had beds available.

4. Another organizational factor that needed to be modified before implementation of the technology was the transport system. As previously mentioned, because the NICU is a regional center, transport for infants from network hospitals is provided 24 hours per day. In this instance infants were received from other tertiary units both within and outside our tristate area as well as from other ECMO programs outside the metropolitan area. Some tertiary units had their own transport system and thus were able to transport such infants with their own transport team. For tertiary units that did not have transport systems, it was necessary to provide transport. This requirement demanded interaction with New York City Premature Transport Program, which had the obligation to provide transport for sick infants within the city itself. Permission from the administration of the Preemie Transport System enabled the NICU to assume responsibility for these transports because of the unique nature of the technology.

For infants transferred from outside the metropolitan area, appropriate air transport had to be arranged. Experience of an organ transplant unit provided an appropriate air transport model. After careful consideration, a decision was reached that the NICU role in the transport of patients from outside of New York who would arrive by air was to provide an ambulance, a nurse, and a physician to meet the transporting teams at the airport and arrange transport of the infant from the airplane to the transport ambulance. Transfer of responsibility for the patient, however, would not occur until they arrived in our unit. Transfer of responsibility for an acutely ill infant would more safely take place in the intensive care unit than at the airport site.

5. The site for ECMO was another organizational factor that was considered before implementation of the technology. Because of the bulkiness of the equipment and the uniqueness of the situation, it was decided to use a room directly adjacent to the unit but yet separate from the unit. This would allow the physicians and the single nurse who was assigned to this infant 24 hours a day to work somewhat in isolation yet enjoy the full support of the unit. This "isolation" from the unit remains an administrative problem to this moment and will be discussed later under unanticipated effects.

6. Finally, it was important to the neonatal intensive care unit

staff and their surgical colleagues to be aware at the outset that there would be infants placed on ECMO who would be unresponsive to therapy immediately or late and expire in the early or late stages of treatment. For others the therapy would need to be discontinued because of complications or because after 10 or 12 days on the technique they did not respond. Each of these issues was discussed before implementation of the program, but until a team has faced the dilemma it is impossible to anticipate group reaction. However, because the neonatal team had prior experience with the discontinuation of medical therapy both in full-term and premature infants, decision making was not new and there were acceptable standards in place to provide the basis for making these decisions.

## Ongoing Evaluation

With regard to the management of setbacks and failures, it was decided that each case should be reviewed both prospectively and retrospectively to decide what had gone wrong, if anything, and why. In each instance these reviews involved the pediatric surgeons, the neonatologist assigned to the case, and the nursing staff. Where organizational defects had been detected in the management of an individual infant, the review took place at the level of the director of the newborn intensive care unit and all services to isolate the problem. To prevent its recurrence, it was necessary to make appropriate modification in the operating policies and procedures. In the beginning, quite understandably, the problems were often administrative, and changes were made to facilitate process, whether it was movement of the infant from one institution to another, shortening the time required to place an infant on ECMO once a decision had been made, or transfer of information to the referring institution. Reviews were conducted by the pediatric surgeon directing the program. They were critical and constructive, and the only goal was to improve the operation. The team was aware of the intensity of the experience, particularly the critical nature of time, rapid decision making, and risk to the infant involved.

Broad measures were also used to monitor the consequences of this innovation, including mortality and longitudinal morbidity, which are essential markers measuring the consequences of instituting a new therapy. In addition, both the pediatric surgeon involved and the hospital monitor the cost of the new innovation. The pediatric surgeon also maintains a log of all requests as a means of monitoring the ability of the unit to accept patients in transfer.

## Staffing

After the initial experience with ECMO, it became obvious that one problem was the availability of sufficient additional nursing manpower to allow one-on-one nursing care for the sick infant. At times, depending on number of infants in the intensive care unit, there were not sufficient personnel to remove a nurse from the existing staff and to assign that professional to the case. Once this situation was recognized, the institution approved two new nursing positions that would be assigned to the ECMO program and that would provide the basis for an on-call system for nurses. With the on-call system, the unit then had the potential addition of a nurse for ECMO as the demand arose. Thus, the administration of nursing was not required to change schedules based on the potential needs of ECMO. Costs involved in this on-call system and in providing additional nurses were borne by the hospital.

## Control

ECMO represented the introduction of a brand new technology. The adoption did not require the acquisition of new technical knowledge for the nursing staff or the neonatologists, however, nor the abandonment of prior knowledge. Rather modification of existing knowledge was needed to aid the technology. For the first time, the nursing and medical staffs did not have total control over the clinical care of the patient. In almost every other treatment, they might relinquish control for brief periods of time, for example, during surgery, but control was resumed when the infants returned to the NICU from the operating room. This loss of control had the anticipated effects on both the nursing and the medical staffs.

At the outset there were only two physicians involved in this program. When an infant was selected for ECMO the pediatric surgeon and his fellow were at the bedside continuously while the infant was on ECMO. For some infants this was a relatively short period of time—two or three days—but for others it was for as long as 10 or 12 days. The dedication and endurance of these two physicians ensured consistency in decision making and continuity in the care of the patients. It also allowed the nursing staff to become accustomed to dealing with the same individuals in these recurring clinical situations.

After a year of using this approach, however, it became obvious that the enormous time commitment from the pediatric surgeons could not be maintained. The physical presence of a pediatric surgeon at a patient's bedside throughout the period of ECMO was no longer possible. At that point it became necessary to introduce the perfusionists, another group of professionals previously not exposed to the NICU and vice versa. They would be responsible for the maintenance of the machine once the infant was placed on ECMO. The introduction of these new professionals was discussed at length before the change. The nursing and medical staffs were informed, and there was anxiety from all involved about the introduction of this change. A new unproven, unknown professional was introduced into a high-tech process, where there were great risks to the infant involved and where the medical and nursing staffs were not at ease with the technology.

Despite the attempts of the leadership to alleviate this anxiety and to provide a smooth transition, there were major problems of staff confidence and implementation of the new system. This alteration required a series of meetings with the medical and nursing staffs to assure them of the new professional's competence and to explain the exact role of the new participant. The pediatric surgeon was still available 24 hours a day. The perfusionist was included in the administrative hierarchy of the unit related to ECMO patients and this contact, although infrequent, increased the confidence in another group of professionals and a smoother transition to the new system.

## RESULTS

### Goals

The purpose of the ECMO program was to determine whether the new technology would in fact reduce mortality and whether the surviving infant would have an acceptable morbidity at one and two years of age. It was also the intent of the organization to be an educational resource and provide this service on a regional basis, since the only other programs were in Ann Arbor and Pittsburgh.

ECMO has been successful in accomplishing the first two purposes. Infants who previously expired with diaphragmatic hernia and meconium aspiration now survive. The survival rate to date involving 51 patients is 84 percent. The effectiveness of ECMO in terms of mortality is easy to measure, but an equally important question is the longitudinal development of the infants. That information is being collected as we proceed and to date approximately 80 to 85 percent of the infants who have required ECMO are considered normal at two years of age. Educationally, the program has been an asset to both neonatal and pediatric surgical programs, and as a university hospital the program has provided another arena of clinical investigation.

With regard to the third purpose, providing the technology on a region-wide basis, the program has not been totally successful. The success has been limited primarily by availability of beds and availability of nursing. The neonatal intensive care unit has had increasing demands for its services related to the crack epidemic currently afflicting NYC and particularly Washington Heights, the immediate environment of the institution. The delivery rate in the institution has increased to 5,300 on a delivery service that was designed for roughly 3,500 mothers. This unexpected increase in delivery rate has stretched the resources of the neonatal intensive care unit to the point at which it has been required to transfer sick infants born in the institution to other neonatal intensive care units within the metropolitan area.

Increased occupancy has become a regional problem with the insufficient beds available to provide for sick infants in the region. The lack of beds along with the recent implementation of Diagnostic Related Groups has created an economic environment that is threatening to every hospital in New York State and has inhibited development of an orderly plan to meet the crisis of bed availability. This problem is being dealt with by the New York City Health Department and the State Department of Health.

The increasing crisis with regard to beds has forced the NICU to deploy new resources to meet demands of patients born in the institution. Included in this process is the opening of a transitional nursery in the delivery room around the clock rather than as a triage area for the care of infants. This physical unit often requires the presence of a nurse 24 hours a day, further stretching an already stressed nursing staff. It also pulls a nurse from the nursing pool and prohibits the opening of the ECMO room when a request for transfer occurs. The number of nurses does not allow the simultaneous operation of the newborn intensive care unit, the transitional nursery, and acceptance of an ECMO patient.

In late fall 1988 the crisis reached enormous proportions, and a large number of requests for ECMO were not accepted. The rejection of requests creates not only institutional problems but also regional problems. Even though the surgical team located beds for the requested transfers, in each instance the logistic problems involved in moving a sick infant out of the metropolitan area to either Boston, Pittsburgh, or Washington, D.C., were enormous. The credibility of the program is threatened and colleagues will begin to look elsewhere for their patients. Another issue is the development of other ECMO programs to serve the tristate region as a result of NICU's inability to meet requests for transfer. This is a logical step for other institutions to take although fiscally and organizationally the need for more than one unit in the area has not been demonstrated. Although the program has achieved its intended purpose in the survival of infants placed on ECMO with good longitudinal outcome, the goal of serving as a regional resource has not been accomplished.

## Unanticipated Effects

There are always surprises when anything novel is introduced into an organization. Perhaps most surprising at the human level is that, despite successful implementation of ECMO, a certain amount of resistance and antagonism persists. Strong initial resistance to this invasive high-risk therapy has abated as the success of the technique accumulated. Some resistance continues, however, because the process is labor intensive and the technology still resides in the hands of surgical colleagues and therefore retains some degree of intimidation on the part of both the medical and the nursing staffs.

The assumption also remains among the professionals involved that a pharmacological approach to the treatment of these infants may be possible with proper investigation and research into the development of respiratory failure. ECMO programs may no longer be necessary once the key developments in research have occurred and the appropriate drugs for treatment are in place. Thus it may be that ECMO is a transient technology that would allow survival of infants while research develops a less invasive approach to treatment of the related disorders.

The "isolation" of the professionals treating an infant on ECMO was also not anticipated. Out of sight/out of mind mentality permeated the behavior of the staff not directly involved. The significance of this isolation cannot be overestimated. Movement of the patient into the main unit would not require further reduction of census, since NICU census is reduced by one bed when an ECMO infant is accepted.  In a sense, it is time for ECMO to join the unit and for us to determine the benefits of a move of six feet on staff morale!

## Alternatives

There are a number of changes that would be appropriate if this system were implemented anew.  More time should be devoted to the development of consensus before the implementation of a new technology.  Where consensus cannot be achieved before implementation, the assignment of a core group of individuals at the professional level who are enthusiastic supporters of the technique would contribute to a smoother transition in the application of the technology.  Once the technique has proven beneficial, then extension of responsibility to other members who have been previously resistent would be simplified.

It is also obvious, retrospectively, that we should have had a greater degree of institutional commitment to the enormous resources involved.  However, the enthusiasm of the surgical staff to implement the program led them to assume fiscal and physical responsibilities above and beyond those for any professional or division.  At a time of cost containment, and particularly with the implementation of the Diagnostic Related Groups in New York State, the fiscal problems associated with the implementation of a new program should have been more clearly anticipated and dealt with in a prospective fashion.

Now some five years after institution of ECMO, the staff more readily accepts the benefits of the procedure to infants selected for ECMO, but continues to have questions about the technology. In light of the success of ECMO, this continuing concern with regard to the technology and the lack of control of that technology on the part of neonatal nursing and medical service remain an enigma.  Perhaps as we move further from the second transition to the use of perfusionists, and as those professionals interact with our staff more regularly, the concern about technology will fade.  It may well be, however, that until the nursing staff and medical staff are more familiar with the technology in a hands-on fashion, this concern will not be totally alleviated.

The joint leadership of the ICU and the ECMO program will now request outside assistance in addressing the issues that in both measurable and unmeasurable ways continue to affect on the smooth operation of the ECMO program, particularly the continued staff resistance.  Under immediate consideration is the issue of how much the neonatal nursing and attending staffs should learn about hands-on application of the technology. The final decisions with regard to this issue have not been reached.

## ENDURING SOCIAL EFFECTS

Retrospectively, the expectations of the professionals responsible for the implementation of the program have been realized in terms of improved survival for the infants selected for ECMO. Concerns about the potential neurologic complications for these infants have been alleviated. The favorable development of infants who have been on ECMO has served to reduce the concerns of both medical and nursing staffs about the potential complications of the procedure itself on the developing central nervous system. These outcomes could not have been accurately predicted, because the experience at the national level was still relatively limited at the time the program was implemented.

These results confirm more recent national findings. An increasing number of infants are being treated with ECMO and surviving as more centers report their experience. The most recent report from the ECMO central registry described 2,528 newborn patients with respiratory failure supported by ECMO from the 56 reporting centers. The patients were treated between 1980 and 1989. Eighty-three percent of these patients survived. It is important to remember that before the introduction of this technology, the mortality rate for these infants was 90 percent. These results indicate that ECMO and lung rest are an appropriate and successful treatment for the newborn with respiratory failure that has been unresponsive to other means of treatment.

The introduction of ECMO into an established neonatal intensive care unit has been successful in reducing mortality, with acceptable longitudinal outcomes for the high-risk infants. The unexpected fiscal and manpower costs were not reasonably estimated in the beginning and continue to be a problem for pediatric surgery, the institution, and the neonatal intensive care unit. The interaction of the professionals involved has improved substantially over the course of the program, but the lack of control of the technology by the neonatal nursing and medical staffs remains a major problem. The concurrent development of an unexpectedly high delivery rate and a nursing shortage have obstructed the goal of serving as resource for the tristate area. The recent changes and the addition of new beds may allow achievement of this last goal. In short, the introduction of ECMO has been successful in saving lives previously lost, but costly and not yet fully implemented as a regional resource. The process is in place, however, to modify the system and to resolve remaining problems.

## REFERENCES

Bartlett, R. H., A. B. Guzzaniger, R. F. Huxtable, H. C. Schippes, M. J. O'Connor, and M. R. Jefferiar. 1977. Extracorporeal circulation in neonatal respiratory failure (ECMO). Journal of Cardiovascic Surgery 74:826–833.
White, J. J., H. G. Andrews, H. Rosenberg, and D. Mazun. 1971. Prolonged respiratory support in newborn infants with a membrane oxygenator. Surgery 70:288–296.

People and Technology in the Workplace. 1991.
Pp. 189–225. Washington, D.C:
National Academy Press.

# Operations Research in
# Nurse Scheduling

THOMAS CHOI, HELEN JAMESON, AND MILO L. BREKKE

Among all the problems that currently plague the nation's health profession, perhaps none is so obvious and detrimental as the much publicized nursing shortage. At a time when hospitalization policies mean only the very sick patients are admitted, the retention of nurses, especially qualified nurses, is paramount. Nurses are the largest work force in any hospital and are basic to the operation—but in recent years their turnover rate has been as high as 50 percent (Prescott and Bowen, 1987). An inability to maintain nursing manpower can radically affect quality of care. Clearly it is imperative that ways be found to increase job satisfaction, and thus retention, for qualified nurses.

What makes nurses resign? Previous studies have shown that discrepancies or disappointments between what nurses expect of their work schedules and what they experience are strong predictors of their intent to resign. This is because work schedules impose far-reaching constraints on the nurses' professional and social lives (Choi et al., 1986, 1989). So from 1983 to 1985, Rochester Methodist Hospital in Minnesota conducted an experiment with nurse scheduling to assess how various schedules might affect the retention of nurses.

The hospital's report of that experiment showed that various schedules did indeed reduce the nurses' job disappointment. But equally interesting is the behind-the-scenes report of the organization that elected to try such an experiment, and how it attempted to reconcile good management with the sometimes-

189

frustrating dictates imposed by "good science," or the experimental method. Both reports together tell an evolving tale of organizational change.

## ROCHESTER METHODIST HOSPITAL

In many ways Rochester Methodist Hospital was an ideal site for such an experiment. Rochester Methodist Hospital, affiliated with the Mayo Clinic, was founded in 1954 as an acute-care facility. Methodist Hospital has always been staffed by only Mayo clinic physicians. The present facility with 791 licensed beds was designed in part for research (Sturdavant, 1960). The hospital was built as a "laboratory in which to study alternative designs of nursing units, hospital systems, and organization" (Trites et al., 1969).

The Mayo Medical Center and Methodist Hospital's reputation for quality of care and productivity is well known (Dietrich and Biddle, 1986; Fifield, 1988; Sunshine and Wright, 1987).

Methodist is more stable than many hospitals because it does not compete for patients. Mayo Clinic allocates admissions between Methodist and St. Mary's Hospital. During the period of the experiment, patient census declined from 85.3 percent occupancy to 65.5 percent, reflecting a national trend.

The nursing department at Methodist Hospital was also recognized for its leadership. The organization of the nonunionized department was traditional, with centralization of major functions such as scheduling, budgeting, and education. However, despite centralization, communication "from the bottom up" was consistently encouraged by top management, and nurses' suggestions were shared through the line managers.

Nurse turnover had been gradually reduced from 39.1 percent in 1974 for full-time nurses to 12 percent in 1983 (the beginning of the scheduling experiment), a time when many hospitals nationally were still having greater than 50 percent turnover (Prescott and Brown, 1987). Methodist's nursing success was documented in the 1983 report *Magnet Hospitals*, in which it was named one of the 41 "magnet hospitals" in the United States that had demonstrated outstanding success in attracting and retaining professional nurses (McClure et al., 1983). According to the study, conducted by the Academy of Nursing of the American Nurses' Association, these 41 hospitals are set apart by three common denominators:

• Knowledgeable leadership providing for nursing input in policies affecting their practice,

- Opportunity to practice professional nursing, and
- Provision for professional growth.

The nursing department staff was also clearly interested in research. Methodist Hospital's philosophy read, "The institution has an obligation to its patients and professional groups to seek new knowledge and skills in the health care field." This hospital mission and nursing department staff's interest in research resulted in a 1978 study to review the feasibility of developing a nursing department program for systematic studies at Methodist Hospital (Egan et al., 1981). Several enabling factors were identified in that study, which suggested Methodist Hospital had the right climate for conducting research and implementing research results.

When the 1983 research project on nurse scheduling was approved, Methodist Hospital was governed by its own board of directors, whose backgrounds were primarily in fields of medicine, business, and law. The board was supportive of the nursing department, both having worked together for years, and recognized the department's accomplishments in the delivery of quality care, productivity, and nurse retention. All in all, Rochester Methodist Hospital was a progressive and even idyllic place in which to run an experiment.

## THE TURNOVER PROBLEM

The scheduling problem addressed in the research project was how to maintain a qualified work force. This was not an immediate problem for Methodist Hospital, since its nurse turnover rate in 1983 was only 12 percent. However, there were undeniable signals that suggested a likely recurrence of a nursing shortage; one which would be of much longer duration than the cyclical shortages of the past.

Inability to maintain nursing manpower would affect quality of care. Patients coming from around the world to this tertiary care setting expected a competent nursing staff. Methodist's need to schedule and staff 35 nursing units 7 days a week, 24 hours a day, with limited turnover seemed difficult for those outside of nursing to understand. But the fact that companies like Atwork, which developed the scheduling software used by Methodist Hospital,[1] spent years in developing these computer programs for nurses attests to the complexity that must be taken into account for quality patient care, concern for employees, and the maintaining of a budget.

Mayo Medical Center had experienced a nursing shortage in the early 1970s that precipitated the unprecedented action of closing hospital beds. This was difficult for the physicians. Studies in Minnesota and nationally predicted another shortage of nurses in the 1980s. These studies were conducted by such groups as the Minnesota Higher Education Coordinating Board and the Special Governor's Task Force on Nursing (1982). The report of the Governor's Task Force on Nursing called for "the health care industry to do a better job of retaining nurses in active practice if Minnesota is to deliver quality, cost-effective health care in the 1980's and beyond." The same task force listed the following trends indicating an upcoming nurse shortage:

• the increasing demand for nurses to work in hospitals and nursing homes,

• changes in hospital staffing patterns in response to technological and clinical development,

• the decreasing population of high school graduates (predicted decrease of 34 percent between 1980 and 1992), and

• the decrease in number of high school graduates who express an interest in nursing as a career.

The human-resource prediction model that was developed at Methodist also indicated a nursing shortage at the hospital unless retention could be maintained or improved upon.

The decision to go with the scheduling experiment was greatly influenced by the minutes of the Nurse Research Committee, which consisted of representatives from a cross section of nurses in the hospital. The minutes recalled that this research idea was not new:

> In 1980, a Nursing Research Advisory Task Force was established with the purpose of identifying research study topics which would provide the most potential benefits to the Nursing Service Department, and to develop a framework for a Nursing Studies Department. The idea of a research project related to retention first appeared in the Research Advisory Task Force Minutes of October 1, 1981, when it was listed as a priority for study selection at Rochester Methodist Hospital.

In 1982 the hospital's nursing service department—to which all nurses belong—identified scheduling, continuity of care, and research as areas requiring attention. A number of criteria were also identified that would be applied to any nursing research project:

• each research project would need to be successful and deemed important by the staff at all levels;

- each research project should have some practical results;
- each research results, when implemented, should be visible;
- each research visibility should go beyond the institution;
- each research project should mobilize and set up resources with the hospital, viewed positively by Mayo Clinic;
- each research project should find its own funding; and
- each project should contribute to an evolving and cumulative base for a research department.

As a result of applying these criteria, the immediate objective of Methodist's research was to develop, install, and evaluate alternatives that would improve the scheduling and staffing of nursing personnel in ways that were acceptable to them and that maintained the continuity and quality of patient care.

## CHOOSING THE SCHEDULE

The scheduling research project consisted of the development, implementation, and evaluation of new schedules, or strategies, that would balance the needs and desires of nurses with cost and quality-of-care issues. No one schedule was favored before the research began. However, there was interest in the expanded use of the scheduling department computer.

The Research Steering Committee (consisting of researchers, the hospital administrator, the hospital's human resource director, the director of nursing, and the project coordinator) agreed that a literature review of information on scheduling and staffing be the first step of the research project. The review covered issues of staff morale, community, satisfaction, hospital image, cost, turnover and retention, and quality of care. The review identified 20 schedules or strategies being used in hospitals across the nation. Intense discussions occurred between members of the Research Project Committee (researchers) and the Nursing Executive Committee (nurse managers) regarding those 20 work schedules. In these discussions, the researchers wanted to test new schedules that would have transferability within and outside the organization. Nursing managers agreed, but favored those schedules that would be practical and realistic to implement at Methodist.

The scheduling supervisor described the 20 schedules and used a paper-and-pencil method to test them against a set of criteria previously identified as essential (see Appendix A). The results were brought to the Nursing Executive Committee for action, and 12 schedules were selected for further consideration and evaluation.

The general procedure was first to rank-order the scheduling options in terms of the estimated scores for each of the criterion variables. A sum of ranks across all the criteria was then computed for every scheduling option. Finally, a rank-ordering of those sums effectively enabled the Nursing Executive Committee to sequence the scheduling options from the one most likely to have the best effect on nurses and the quality and cost of care (by comparison with existing schedules) to the one that probably would have the weakest or poorest effects (see Table 1). In making its selection of experimental schedules, the Nursing Executive Committee also sought as much variety as possible among high-ranking schedules.

The Nursing Executive Committee and the Research Project Committees then selected three schedules to be implemented during the experiment: straight shifts, computerized scheduling (compflex), and select-a-plan. These schedules are described in a later section.

## THE FIRST SNAG

It was at this point that the Nursing Executive Committee ran into difficulty with the research. It became clear that in order to test schedules objectively, units would have to be randomly assigned new schedules. This precluded choice or participative involvement—a fact that concerned all levels of nurse managers and nursing staff. The only incentive given to the staff was that if the experimental schedule met the criteria and was preferred over their previous schedules, staff could remain on the new schedule.

Good managers know it is virtually axiomatic that there must be good communication, support, mutual troubleshooting, and problem solving between management and staff. This was in fact the tradition at Methodist, which accounted for the esprit de corps and low turnover in the nursing staff. In sharp contrast, scientific research requires a commitment to an unbiased evaluation of new nurse schedules. Specifically, the experiment must be free of management interference. Otherwise, results of the experiment could be due not only to nurse schedules but also to management behavior.

Herein lies the conflict: Good management does not necessarily allow for good science. Testing new technologies in one's own organizational site has the advantage of ensuring that the technology—in this instance, nurse schedules—fits the setting. The disadvantage is that such a test may severely disrupt normal behav-

**TABLE 1** Example of Comparison of Scheduling Options

| Criterion | Scheduling Option | | | | | | | | | Estimated rank |
|---|---|---|---|---|---|---|---|---|---|---|
| | 1 | 2 | 3 | 4 | 5 | 6 | 7 | 8 | 9 | |
| Continuity | 10% | 27% | 19% | 19% | 25% | 0% | 18% | 0% | 20% | Estimated rank |
| | 4 | 9 | 6.5 | 6.5 | 8 | 3.5 | 5 | 3.5 | 7 | |
| Flexibility | .32 | .89 | .25 | .86 | .41 | .44 | .70 | .76 | .98 | Estimated rank |
| | 2 | 8 | 1 | 7 | 3 | 4 | 5 | 6 | 9 | |
| Quality | 76 | 75.4 | 77.6 | 75.5 | 75.9 | 70.6 | 73.9 | 77.4 | 75.8 | Estimated rank |
| | 7 | 3 | 9 | 4 | 6 | 1 | 2 | 8 | 5 | |
| Sum of ranks for each option | 13 | 20 | 16.5 | 17.5 | 17 | 8.5 | 12 | 17.5 | 21 | |
| Rank order of the sums of ranks | 3 | 8 | 4 | 6 | 5 | 1 | 2 | 7 | 9 | |

ior, which may in fact hurt the very group the technology is intended in help. Thus on the surface, good management and good science seemed to share a common concept, but putting the concept into operation was a different matter.

Despite misgivings, the Nursing Executive Committee decided to go ahead. At the first of what was to be many "update" meetings of all head nurses—first-line managers—random schedule assignments were made. Those head nurses in the selected units (i.e., regular nurse work stations) were given special recognition for their forthcoming participation. This recognition was not particularly well received. Individual reactions among head nurses at the meeting ranged from joy to extreme anger—so much so that the Nursing Executive Committee became apprehensive about the possibility of bias in the experimental outcome. Fortunately, however, true to their professionalism, each head nurse presented the new schedules fairly, with assistance from the scheduling department. The nursing staff reacted with the same range of emotions.

Because of these strong reactions, an unplanned facet to the research was added, which was to allow head nurses and staff the opportunity to submit anonymous comments about their schedules. The research coordinator on the experiment assembled the comments and shared them with the Nursing Executive Committee. The key to surviving a possible breakdown in morale at this point was trust in the dedication of the manager and the leadership of the department. These comments continued for the nine months of the intervention phase—that is, trying out new schedules—of the experiment. A review of the comments after the experiment still evoked pain on the part of the managers. These comments described the emotions of experiencing change at the personal, staff, and organizational levels.

The head nurses were definite losers in this change. They not only lost control of selecting schedules for their unit but also were placed in the most difficult position of bridging between employees and management. Although this situation improved with time, it contributed to stressful relations.

## OTHER GLITCHES

After the research project started in 1983, four activities took place that significantly affected the hospital employees. These activities were important to the research project in terms of time commitments, potential employee morale problems, and lowering of managers' willingness to take risks.

First, pressure increased for immediate action on nurse scheduling. The hospital management and Board of Governors decided in 1983 to develop and conduct the first hospital-wide employee opinion survey. The results were generally positive and management was viewed favorably. However, the additional comment section contained 23 negative remarks (6 percent of the comments) about nurse scheduling. The implication of conducting an opinion survey was that the employees could expect immediate action in response to their comments; therefore, a scheduling experiment could have been seen by staff nurses as an unnecessary delay.

Second, the nursing department picked this time to computerize. Although the department had centralized scheduling in 1968, except for the schedules themselves, the department had kept limited data for managing projections. In the mid-1970s, increased record keeping of nurse statistics, such as turnover, manpower requirements, and costs, was begun; and by 1983 it was determined that some data automation was essential to manage this department of more than 1,000 employees. Therefore, in 1983, the nursing and management services departments began investigating scheduling systems that would produce reports, assist in nursing department record keeping, and automate the present schedules. Before this time, there had been no computer programs that could totally automate scheduling. In May 1984 a contract was signed with Atwork for the Automated Nurse Scheduling System (ANSOS) computer program. The nursing management team had been consistently informed of the investigation into this system but choose not to involve staff nurses because it did not anticipate that the change would negatively affect the staff.

They were wrong. Implementation of change without staff involvement taught an invaluable lesson. Initially, ANSOS could not accommodate the size of the nursing staff. Therefore, it became necessary to use two separate programs, which precluded computer tracking of staff between the two programs. The lack of flexibility and integration resulting from this use of two independent computer programs fragmented the hospital into two separate systems, thereby affecting employee schedule exchanges and employees' ability to float or move to all units. The unexpected consequence of this change, in which the nursing staff viewed the computer as deciding their lives, was especially negative. The nurses became skeptical of the use of computers for scheduling.

The third activity that affected the research project was the implementation of the government's program of prospective diagnostic related groupings (DRGs) in October 1984. This program should have had little effect on the already short length of hospital stays at Methodist. The effect it did have, however, was only to postpone the inevitable nursing shortage. This shortage came about because the decrease in the number of beds occupied (to 65 percent) and the length of inpatient hospital stay (by 0.3 days) caused nursing units to close. The hospital decided not to resort to layoffs. Soon, however, trying to stay on budget with too many nurses was one more problem for management to resolve.

Fourth was the prospect of a merger of Mayo Clinic, Rochester Methodist Hospital, and Saint Mary's Hospital. The potential merger was announced in 1985 during the study on scheduling and was completed in 1986. The major change was to form a common governance structure.

Nurse managers coping with the three other new activities just described, in addition to their normal activities and scheduling research, questioned whether the scheduling experiment should be continued. For this kind of research (and the implementation of its results) to work in a hospital, management needed to be strongly committed to the activity. As discussed, the requirements of good management and good research came into conflict.

## NATURE OF THE NURSE SCHEDULING EXPERIMENT

As mentioned at the outset of this discussion, disappointment in nurse scheduling indicates the process leading to resignation. Figure 1 shows how disappointments and discrepancies between what nurses expect and experience of their work schedules are strong predictors of nurses' intent to resign (Choi et al., 1989). Intention to resign has also been shown to have a direct and significant effect on turnover (Weisman et al., 1981). Satisfaction affects turnover through intention to resign (Weisman et al., 1981). Therefore, intention to leave is a critical intervening variable between satisfaction and actual turnover. Expressed by means of a parsimonious model, nurse turnover is a consequence of intention to resign, which is precipitated by dissatisfaction and discrepancies. Dissatisfaction itself is also a consequence of discrepancies.

Each discrepancy variable is a continuum, the two poles of which are represented by disappointment, which stems from expectation exceeding experience, and contentment, from experience superseding expectation. In the larger context of social theories, Davis (1962) and Durkheim (1951) both indicated that attitudes most likely to trigger action have to do with perceived discrepancy between a person's expectations and experiences, or the lack of

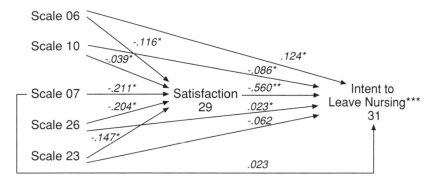

FIGURE 1    Operational model—predicting intention of nurses to leave nursing. Key: Scale 06: Discrepancy concerning work schedules creating a climate for ideal professional nursing.    Scale 10: Discrepancy concerning work schedules allowing freedom for personal business.    Scale 07: Discrepancy concerning work schedules that are predictable.    Scale 26: Discrepancy concerning work schedules allowing social activities outside the hospital.    Scale 23: Discrepancy concerning work schedules fostering relationships at and outside of work.    Scale 29: General satisfaction. Scale 31: Intent to leave nursing altogether because of scheduling dissatisfaction.   $^AP < .01$, $^{**}P < .001$, and $^{***}r^2 = .3085$.

integration between ends conceived and means available to achieve them.   That is, dissatisfaction resulting from failing expectations— jolts that create disequilibrium—may very well induce change-seeking behavior.

Low nurse turnover, especially when the economy is sluggish, may lead to the mistaken conclusion that root causes of nurse turnover—schedule-induced dissatisfaction and disappointment— have vanished.   The combination of uncorrected root causes and an improved economy would instigate nurse turnover.   But redesigning work schedules may increase satisfaction and contentment, hence retention.

## RESEARCH METHODS

To evaluate how different schedules affect retention, the research project committee and the nursing executive committee designed an experiment calling for three experimental groups and one control group.   Each experimental and control group in turn consisted of three randomly selected nursing units.   All told, 12 randomly chosen units were involved (random sampling process described later). Two of the randomly selected experimental groups were randomly assigned a schedule; the remaining experimental group was assigned to design a schedule using its own criteria. Although the control group served only as a reference for comparison with the experimental groups, subjects in this group were administered similar data collection instruments and given the same opportunity to deliver anonymous comments about the experimental process. The experimental treatment was administered over a 40-week period. By staying within one hospital, experimental results would most likely not be confounded by differing hospital policies and management styles. Results reported here are from data collected before and after the full implementation of experimental schedules.

## Three Experimental Schedules

The three experimental schedules were selected after a long process of examination and deliberation. Part of this process was discussed earlier. The first two experimental groups were assigned either straight shifts or computer-assigned scheduling (compflex). The third group designed its own schedule, labeled select-a-plan. To make the experiment as realistic as possible, none of the stations in the three experimental groups was allowed to exceed the normal budget; thus, results of the experiment did not involve a cost increase.

Under the straight-shift schedule, virtually all staff members of nursing units worked straight days, evenings, or nights. Staff members working days were expected to cover the evening and night shifts when vacancies occurred (e.g., during vacations). There were 63 nurses under the straight-shift treatment, of which 42 (67 percent) were registered nurses (RNs), the rest were licensed practical nurses (LPNs). The intent of the straight shift was to provide nurses with predictability and regularity, the lack of which threw their daily living out of synchronization.

The second schedule, compflex, aimed to provide both flexibility and control so that nurses could individually plan for their own schedules. Under the compflex schedule, a computerized system was used to generate a monthly schedule based on a combination of the unit's daily needs for the unit and staff requests. Staff members were allowed unlimited requests, though they soon demanded that a policy be implemented allowing for no more than one Friday evening or one Saturday night off per month. The requests were incorporated into the system; the schedule was computerized. The scheduling department then reviewed the schedule to ensure that patient care needs would be met, and, if so, requests were granted on a first-come, first-served basis. This type of schedule did not have the predictability of a cyclical schedule but allowed for a great deal of input by individual nurses. Sixty-eight nurses were under this treatment of which 48 (72 percent) were RNs and the rest were LPNs.

Unlike the other two treatments, select-a-plan may be seen as much as a process as a schedule. Under the select-a-plan schedule, the staff on each of the stations developed from scratch the type of schedule to be used on that station. Each station selected two RNs and one LPN to develop the schedule based on the group's ideas. Minimum guidelines on budget and legal constraints were given to each work station, and assistance was offered by the nursing administration if the treatment group needed help. The schedule arrangement had to be voted and agreed upon by at least 80 percent of the nurses on each station.

Each of the three select-a-plan stations elected various combinations of 8- and 12-hour shifts. A certain portion of the staff had schedules of 8-hour shifts during the week and 12-hour shifts on the weekend. In those schedules, the staff worked every third weekend. Some stations also used a portion of straight days; others, a limited number of 12-hour shifts. All had some 8-hour shifts on rotating schedules. There were 59 nurses under this treatment: 30 (66 percent) RNs, the rest LPNs.

The nursing stations under the control plan continued to use the schedules as before the experiment. These schedules included 8-hour rotating shifts of day and evening, days and nights, and a limited number of straight evenings or nights. All staff members worked every other weekend.

## Random Sampling

Data were collected from all RNs and LPNs regularly assigned to nursing stations. This intervention was primarily intended to monitor nurses on a station; thus random sampling was used for stations, not specific individuals.

Three general types of nursing units were identified through hierarchical cluster analyses of some 37 characteristics of each unit that were judged by head nurses and nursing administrators to be relevant to the scheduling of nurses. The analyses were performed using the CLUSTER program with the Statistical Analysis System (SAS) programming language (Anderberg, 1973; Milligan,

1980). Appendix B lists those 37 characteristics that were responsible for the cluster content in a statistically significant way. The sampling frame consisted of 18 medical and surgical nursing units stratified by general type of unit (clusters of 4, 7, and 7 units of types A, B, and C, respectively). Some highly specialized units such as intensive care and obstetrics and gynecology were excluded from the final sampling frame because there were too few of each to allow assignment of at least one unit to each of one control group and three experimental groups.

As many unit characteristics as possible were included to maximize the generalizability of study results. The units of each type also were stratified both by kind of floor architecture (circular or linear) and kind of care (medical or surgical). Type A units were all circular and surgical. Type B units were predominately surgical (5 of 7) and more frequently circular (4 of 7). Thus, a completely balanced sampling across the three stratification variables was not possible.

A stratified random sample of 12 units (three for each experimental and control group) was selected in such a way that each level of each stratification variable was represented at least once within each experimental and control group. That is, among the three units assigned to each group, the following unit characteristics were represented at least once: type A, type B, type C, medical, and surgical. Circular or linear types were represented more than once in each group.

### Scales Used to Assess Experimental and Control Differences

Effects of treatment on the experimental groups relative to the control were gauged according to scores on 36 reliable scales (Appendix C). All scales, designed to be critical and relevant to scheduling-related issues and retention, were constructed through item analysis (Carmines and Zeller, 1979). The analysis consisted of reliability tests and factor analysis of questionnaire responses from all of the nurses ($n$ = 792, 98 percent response rate) employed at the study hospital. The questions were developed with the help of two expert panels representing nursing education, scheduling, operations, and administration.

Each discrepancy scale score was derived from the sum of differences between nurses' own ratings on expectation and on experience for items specific to that scale. The direction and degree of difference across all items would indicate the level of disappointment or contentment.

## Data Analysis

Beyond assessment and refinement of scale reliability, an analysis of variance was performed to ascertain that the experimental groups were significantly different from the control group, before and after implementing the experimental treatment.

## FINDINGS

### Immediate Results

Results shown in Table 2 indicate that there were significant differences in scores across 6 of the 36 scales between the experimental and control groups after the experimental treatments were administered. In contrast, before the intervention, there was a difference in only one scale—experience in privacy of work—which was judged to be inconsequential. The composition and reliability of each scale, out of the total of 36 that discriminated significantly between the groups, is shown in Appendix D.

The select-a-plan scheduling group was significantly different from the control in four of the 36 scales: expectation of a work schedule that allows for communication with day department (scale

**TABLE 2** Significant Differences Across 36 Scales Relative to the Control Group: RNs and LPNs

|  | Before Treatment | After Treatment |
|---|---|---|
| Straight shift |  | Scale 2 (+)  Scale 3 (–) |
| Compflex |  | Scale 2 (+)  Scale 3 (–) |
| Select-a-plan | Scale 1 (+) | Scale 4 (–)  Scale 5 (–) |
|  |  | Scale 6 (–)[a] Scale 7 (–)[a] |

Key: Scale 1 = experience of a work schedule that allows privacy at work; Scale 2 = sense of one's own marketability; Scale 3 = experience of a work schedule that fosters staff teamwork and friendship on the unit; Scale 4 = expectation of work schedule that allows communication with key departments; Scale 5 = expectation of being able to control one's schedule; Scale 6 = discrepancy concerning work schedules creating a climate for ideal professional nursing; and Scale 7 = discrepancy concerning work schedules that are predictable.

(+) = scored higher than control

(–) = scored lower than control.

[a]Indicates less disappointment or more contentment.

4), expectation of being able to control one's schedule (scale 5), discrepancy concerning work schedules creating a climate for ideal professional nursing (scale 6), and discrepancy concerning work schedules that are predictable (scale 7) (see Table 2). The compflex and straight-shift groups were significantly different from the control group in two identical scales: sense of one's own marketability (scale 2) and expectation of staff teamwork and friendship (scale 3). Thus, the select-a-plan group was affected most by the experiment.

When compared with the other two groups, the select-a-plan group also showed significantly less disappointment (discrepancy) in a key variable—discrepancy concerning work schedules creating a climate for ideal professional nursing (scale 6). This particular scale was shown previously to have a direct and significant effect on the intention to leave nursing (see Figure 1). The select-a-plan group showed no increase in sense of marketability and had lower levels of expectation in communications with other departments. The select-a-plan group also showed less disappointment, previously shown to be a predictor of intention to resign (Figure 1).

When the groups were stratified into RNs and LPNs, the RNs in the experimental group scored differently from the RNs in the control group on two of the 36 scales (see Table 3). When RNs from all three experimental groups were treated as a group, they perceived a greater sense of their own marketability (scale 2). On a group-to-group comparison, only compflex RNs were shown to have a significantly higher sense of marketability than the control. They also had greater expectation of a schedule that allowed more continuity of care (scale 8).

In contrast, Table 4 shows that LPNs in the experimental groups differed from LPNs in the control group on four scales: less expec-

**TABLE 3**   Significant Differences Across 36 Scales Relative to the Control Group:  RNs Only

|  | Before Treatment | After Treatment |
|---|---|---|
| Straight Shift |  |  |
| Compflex |  | Scale 2 (+) Scale 8 (−) |
| Select-A-Plan |  |  |

Key:  Scale 2 = sense of one's own marketability; and Scale 8 = expectation of a work schedule that allows continuity of care.
   (+) = scored higher than control.
   (−) = scored lower than control.

**TABLE 4**  Significant Differences Across 36 Scales Relative to the Control Group:  LPNs Only

|  | Before Treatment | After Treatment |
|---|---|---|
| Straight Shift |  |  |
| Compflex |  | Scale 9 (–) Scale 10 (–)[a] |
| Select-A-Plan | Scale 1 (+) Scale 11 (+) | Scale 9 (–) Scale 5 (–) |
|  |  | Scale 7 (–)[a] |

Key:  Scale 1 = experience of a work schedule that allows privacy at work; Scale 5 = expectation of being able to control one's schedule; Scale 7 = discrepancy concerning work schedules that are predictable; Scale 9 = expectation of a work schedule that fosters relationships at and outside of work; Scale 10 = discrepancy concerning work schedules allowing freedom for personal business; and Scale 11 = expectation of a work schedule that allows privacy at work.
(+) = scored higher than control.
(–) = scored lower than control.
[a]Indicates less disappointment or more contentment.

tation of being able to control one's schedule (scale 5), less disappointment (discrepancy) in the predictability of work schedules (scale 7), less expectation of work schedule that fosters relationships at and outside of work (scale 9), and less disappointment (discrepancy) concerning work schedules allowing freedom of personal business (scale 10).

## Later Results

The immediate results just discussed, which reflect what happened shortly after the experiment was implemented, were consistent over time; disappointments were lowered and satisfaction with other facets of nursing were increased in the experimental groups relative to the control groups. Over time, lower teamwork and a higher sense of one's marketability—two unintended negative consequences—disappeared.

A particularly important finding was that there were no significant statistical differences in actual turnover between experimental and control groups after the treatments. (Turnover data included transfers to another nursing unit within the hospital as well as voluntary resignations from the hospital.)  The range of transfers for all groups was between 7 percent and 8 percent; resignations were between 2 percent and 4 percent for the experimental groups, but 7 percent for the control group.  Although the data seemed to favor retention in experimental groups, the number of turnover cases was too small to generalize with statistical confidence.

The actual turnover numbers continued to favor the experimental groups two years after the experiment was completed. Again the numbers were too small for statistical tests. By the third year the actual turnover rate became similar between the experimental and control groups.

The study also examined the relationships between scheduling, cost of care, and quality of care. These relationships are complex and go beyond the scope of this paper. In brief, the study showed that staffing, not scheduling, affected cost of care. Scheduling also had little impact on continuity of care, the proxy that was used to measure quality.

## DISCUSSION

Overall, the experiment was effective in that varying work schedules produced different consequences. Virtually no difference existed between the study groups (all randomly selected) before the intervention began. The differences between experimental and control groups after intervention attest to the importance of schedules or schedule-related issues. The select-a-plan treatment showed the greatest experimental impact, judging by the number of changes on the units detected by the scales. By the end of the interventions after roughly 40 weeks, all but one of the nine experimental stations voted to continue their respective experimental schedules. The lone exception was a straight-shift station. Furthermore, none of the three types of experimental schedules appeared to have been viewed negatively by the nursing staff. This conclusion was supported further by a very low turnover rate. This low rate may be due in part to the poor job market when the experiment took place in 1984–1985. Of greater significance, perhaps, was that some of the root causes of turnover—two of the five discrepancy variables—were affected by the experiment in such a way that would favor retention (Figure 1).

One of the unanticipated consequences that appeared shortly after the experiment began was the nurses' increased sense of their own marketability in two of the three study groups. Thus, ironically, an experiment that was intended to find ways to retain nurses may have also encouraged some nurses to seek employment elsewhere. Why nurses in the two experimental groups felt more marketable is a matter of speculation. The classic Hawthorne effect may be ruled out as a cause because all of the groups, including the control, received about the same amount of research attention. A more likely explanation might be that the nurses in the compflex group were reinforced by a new sense of control derived from the legitimatized right to negotiate their own work schedule. They probably also chose to be on new schedule(s) that gave them positive experiences, which in turn, enhanced their self-esteem and sense of marketability.

While choice of schedule may be relatively limited for some under the straight-shift format, for others, being on a straight-shift schedule may have approximated the "ideal" work schedule. (For example, straight days are more likely to be synchronized with the schedules of people outside the hospital.) At a minimum, straight shifts offered a regular work schedule whether it was day, evening, or night. There were those nurses on straight evenings or straight nights who preferred such shifts because they coincided with the work hours of their spouses or because shifts had smaller and potentially more cohesive work groups. Perhaps most important is that straight shifts allowed for a less ambiguous relationship between seniority and attainment of an ideal schedule. These combined factors possibly enhanced the self-esteem of nurses, which in turn may have heightened self-perceived marketability as well.

Another consequence of the experiment was a lessening of teamwork under compflex and straight-shift schedules. This may be explained again by an individual's increased power to negotiate one's schedule without consulting other nurses on the unit. Under the straight-shift schedule, it could also be explained by the lack of continuity in nurses between shifts. That is, in the strictest sense, straight shifts fostered a sense of nursing identity by shifts rather than by units. Because nurses did not span shifts, the overall cooperation on the unit suffered.

Over time, the lack of teamwork and the increased sense of marketability disappeared. Returning teamwork and nurses' sense of marketability to their former states had to do with a deeper understanding of how one's schedule changes affected others on the unit. Once the process was understood, teamwork improved again and the nurses' own sense of marketability also returned to the normal level.

Over time, straight shifts could not be kept in the strictest sense at this acute-care hospital because nursing management desired experienced nurses on all shifts. The decision to honor seniority—that is, senior nurses having first pick of schedules—

ran counter to the need to schedule experienced nurses on all shifts. Methodist nursing units were small, 14-30 beds, which required a small staff and, thus, less flexibility. Therefore, an increased budget or overhiring would have been required to remain on a strict straight shift. By rotating some skilled nurses across shifts so that none was assigned exclusively to a particular shift, the we/they dichotomy between nurses on different shifts of the same stations disappeared. Thus, the necessary continuity between shifts was restored, but the straight shift became less attractive to the nurses who had to rotate to fill in for vacancies.

The intended effect of the entire experiment was, in part, to reduce discrepancies between nurses' experiences and expectations of their jobs, root causes of turnover. Less disappointment, or more contentment, was most evident with the select-a-plan group, which improved its discrepancy scores over the course of the experiment by lowering expectation scores relative to that of experience. That group showed less of the disappointment (scale 6) that contributed directly to the intention to resign. Data taken before the experiment had shown a high level of expectation—and experience as well—among the majority of the nurses. A scheduling experiment would have had to be very powerful before it could have improved on the already high scores on expectation and experience among this group of nurses. Quite unexpectedly, however, discrepancy scores did improve—that is, experience superseded expectation—by the lowering of nurses' expectation scores. When nurses lowered their high expectations, this may have been a healthy sign that individual nurses believed they could bring about greater consistency between expectation and experience. Despite the generally high score of the nurses in expectation, experience, and satisfaction, scheduling as an experimental treatment was able to bring about several significant changes; this attests to the importance of scheduling to nurses.

The after-treatment differences of select-a-plan relative to the other two experimental groups shows that select-a-plan appeared to have best met the objective of retaining nurses without increasing costs. The select-a-plan group was able to reduce discrepancies (disappointments) because the nurses significantly lowered their expectations of being able to (1) control their own schedules (scale 5), and (2) communicate with other departments (scale 4). These lowered expectations for the select-a-plan group may be a consequence of the group's having to construct a work schedule that was approved by at least 80 percent of the group. This process of deliberation may have exposed the nurses to the difficulties of making a schedule work. Thus, mere exposure might have led to a certain understanding, if not acceptance, that some elements in the practice of clinical nursing might elude personal control. Perhaps these sets of experiences and exposures, particularly obvious through the select-a-plan group process, contributed to the lowering of expectations and, as a result, reduced disappointments.

The three experimental treatments did not have a statistically significant direct effect on retention (as measured by different indices of intention to resign), although the experiment did have significant effects on predictors, or root causes, of intention to resign. Several factors may have mitigated the direct effect of the experiment on resigning: (1) the period of experimentation with the new schedules (1984–1985) was characterized by a poor job market, which made job changes less feasible; (2) nurses in the study knew that despite their desire for immediate changes, the experimental schedules were to last no longer than 9 months; and (3) the nurses in the study understood that a primary purpose of the experiment was to improve the quality of their professional and personal lives. Although circumstances discouraged nurses from actually resigning, the experiment did significantly affect root causes of potential resignations. It may be possible to infer from this that if the experiment had been continued, significant differences in retention between nursing units in the study would have been evident.

The lower turnover rate among the experimental groups two years after the experiment—including the one straight-shift station that voted against continuance after the experiment—speaks to the importance of scheduling. But the turnover rate was more similar across all study groups by the third year (1988) after the experiment. It should be noted that nursing management had expected a greater increase in nurse turnover on a hospital-wide basis in 1988, since many of the requested schedules had not been implemented. However, the following reasons may account for the less-than-expected turnover: the scheduling task force became a permanent scheduling advisory committee with representation from all service areas; units felt there was a more flexible attitude in the scheduling department despite limited changes in policy; nurses were aware of a scheduling task force between the two merged hospitals and their efforts to find means of implementing new schedules; and some staff energy was diverted away from scheduling to the ongoing merger. Thus, nurses may have adopted a wait-and-see attitude.

Of interest was the influence of the treatments on RNs in the experimental groups compared with RNs in the control group. RNs showed changes on only two scales. But LPNs in the experimental groups relative to their counterparts in the control group showed four scale changes. The relative marketability of RNs to that of LPNs may explain the difference in the effects of the scheduling changes. Hence, the changes may have greater impact on LPNs than RNs.

## POLICY IMPLICATIONS

From the perspective of hospital administration and policy, it should be clear that the experiment did not cause significant nurse turnover. The experiment answered the feasibility question positively and also indicated that none of the three new schedules is likely to be negatively received by nursing personnel. This latter feature is particularly important considering the frequency with which well-meaning interventions unintentionally hurt the very target population they are designed to help.

Results of this experiment should give hospital administrators confidence to proceed in implementing new types of schedules, knowing that cost and turnover probably will not be affected when conditions are stated beforehand to the staff. Results should also alert decision makers to be aware of the potential risks involved—for example, enhancing nurses' sense of marketability, which indeed may lead to turnover—when the reduction of discrepancies between job expectations and experience (disappointments) becomes especially successful.

The three experimental schedules provide variety and give hospitals different options. Variety may be crucial even for just one hospital to accommodate the diverse units of modern hospitals. A single-schedule format would probably not suffice to meet the many different needs of patients and staff.

Of the three experimental schedules, select-a-plan offered the most flexibility in tailoring a schedule for nurses on a unit. The results of this treatment also appeared particularly encouraging in inhibiting intention to resign. Overall, the success of select-a-plan proved the soundness of allowing nurses to design their own schedules. However, this success is not inevitable. Clear goals, criteria, and boundaries, for example, emphasis on budget limitations and quality of care must be communicated first. A successful implementation is predicated on the assumption that nurses on the unit are willing and able to design and agree upon a schedule. The degree to which such an assumption can be met depends on the specific unit involved and the time allotted to the unit for such activity.

The results of the experiment did not induce widespread changes as gauged by the 36 scales that measured job satisfaction. From a policy perspective, it may be concluded that this was a positive sign, because the experiment did not induce large-scale upheaval. Changes that were statistically significant involved a few variables, some of which were particularly relevant to retention. However, had the study been conducted in a hospital where nurses were less content, there could indeed have been more significant changes.

## CURRENT SITUATION

After the experiment, 16 nursing units requested to design and implement their own select-a-plan schedules. These schedules allowed more ways for nurses to try new ideas and provided for a variety of schedules.

However, two factors have delayed the implementation. First, federal wage and hour regulations have been tightened for nonexempt employees' so that the desired select-a-plan schedule would cost, for the entire nursing department (RNs, LPNs, and ward secretaries), $700,000 more in 1989 than in 1988 and would escalate each year with salary increases. Hospital decision makers are exploring solutions such as going exempt and changing the starting day of the work week. Second, a consequence of the hospital merger requires that new and innovative scheduling decisions be jointly made between the two hospitals. This arrangement could curtail the nursing department's ability to develop its own schedules.

Other hospitals are using variations of the select-a-plan process. The difference is that they may not have applied the aforementioned criteria (see Appendix A) used in the initial evaluative review of schedules. This evaluation is critical because it identified the potential problems and necessary corrective steps that were then suggested by hospital management, the human resource department, and nursing management.

## A LAST WORD ON MANAGEMENT

### The Head Nurse

It bears repeating that it is crucial for the head nurse to be involved in, and committed to, both planning and implementa-

tion.    Regardless of the type of organization, the nursing staff
needs a regular, consistent process of communication between
various departments.  The head nurses, as first-line managers, are
the necessary link for the following reasons.

The new schedules, especially select-a-plan, reflected decentralization, which made frequent communication all the more necessary between management and staff nurses.  Head nurses were
the critical link between the key parties.

Decentralization also represented change, which many employees resented even though quality of care and services continued.
The resentment against change demonstrated that upper management could not predict employee response as well as the head
nurses could.  For example, it seemed logical to outside nursing
managers that a schedule that gave each employee freedom to
make unlimited requests for changes (compflex) had to be attractive to nurses.  But upper management failed to recognize that
schedules needed to be predictable, and that more aggressive employees took advantage of the freedom, causing resentment in
others.  Only the head nurses, who knew their employees personally, could and did accurately predict staff reaction.

## WHY THE NEW SCHEDULES WORKED

There are strong disincentives for hospitals to adopt new schedules. The planning process, assessment of readiness, and achieving consensus on what schedule to implement are time-consum-
ing and stressful and compete with other demands.  As a result,
there is a built-in reluctance to commit to such an endeavor.

In retrospect, on this project, management was less involved in
solving a problem than it was in preventing a problem from happening.  Through the process of experimentation, the potential for
disaster was so apparent that the following ingredients appeared
essential for the project to succeed: (1) leader commitment to take
risks, (2) a steadfast vision of what is feasible and desirable, and
(3) a steadfast support of personnel undergoing change. Also critical to the process was that Methodist was not fighting for survival. It had the freedom to find ways to make improvements.

Again in retrospect, it also became apparent that a minimum of
nine months was needed for implementation and adjustment of
schedule changes. Commitment and continuity are key ingredients.  Such a project should probably not be attempted if top-level
management is undergoing personnel changes. When change can
be implemented along regular channels without having to create

new or temporary structures, communication and trust are more likely to result.

Some of the changes in schedules and scheduling were not planned but evolved by trial and error. Both select-a-plan and compflex tried various combinations of scheduling arrangements. The evolution was aided by the scheduling department and by computer-scheduling software, which were essential to the realization of select-a-plan and compflex schedules.

Because specific criteria of schedule selection and implementation were put in place for the select-a-plan group, the risk to management of allowing staff freedom to develop these schedules was lessened. The trust in staff to respect limits imposed by the criteria paid off.

Several other organizational factors were important, and these were considered before the experiment was implemented. First, it was recognized from the start that nurse scheduling and staffing was an issue of concern to every new employee. Thus, an experiment on scheduling would probably be well received. Second, it was recognized that management staff working on the research was already assigned a heavy workload. Even with the employment of a full-time coordinator, extra time would most likely be needed from specific staff members for the project to succeed. Third, the diverse composition of Methodist's nurses made fair play a challenge in implementing schedule changes. The experimental schedules were designed as much as possible to give nurses with seniority the first pick, even though some of these nurses had been at the hospital for 10 or more years and were unlikely to leave. The recognition of seniority and respect for fair play may also have contributed to the acceptance of the experiment.

For the future, two changes are foreseen. If new schedules continue to evolve at Methodist they will be kept, provided that they demonstrate improvement over existing schedules. It is possible then to have a large variety of schedules at the hospital rather than the standard two before the experiment started. The other anticipated change is an increasingly stronger role for head nurses in schedule selection. This should reduce the erosion of authority as a result of implementing new schedules.

## NOTES

1. Atwork, Inc., in 1982 used information developed by Michael Warner (1976).

2. Nonexempt employees, in accordance with the 1938 Fair Labor Standards

Act and the subsequent amendment of 1986—which applies to hospitals—are paid by the hour and entitled to overtime pay. Exempt and nonexempt statuses are conferred based on the nature of work, responsibility, and salary. Most nurses at Rochester Methodist Hospital are of nonexempt status. But they are eligible for exempt status, which is generally, though not always, represented by executive nurses or nurses with a certain level of education (e.g., RNs).

By regulation, there is less flexibility allowed by the Fair Labor Standards Act for nonexempt employees. Thus, despite the attractiveness of the select-a-plan (SAP) to the nurses—because of its flexibility—and the willingness of the hospital administration for nurses to adopt SAP, accommodating the constraints imposed by nonexempt status and flexibility inherent in SAP presents continuous challenges yet to be fully met. For a comprehensive treatment of exempt and nonexempt status, refer to Murphy and Azoff (1987).

## REFERENCES

Academy names 41 "magnet" hospitals because of their "demonstrated success" in attracting and retaining nurses. 1983. American Nurse 15(2):1.

Anderberg, M. R. 1973. Cluster Analysis for Applications. New York: Academic Press.

Carmines, E. G., and R. Zeller. 1979. Reliability and Validity Assessment. Beverly Hills, Calif.: Sage Publications.

Choi, T., H. Jameson, M. L. Brekke, R. O. Podratz, and H. Mundahl. 1986. Effects on nurse retention: An experiment with scheduling. Medical Care 24(11):1029–1043.

Choi T., H. Jameson, M. L. Brekke, J. G. Anderson, and R. O. Podratz. 1989. Schedule related effects on nurse retention. Western Journal of Nursing Research 11(1):92–107.

Davis, J. C. 1962. Toward a theory of revolution. American Sociological Review 27:5–19.

Dietrich, H. J., and V. H. Biddle, eds. 1986. The Best in Medicine. New York: Harmony Books.

Durkheim, E. 1951. Suicide (J. A. Spaulding and G. Simpson, translators) New York: Free Press.

Egan, E., B. McElmurry, and H. Jameson. 1981. Practice-based research: Assessing your department's readiness. Journal of Nursing Administration 11(10):26–32.

Fifield, F. F. 1988. What is a productivity-excellent hospital? Nursing Management 19(4):32–40.

Final Report and Recommendations. 1982. Governor's Task Force on Nursing, State of Minnesota, p. 1.

Higher Education Coordinating Board (HECB). 1982. Post-Secondary Education Enrollment Projection, St. Paul, Minnesota.

McClure, M., Paulin, Sovie and Wandelt. 1983. Magnet Hospitals: At-traction and Retention of Professional Nurses. Kansas City, Mo.: American Nurses' Association.

Milligan, G. W. 1980. An examination of the effect of six types of error perturbation on clustering algorithms. Psychometrika 45:325.

Murphy, B. S., and E. S. Azoff. 1987. Guide to Wage and Hour Regulation: A Practical Guide for the Corporate Counselor. Washington, D.C.: Bureau of National Affairs.

Prescott, P. A., and S. A. Bowen. 1987. Controlling nursing turnover. Nursing Management 18(6):60–66.

Sturdavant, M. 1960. Intensive nursing service in circular and rectangular units compared. Hospitals 34(14):46–48ff.

Sunshine, L., and J. W. Wright. 1987. The Best Hospitals in America: The Mayo Clinic and Hospitals. Henry Holt and Company: New York. pp. 178–184.

Trites, D. K., F. Galbraith, J. Leckwart, and M. Sturdavant. 1969. Radial nursing units prove best in controlled study. Modern Hospital 112(4): 94–99.

Warner, M. 1976. Scheduling nursing personnel according to nursing preference: Mathematical programming approach. Operations Research 24(5):842–857.

Weisman, C. S., C. Alexander, and G. Chase. 1981. Determinants of hospital staff turnover. Medical Care 19:431.

# APPENDIX A

## Criteria Used to Evaluate Schedules

1. Continuity of schedule:
   An estimate of the number of times an employee was scheduled to work consecutive days. A base standard of minimal continuity was identified as three consecutively scheduled days. The scale score ranged from 1 (low continuity) to 7 (high continuity).

2. Cost of schedule:
   An estimate to determine the compliance with the budget standard set for the unit. The number of full-time equivalents (FTEs) required for adequate unit coverage was determined and the impact of the schedule on benefits for staff was calculated. The schedules were listed in the order of low to high cost.

3. Ease of hiring:
   An estimate of the ease of hiring nurses into the positions (shift rotation patterns and number of days to work within a pay period) dictated by the schedule. Each position, which consisted of a pattern of hours worked, was given a score from

1 (low) to 7 (high) and these scores were added together for a unit score.

4. Unit internal community:
   An estimate to determine the maximum and minimum number of potential staff an employee would work with on the unit.
5. Schedule management:
   An estimate of the amount of time for ongoing management of the schedule. (Included time for manual work by personnel/payroll and time necessary to keep the schedule operational).
6. Quality of care:
   Estimates were made of the scores on six scales that would be used to measure quality of care on nursing units after the schedules were implemented. Quality scales included items on physical care, assessment, non-physical care, evaluation of care, etc.
7. Staff morale:
   An estimate of the effect of the new schedule on staff morale and satisfaction. Behaviorally anchored scales were developed that allowed for varying levels of nurse behavior ranging from 1 (low morale) to 9 (high morale).
8. Schedule flexibility:
   An estimate of the ability of staff to change schedules through exchanges, etc. The scale ranged from 0 (meaning no flexibility) to 1 (meaning maximum flexibility).
9. Schedule satisfiers/dissatisfiers:
   An estimate of the number of satisfiers and dissatisfiers within each schedule. The range was from –5 (meaning many dissatisfiers) to +5 (meaning many satisfiers). An example of a satisfier was straight-day shifts with the weekend off. An example of a dissatisfier was working a day/evening rotating shift and working every Friday evening before a weekend off.
10. Schedule implementation:
    An estimate of the amount of time needed to implement a schedule on the unit. Included were hiring of new staff to fill positions, developing the base pattern, determining the number of full-time and part-time employees for the schedule, etc.
11. Compliance with personnel policies and regulatory requirements:
    An evaluation of compliance/noncompliance of each work schedule with department policies and regulatory requirements.

# APPENDIX B

*Significant Characteristics of Nursing Units*
*That Were Used to Identify Empirical Types*
*of Nursing Units by Means of Cluster Analyses*

1. Ways that ward secretarial services are provided
2. Percent and FTE budgeted by job category (RN/LPN/NA)
3. Average number of patient admissions
4. Average acuity
5. Percent and FTE actual cost by category (RN/LPN/NA)
6. Actual hours per workload index
7. Average patient census
8. Average number of patients of types 1, 2, 3, and 4
9. Total number of beds on the unit
10. Percent shifts on days, evenings, nights
11. Average percent patient occupancy
12. Average number of patient dismissals/day
13. Percent full-time and part-time by category (RN/LPN/NA)
14. Unit architectural design
15. Percent rotating shifts
16. Average number shifts floated in by category (RN/LPN/NA)
17. Average number shifts floated out by category (RN/LPN/NA)
18. Average number of patients over 65
19. Average length of stay of nurse staff
20. Percent straight shifts
21. Average number of tests done at Mayo Clinic
22. Average number of patient transfers/day
23. Percent and number of employees hired into unit
24. Percent and number of employees terminating from unit
25. Percent and number of employees transferred out of unit
26. Percent and number of employees on LOA by job category (RN/LPN/NA)
27. Average number of clinical tests done for patients while hospitalized
28. Frequency and number of student nurses on unit
29. Percent and number of employees transferred into unit
30. Average length of stay of patients
31. Length of stay of Head Nurse
32. Number of patient referrals
33. Number of physician services assigned to unit
34. Mayo Clinic support services

35. Primary physician services assigned to unit
36. Medicus unit quality assurance scores
37. Average number of patient falls

## APPENDIX C

*Questionnaire Scales Reliability Related to Job Satisfaction*

Scale 1:   Experience of a work schedule that allows privacy at
           work
           Reliability = .92
Scale 2:   Sense of one's own marketability
           Reliability = .86
Scale 3:   Experience of a work schedule that fosters staff team
           work and friendship on the unit
           Reliability = .80
Scale 4:   Expectation of a work schedule that allows communi-
           cation with key departments
           Reliability = .93
Scale 5:   Expectation of being able to control one's schedule
           Reliability = *
Scale 6:   Discrepancy concerning work schedules creating a
           climate for ideal professional nursing
           Reliability = .91
Scale 7:   Discrepancy concerning work schedules that are
           predictable
           Reliability = .80
Scale 8:   Expectation of a work schedule that allows continuity
           of care
           Reliability = .70
Scale 9:   Expectation of a work schedule that fosters relation-
           ships at and outside of work
           Reliability = .88
Scale 10: Discrepancy concerning work schedules allowing
           freedom for personal business
           Reliability = .87
Scale 11: Expectation of a work schedule that allows privacy at
           work
           Reliability = .95

---

*Reliability coefficient, using Cronbach's alpha, less than .70; but single factor
solution was obtained through factor analysis.

Scale 12: Expectation of a work schedule that creates a climate for ideal professional nursing
Reliability = .96

Scale 13: Experience of a work schedule that creates a climate for ideal professional nursing
Reliability = .88

Scale 14: Experience of a work schedule that allows communication with key departments
Reliability = .92

Scale 15: Discrepancy concerning work schedules allowing communication with key departments
Reliability = .91

Scale 16: Expectation of a work schedule that allows freedom for personal business
Reliability = .92

Scale 17: Experience of a work schedule that allows freedom for personal business
Reliability = .93

Scale 18: Discrepancy concerning work schedules allowing privacy at work
Reliability = .90

Scale 19: Expectation of a work schedule that is ideal for what I want
Reliability = .80

Scale 20: Expectation of a work schedule that fosters communication and teamwork on the unit
Reliability = .90

Scale 21: Discrepancy concerning work schedules fostering communication and teamwork on the unit
Reliability = .86

Scale 22: Experience of a work schedule that fosters relation ships outside of work
Reliability = .84

Scale 23: Discrepancy concerning work schedules fostering relationships outside of work
Reliability = .88

Scale 24: Expectation of a work schedule that does not get in the way of social activities outside of the hospital
Reliability = .85

Scale 25: Experience of a work schedule that allows social activities outside the hospital
Reliability = .83

Scale 26:  Discrepancy concerning work schedules allowing
           social activities outside the hospital
Scale 27:  Perceptions that work schedules reflect respect and
           sensitivity toward work and personal lives of nurses
           Reliability = .91
Scale 28:  Perceptions that hospital provides potential for nurses,
           professional growth
           Reliability = .86
Scale 29:  General satisfaction
           Reliability = .85
Scale 30:  Satisfaction with being a nurse
           Reliability = .84
Scale 31:  Intent to leave nursing altogether
           Reliability = .91
Scale 32:  Intent to change nursing jobs within or outside hospital
           Reliability = .89
Scale 33:  Intent to leave hospital, but not due to dissatisfaction
           Reliability = .95
Scale 34:  Intent to resign job
           Reliability = .82
Scale 35:  Expectation of being able to change one's own schedule
           Reliability = *
Scale 36:  Experience of a work schedule that may influence my
           leaving the hospital or nursing
           Reliability = *

---

*Reliability coefficient, using Cronbach's alpha, less than .70; but single factor solution was obtained through factor analysis.

## APPENDIX D

*Scales That Discriminated Significantly Between
Experimental and Control Groups*

Scale 1. Experience of a Work Schedule That Allows Privacy at
Work (Reliability = .92)

---

I experience this at the hospital:  A work schedule that
allows me time away from

a. nurses on my unit
b. the head nurse on my unit

c. patients on my unit
d. supervisors on my unit
e. physicians on my unit
f. unit activities

## Scale 2. Sense of One's Own Marketability (Reliability = .86)

Without relocating, what are the chances that you could

a. obtain another job that uses your skills and abilities?
b. obtain another job that pays as much as your present job?
c. obtain another job that is as easy or easier to commute to as your present job?
d. obtain another job that has similar or better hours than your present job?
e. obtain another job that has similar or better working conditions than your present job?

## Scale 3. Experience of a Work Schedule That Fosters Staff Teamwork and Friendship on the Unit (Reliability = .80)

I experience this at the hospital:

a. staff members on my unit that enjoy working with each other
b. a work schedule that fosters a sense of belonging on my unit
c. a work schedule that promotes loyalty among staff on the unit
d. a clear idea of what to expect from the staff with whom I work
e. a work schedule that fosters my sense of teamwork on the unit
f. a work schedule that helps friendships form on the unit

Scale 4. Expectation of a Work Schedule That Allows Communication with Key Departments (Reliability = .93)

---

I currently expect this from a first-rate hospital:  A work schedule that allows me the opportunity to communicate with

a. personnel department
b. health services
c. nursing education
d. nursing administration
e. nursing library
f. community agencies

Scale 5. Expectation of Being Able to Control One's Schedule (Reliability = .80)

---

I currently expect this from a first-rate hospital:

a. a work schedule in which I am able to make changes by negotiating with other staff nurses
b. a work schedule that is more likely to be determined by the exchanges I make with my co-workers than by the scheduling department
c. a level of satisfaction, while working on my unit, that is dependent more on day-to-day staffing than on the work schedule assigned to me by the scheduling department
d. opportunity for me to suggest adjustments to my work schedule before it is finalized by the scheduling department
e. a work schedule in which I am able to make changes by negotiating with my head nurse

Scale 6. Discrepancy Concerning Work Schedules That Create a Climate for Ideal Professional Nursing (Reliability = .91)

---

Discrepancy between expectation and experience concerning

a. sufficient staff when I am on duty for me to provide quality of care
b. a work schedule that allows me to obtain information that is necessary to my providing care
c. replacement by a nurse when someone on my unit is absent (due to illness, vacations, etc.)
d. sufficient equipment on any work schedule, including weekends, for me to provide quality care
e. a work schedule that allows for the right balance of independence and supervision when I am providing care
f. a flexible work schedule without jeopardizing cost and quality of care
g. a clear idea of what to expect from staff with whom I work
h. a work schedule that allows me to give the most efficient care to my patients
i. a work schedule that allows me to get adequate rest
j. a work schedule that will not lower the quality of care I can provide
k. a work schedule that allows me time to consult with other health professionals
l. a work schedule that allows me to do dismissal planning for patients
m. good supervision even if my head nurse is not there
n. a work schedule that facilitates the opportunity to communicate directly with other nurses regarding the plan for my patients
o. clinically competent staff nurses on my unit
p. a work schedule that is practical
q. a work schedule that allows me to give nursing care the way I choose

Scale 7. Discrepancy Concerning Work Schedules That are Predictable (Reliability = .80)

---

Discrepancy betwcen expectation and experience concerning a work schedule that

a. is regular
b. is predictable
c. allows me to plan months in advance

Scale 8. Expectation of a Work Schedule That Allows Continuity of Care (Reliability = .70)

---

I currently expect this from a first-rate hospital:

a. a work schedule that is flexible enough to allow me to care for the same patients several days in a row, if I am willing to change my personal plans in order to provide such care
b. a work schedule that allows patients to receive care from the same nurse on the same shift for several days in a row
c. a work schedule that allows me consistent contact with the same patients during their hospital stay

Scale 9. Expectation of a Work Schedule That Fosters Relationships at and Outside of Work (Reliability = .88)

---

I currently expect this from a first-rate hospital:

A work schedule that fosters relationships outside of work that are a positive influence on my personal life and make me happy

A work schedule that fosters relationships outside of work that

a. are a positive influence on my work
b. are a positive influence on my personal life
c. make me happy
d. make me want to stay in the hospital

Scale 10. Discrepancy Concerning Work Schedules Allowing Freedom for Personal Business (Reliability = .87)

A work schedule that does not get in the way of

a. doing banking
b. going out for snacks, dinners
c. seeing a lawyer, tax accountant
d. shopping for clothes, housewares, hardware
e. getting the house/apartment repaired/refurnished

Scale 11. Expectation of a Work Schedule That Allows Privacy at Work (Reliability = .95)

I currently expect this from a first-rate hospital: A work schedule that allows me time away from

a. nurses on my unit
b. the head nurse on my unit
c. patients on my unit
d. supervisors on my unit
e. physicians on my unit
f. unit activities

# 3

*Office Automation Technologies*

People and Technology in the Workplace. 1991.
Pp. 229–252. Washington, D.C:
National Academy Press.

# Integrating New Tools into Information Work: Technology Transfer as a Framework for Understanding Success

T. K. BIKSON AND J. D. EVELAND

A major thesis guiding current research on social aspects of computerization is that it can be understood as an instance of technological innovation in organizations. If so, much of what has been learned about the successful transfer and use of other new technologies can be applied to understanding how best to introduce new computer-based tools into information-intensive work. In this chapter, we propose a technology transfer framework as an appropriate model for understanding this process. This framework incorporates three key sources of effect: features of the new technology; characteristics of the organization; and properties of the implementation process.

The chief conclusion from research based on this conceptual framework is that properties of the implementation process—the sequence of events that starts with the selection of a new tool and ends with its incorporation into ongoing work—are strong predictors of subsequent organizational outcomes. They predict what individuals and work groups will do with or to new tools, and what will happen to the organization as a result.

In what follows we briefly explain why characteristics of the change process are critical determinants of the social impacts of computerization. Then we describe the technology transfer framework in more detail, reviewing research results that have helped to corroborate and refine it, and identify implementation process variables predictive of successful outcomes; namely, people effectively using new computer tools in the office setting.

## FOCUS ON THE IMPLEMENTATION PROCESS

The study of technological innovation has a long history of its own and has been the subject of a number of critical reviews (Berman and McLaughlin, 1978; Bikson and Eveland, 1986; Bikson et al., 1981; Rogers, 1983; Tornatzky et al., 1983; Tornatzky and Fleischer, 1990; Yin et al., 1977). Traditionally innovation has been seen as a process that occurs in the stages depicted in Figure 1.

Under the usual assumptions of this framework, the organization is supposed to be in a state of equilibrium before the decision to adopt a new technology. By contrast, the period that immediately follows is expected to involve major changes as the innovation is being implemented. If all goes well, however, this stage should give way to a new stasis as the technology becomes fully routinized in day-to-day work.

In applying this theory to research on computerization, researchers have expected to find that the point of adoption (e.g.,

FIGURE 1 Organizational performance over time.

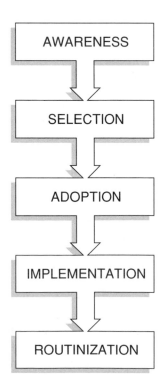

early or late) and correlates of the adoption decision (e.g., reasons for adopting) were critical predictors of successful innovation. In fact, research generally fails to find any real "point" of adoption, and "the adoption decision" is not a single event at a specifiable time (see Bikson et al., 1987). Rather, adoption of computer-based tools is better understood as a more extended process that involves agenda setting, negotiating, experimenting, and the like as well as decision making (see Eveland, 1979). It is difficult to know, either conceptually or empirically, where adoption leaves off and implementation begins. Both the *LA Times* case and the U.S. Forest Service case exemplify this lengthy process when complex systems are undertaken.

A second hypothesis generated by the traditional view is that the mark of successful implementation is stasis; innovation ends with improved organizational routines. In contrast, research suggests that there is no end to implementation processes while the technological state of the art is rapidly advancing (see Bikson, 1987; Bikson et al., 1985). Successful transfer of flexible interactive tools is associated with continued and reciprocal changes in tasks and their supporting technologies, as demonstrated by the four case studies in this volume, while unchanging routines are more likely to signal failure.

The traditional view of information technology utilization, then, has been characterized by an emphasis on the dimensions of *time* (when something gets used, particularly relative to other users, and how long it has been used); *fidelity* (degree of adaptation, usually with an emphasis on the dangers of changing a prototype that works); and *institutionalization* (the degree of stability achieved by the change over time). While these variables serve well to describe a certain range of technological changes, they generally fail to tap the key element of information systems use—namely, its *transactional* character. The dynamics of innovation in computerization require an analytical framework that emphasizes interaction over structure. Accordingly, we propose here a framework drawing explicitly on technology transfer as a way of overcoming some of these key problems with more traditional modes of analysis.

## TECHNOLOGY TRANSFER FRAMEWORK

Across varied types of innovations and a diverse range of organizational settings, common factors consistently emerge in research addressed to technology transfer and utilization. As Figure 2 shows, an adequate conceptual framework for understanding the

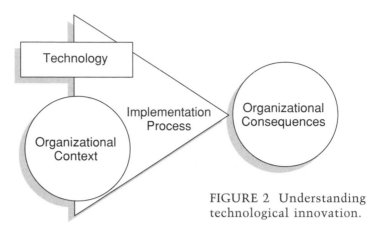

FIGURE 2  Understanding technological innovation.

impacts of new technologies in organizations must include three major components: the technology itself, the organizational context into which it is being introduced, and the process of embedding the technology in the context—the implementation process. Further, research supports the inherent interrelatedness of the three components (Bikson and Eveland, 1986; Stasz et al., 1986).

The conceptual nature of this model must be emphasized. It does not claim to be a complete "checklist" that will inevitably guide correct choices when accurate information for specific situations is plugged in. Rather, it is a sort of map to help understand how different components of technology transfer processes are likely to affect the resulting information systems and how they are used by the people involved. These components are reviewed in detail below.

## PROPERTIES OF THE TECHNOLOGY

Tools are modifiable, but not indefinitely so. Some aspects of technology that need to be understood are its range of potential applicability (i.e., how much its use is constrained by its very nature), its degree of hardware dependence, its potential for adaptability, and aspects of its "packaging" (i.e., how the different parts are put together and sold). Unlike computer technologies that are heavily bound up with specific pieces of equipment (for example, industrial robots or chips embedded in automobile controls), information technology is generally characterized by a high degree of flexibility, modularity, and adaptability. These very properties, however, make it difficult to test and predict successful implementation. From this standpoint, it is worthwhile to consider briefly how information technology is and is not like other technologies.

## Validity and Efficacy

In considering the validity and efficacy of technology, the basic question is whether it works—and if so, with what degree of consistency. Another question is *how* we know—against what criteria is efficacy determined? It would seem essential that for any technology to be successfully transferable from developers to users, it must actually do what it says it will do, with reasonable predictability and few possibilities for catastrophic failure. Yet these conditions are not easy to achieve, especially with information technologies.

Some of the difficulty has to do with the different environments experienced by the developers and the users. Unfortunately, performance in an R&D lab or vendor demonstration is seldom a predictor of performance anywhere else. An information tool that performs reliably in one setting may not perform equally well in another setting because of greater work load in the real world, less predictable user demands, a more heterogeneous base of installed hardware and software into which the new tool must be integrated, and other context-specific factors. A good deal of the empirical analysis of technologies in terms of transferability has to do with determining performance limits—the conditions that bound effective functioning.

The environment for new computer-based information tools has proved to be too rich, variable, and uncontrolled for the technology to be deployed uniformly. This has posed difficult challenges for behavioral scientists attempting to predict what individuals, work groups, and organizations will do. This should not be interpreted as a criticism of the effort to create a behavioral science base for interactive information technologies; rather, it is to say that as yet such a science has not progressed to the point where it can make reliable predictions about the effects of new computer-based tools.

This element of variability has proved both a blessing and a curse. As is clear, information technology can be applied to a great many parts of human activity, and there is little inherent in the tools themselves that conditions how they are to be used. By the same token, however, there are relatively few cues provided by the tools themselves as to their use, and the burden falls on their adopters (perhaps with the aid of developers or implementers) to create patterns of effective use. Thus the effective use of information tools typically requires more creativity—and more introspection into the user context—than many other types of technology.

### Scope, Testing, and Scale

The scope, testability, and scale of a new technology are interrelated features that have to do with how broadly a technology will be applied, how much of the user organization it could potentially affect, over what time frame, and how one might go about finding out. It is noteworthy that all judgments about scope, or how substantially an innovation will affect a particular kind of user, are subject to a very high margin of error. It is one of the aspects of new technologies that is the hardest for either developers or users to assess. It is not hard to see why—it requires looking at a very complex, working whole and visualizing something else. Because new elements in the way work is done reposition existing elements, there is no way to anticipate with confidence how matters are likely to evolve.

Differences between anticipated and realized scope may operate in either direction. A technology that is anticipated to have major repercussions may turn out to be useful only in a limited context (e.g., teleconferencing); or one originally thought to be of relatively limited effect may turn out to be revolutionary (e.g., personal computers). Moreover, these differences—in either direction—may be evaluated rather differently before and after the fact.

To some degree, the unpredictability of scope can be dealt with through trial and experimentation. On the other hand, technologies differ in the degree to which they can be put to meaningful field trials before full deployment. For example, it would be feasible to buy one microcomputer, put it in a room with a lot of conventional office machines such as typewriters and calculators, and evaluate its performance against specified criteria. It is much harder to experiment with, say, integrated local area networks, where the emphasis is on effects that stem from an entire system (see Markus, 1984).

In general, field trials of technologies are progressively less efficient the larger the behavioral or human component of the technology, a fact particularly salient in the implementation of information tools (Johnson and Rice, 1986). Behavior is notoriously context-sensitive, and the context of a trial inevitably differs from the usual world of work. While there is much to be said for careful experimentation with advanced technologies before implementation, most such experiments are difficult at best and misleading at worst; they should be undertaken only with the guidance of extensive prior investigation, as illustrated by the year-long pilot trial of news-editing technology undertaken by the *Los Angeles Times* (in this volume).

A factor that invariably complicates questions of scope and testing is organizational politics, which includes the local standards for handling and distributing costs and benefits among the users of the new system. These accounting mechanisms are essentially opaque to the developers of technologies, who concentrate their attention on context-free criteria of technical performance. On the other hand, they are central to an organization's rationale for installing a new technology and play a key role in the way users absorb the tools.[1] Thus they can play a peculiar role in trials ostensibly aimed at assessing the technical effectiveness of a new information tool. Those responsible for pilot projects would do well to bear such conditions in mind.

Finally, the idea of scale is somewhat similar to scope and testing but more straightforward. Scale refers to how broadly the technology must be applied, how much effort will have to go into using it, and how much it will cost to get started. Some technologies can be applied in limited circumstances with high returns for the organization; others require a broad base and a relatively long time frame for their benefits to be felt. Likewise, economies of scale can be expected to differ significantly. In general, innovations that are limited in scale have a better chance of moving rapidly and incrementally through the organization; by contrast, they may not get the degree of publicity or enthusiasm of more broad-scale innovations.

## Adaptability

The degree to which an innovation can be modified or tailored to its anticipated or actual organizational slot is an extremely critical feature. Any new technology must eventually be mapped into an existing organization with established personnel and procedures. Implementation (see below) is inherently a process of mutual adaptation of the technology to its environment. To the degree that the burden of all changes must be borne by the organization (e.g., by changing tasks to fit the tools or by training or replacing former employees to obtain new skills) rather than being absorbed in part by the technology, the implementation effort is likely to be much more difficult and susceptible to abortion or ultimate failure.

As far as characteristics of the technology are concerned, the key question is the degree to which the tools can in principle be modified by users themselves without damage to their output. Computer-based tools vary in the extent to which their design or implementation imposes a single required method of use. There are differences between product and process innovations on this dimension, although the issue applies to both. That is, the developer of a new microprocessor or a new data base manager undoubtedly takes it for granted that those who buy the product will use it in widely differing ways and for widely differing purposes, by users with strong stylistic preferences for how a given information task should be carried out. Thus, however efficient it may be, a software application that can be used only in one particular way with rigidly prescribed inputs and outputs will be quite limited in the range of sites within which it can be deployed.[2] That is to say, the task of transferring and broadly deploying a non-adaptable technology is likely to be more difficult and require other kinds of mechanisms and resources than are needed with a technology where the user has greater power over how it operates. Much of today's information technology comprises generic process innovations that are designed in almost context-free ways and then deployed into highly variable user contexts (see, for instance, the *Los Angeles Times* and U.S. Forest Service cases in this volume).

The importance of fidelity to the developers' concept of the technology versus the ability of users to adapt and "reinvent" the innovation has engaged lively debate—particularly in relation to process innovations in education (e.g., Berman and McLaughlin, 1974) and health (Kaluzny et al., 1974; Calsyn et al., 1977), and to the use of information technology in a variety of contexts (Eveland et al., 1977; Bikson et al., 1981; Johnson and Rice, 1986). In general, what is important to our analysis at this point is that, other things being equal, adaptability of an innovation both in how it can be used and under what circumstances simplifies the burden on the technology transfer system and increases the chance of success.

### Packaging

The ability of a new technology to be packaged as a salable product reflects the degree to which the subcomponents of the technology—all its different physical elements and associated be-haviors—form "tight" or "loose" bundles, and can be aggregated or disaggregated in the transfer process. Does the user organiza-tion have to acquire an entire system all at once, or can it be bought in stages? Does it have to be purchased up front, or can it be leased without making a final commitment? How extensive a range of associated goods and services—e.g., peripheral equipment, consulting services—will be required to make initial use of the innovation?

Wrapping up innovations in a complete package for "turnkey" deliverability is often a desirable strategy from the point of view of developers. It simplifies their transfer responsibilities, puts the major burden on the marketplace as a technology transfer mecha-nism, and cuts down on the degree of messy involvement with after-sale processes.[3]

For some innovations—primarily those of limited scale and scope, high reliability, low behavioral content, and low adaptability—this approach works well. Users can scan the marketplace and make their decisions to go with one package or another. This strategy does not work nearly so well with more complex tech-nologies—including most information tools—where significant amounts of organizational and social change are likely to accom-pany implementation. The larger the bundle of technical and social components an organization will have to accept, the more difficult the process of making that decision is likely to be. The best illustrations of the problems of trying to deal with complex technologies as single products are to be found in the experiences of large organizations trying to install single, large-scale all-pur-pose information systems. While such efforts can have effective outcomes, the amounts of time and energy expended in trying to keep such complex innovations within the bounds of the package are frequently staggering (Stasz et al., 1986, 1991).

## PROPERTIES OF INVOLVED ORGANIZATIONS

The preceding discussion suggests that in fact there are two aspects of organizational context that influence technology trans-fer and use. First, there is that of the developer or vendor—the set of interrelated goals, rules, expectations, criteria, assumptions, and technical know-how that have shaped the technology. Sec-ond, there is that of the user organization, a similarly compli-cated set of individual and social characteristics that strongly af-fect the ability of work groups to assimilate and use the technology.

Although the two contexts are likely to have a number of features in common, this review gives greatest attention to properties of user organizations that have been shown to influence an organization's capability for technological innovation. While we will single out these properties below, it should be acknowledged that their importance and their consequences depend partly on purely situational factors—how they interact with other characteristics of the user organization and the technology under consideration.

### Organizational Level

The great variety of properties potentially affecting technology transfer operate at one or another of two major levels.

• *Firm level:* Organizational structure and process characteristics include the pattern or arrangement of jobs, authority, work flow, and communications over an organization. They include such variables as size, resources, levels of hierarchy, centralization, and formalization, and need to be assessed as firm-wide properties.

• *Work group level:* Work design variables have to do with the combinations of tasks, skill requirements, responsibility, authority, and other attributes that make up particular jobs. Characteristics such as variety, challenge, autonomy, and rewards fall within this category. They may be assessed at the individual level but are most reliably measured at the work group level.

### Firm

Previous research literature has given greatest attention to properties of a user organization's structure and processes as influences on how it goes about acquiring and introducing new technologies. Four factors appear to be especially salient in shaping an organization's technology transfer stance. These include the organization's size; the resources available (with attention both to resources already committed ["sunk costs"] and those uncommitted ["slack"]); the conceptual rigidity of the organization (e.g., is the "not-invented-here" syndrome a major concern?); and the dependence on technology of the organization specifically and its business sector generally.

This last is an interesting factor. In today's world, most organizations depend on technology to a greater or lesser degree for their competitive edge. These may be production technologies, process technologies, managerial technologies, or others. Some fields are much more dependent than others on a core technology;

if so, they are likely to be responsive to changes in the underlying science. Microelectronics and biotechnology firms, for example, cannot afford to operate with less than leading-edge computer tools. In contrast, a sizable proportion of white-collar enterprises as well as many manufacturing firms can survive happily with technology that is nearer to the lagging edge. The greater the dependence of the firm on its advanced technological position, the more it must scan for and be open to tools developed elsewhere.

On the other hand, size has been a more frequently studied predictor of technological innovation. Typically, large firms are shown to be more likely to adopt and deploy new tools. However, this finding is subject to a number of caveats. First, size is hard to disentangle from other variables (most notably, from available budgetary and human resources). Second, if large firms are quicker to make new procurements, small firms are faster at accomplishing the changes required for a new technology to be fully implemented and diffused throughout the organization (see Tornatzky and Fleischer, 1990). Finally, large organizations—by virtue of having more levels of hierarchy and more entrenched bureaucratic procedures—may be more prone to the conceptual rigidities that impair change.

Finally, there are a host of variables such as centralization, formalization, and specification that appear to be negatively associated with technological innovation. On the other hand, there seems to be a positive association between ability to innovate and such properties as openness of communication and lateral boundary-spanning interactions. While the contrast has some face validity, we cannot draw consistent conclusions. With respect to the rigidity-based properties (e.g., centralization), it is often unclear whether they represent organizational structures or processes; and the flexibility markers (e.g., open communications) are quite clearly process characteristics. But it is not uncommon for de facto processes to take on shapes and patterns not defined by official organization charts (e.g., a highly centralized structure with a lot of lateral interaction). Our own examination of these and other organization-wide properties in a cross-sectional study of innovation found them to be associated with successful outcomes either weakly or not at all (Bikson et al., 1987).

## Work Group

Job design and work group variables make better predictors of the successful incorporation of new tools for ongoing tasks. For example, Bikson et al. (1987) found that a variety of job demands and availability of adequate resources to work group members predict successful innovation at that level for information technology. We believe this reflects the fact that in large organizations, technological innovation starts at different times and proceeds at different rates. Some parts of an organization may be using cutting-edge computer tools (e.g., the R&D department) while other parts are just beginning to use microcomputers. Consequently there may be more variability between departments within large organizations than there is between common types of departments (e.g., legal departments, R&D departments) in different organizations.

### Boundary Phenomena

An important but readily unnoticed part of the framework we have proposed for understanding the transfer and use of new technology is the idea of an organization's boundaries. The notion of transfer implicitly includes boundaries. Most obviously, technology transfer involves moving a new tool out of a developer or vendor organization and into a user organization. But first, boundaries are crossed by information.

Each party going into a technology transfer relationship is presumed to know something about the other participant(s).[4] The key question at this point is, "Who knows what about what?" The question involves not only the amount of relevant knowledge available at any given time but also the ability of the organization to generate new knowledge when it needs it. This in turn requires recognition that not all needed or desired knowledge is currently available.

Consequently an important boundary factor is the capacity of the organization to search outside itself—to engage in systematic environmental scanning. From the perspective of technology developers, this usually takes the form of market research—defining who are likely targets for the technology in question, developing ways of approaching them, and creating an understanding of how the needs of markets should be factored back into the organization's planning strategy. For technology users, scanning means being able to find out what opportunities are becoming available and to help shape their development before they are cast in concrete. Where users are able to interact creatively with technology developers in the early stages of development, both sides benefit (von Hippel, 1988).

Generally in technology transfer, the users seek information about the technology—both its technical and behavioral dimensions. When attained, the information must then be interpreted for the receiving organization. Typically, both parties to the interaction tend to hear what they want to hear. Since developers are generally more comfortable with the technical aspects of their innovations than the behavioral component, they can be expected to hear most questions as technical ones and respond with technical answers. Users, by contrast, are more preoccupied with what they are going to do with the new tool, and have attached social and behavioral meanings to their questions; the mismatch often means they fail to get satisfactory answers. The only solution is frequent communications across the boundaries between developers and users—whether these are boundaries between firms or between departments within large organizations. Frequent iterations are required to get over the information barrier.

Boundary crossing may be regarded as a form of interorganizational interaction in which boundaries become permeable and organizations often in effect "move into" each other. In technology transfer, the boundary crossing may take a variety of forms; but usually one organization crosses farther than the other. For example, a vendor representative who expects to sell the firm's products to a particular organization must know considerably more about that customer than the customer can be expected to know about the vendor. On the other hand, user organizations who know reasonably well what they want may wind up understanding considerably more about the potential products available and those who sell them than any of the potential suppliers know about the client.

Besides informational interactions, market transactions may also be thought as a form of boundary crossing. Market mechanisms are all those that involve reciprocal transactions of value exchange. These include direct sales, technology licensing or leasing, partnerships and cooperative arrangements of varied types, and other exchange processes.[5]

From the perspective of this review, it is sufficient to note that the boundary crossing does not necessarily end when the acquisition decision is made. Particularly with large acquisitions, it is not unusual for members of the user organization to work closely with system developers or integrators. On the other hand, the vendor may work closely with the user to facilitate implementation, training, maintenance, technical help support, and system extension or upgrading. The vendor may well set up an office within the user organization for these purposes, or may take spe-

cial steps to ensure rapid and easy interaction by other means
(e.g., by providing a guest account on its electronic mail system
for the user organization's technical staff or establishing a voice
mail link). Finally, the user organization may come to regard
environmental scanning as a regular part of the way it should
operate.

While the preceding discussion has focused on organizations, it
should be recalled that ultimately it is individual-to-individual
transfer of information and skills that must take place along
with a market transaction. The individuals who make the flow of
information happen between organizations are (for analytical
purposes) generally termed "boundary spanners" in the research
literature. This is seldom, of course, an organizational title. Those
playing this role regularly may be called "salesmen," "field representatives," or "consultants." A number of organizational members have occasion to span boundaries in the course of their ordi-
nary work, usually without thinking much about it. It is a difficult
role to play well. To a significant degree, an effective boundary
spanner must operate in multiple organizations simultaneously—
a position nearly guaranteed to make the participants in each
organization believe this individual has been "co-opted" or some-
how unduly influenced by the other. Few organizations provide
much support for playing the role. On the contrary, many organizations have created barriers to boundary spanning; these may
take the form of specific procedural constraints or may be more
informal cultural inhibitions on interactions that cross organizational lines. Nevertheless, boundary spanning—both laterally within an organization as well as extramurally in the development
community—has long been associated with successful technological innovation.

## PROPERTIES OF IMPLEMENTATION PROCESSES

Implementation refers to the transition from a workable technology idea to its manifestation in day-to-day work. The study of
organizational change suggests that when adopted, most innovations are not new per se but rather are new to a particular user
organization (Tornatzky et al., 1983). Interactive computer tools
of the sort represented by the cases in this volume were not new
inventions; but many organizations were introducing them as tools
for use by white-collar employees who were not computer professionals. Thus, while a great deal was known in general about
computer equipment and software, not much information was avail-

able to any work group about how best to make that knowledge relevant to and operational in the group setting—the heart of an implementation effort.

Implementation variables characterize the processes by which participating groups arrived at their current level of incorporation of computer-based work tools.   There is growing support from both empirical research and case studies for the thesis that the nature of the implementation process itself significantly influences the outcomes of technological innovation efforts (Bikson and Eveland, 1986; Bikson, Gutek, and Mankin, 1981, 1987; Bikson, Stasz, and Eveland, 1990; Johnson, 1985; Tornatzky et al., 1983). While some consistent findings emerge from this literature, they do not rely on a common set of constructs or terminology.  Consequently they are best summarized in terms of the set of themes they embody.

## Planning for Change

In earlier research on innovation processes, perhaps the most widely studied variable was the reason for change (see the review in Bikson et al., 1981).  In general, successful innovation was thought to develop from reasons internal to the organization (e.g., perceived needs rather than technology opportunities) and from positive rather than negative initiatives (e.g., improving performance rather than reducing cost).  With respect to the introduction of computers into office work environments, however, these incentives operate concurrently.  In particular, successful transitions to computerization need to take into account properties of the technology becoming available in the marketplace and characteristics of the organizational setting.  If technology scanning is not part of an organization's planning process, it will not be able to initiate change; rather, it will by default be in a reactive position (typified by fire-fighting or playing catch-up, or both).  Planning initiatives, then, should represent both needs and opportunities.

A second planning variable found to be important in prior innovation research is the thoroughness of the effort.  For instance, the existence of organization-wide policy documents directing the move toward electronic information tools would be treated as an index of careful planning; another index might be the comprehensiveness of the transition (measured, for example, by the proportion of departments or work groups affected by the planned change). Such indicators were associated with positive implementation outcomes in earlier studies; consequently, they were included in large cross-sectional study of the introduction of computers into white-collar work (Bikson et al., 1987).

In this study, slightly more than half the research sites had organization-wide implementation policies, represented in many instances by a formal planning document. Paradoxically, however, the existence of organization-wide change policies in that study was strongly correlated with rigidly detailed, top-down planning and control, and with highly centralized implementation processes; they were not associated with successful outcomes. Flexible approaches to planning are important if an organization is to take advantage of rapid technical developments that threaten to make any long-term blueprint for action obsolete before implementation is completed. Organizations need to be able to make general strategic information technology plans, allowing more detailed decisions to be made at later points in the implementation process.

A final planning theme related to positive outcomes is the extent to which means have been devised in advance to facilitate the assimilation of new work methods by implementing departments. For example, working out procedures for converting manual or batch tasks to interactive systems, and assessing the likely impact of such changes on job design and employee attitudes, are key components of successful planning. However, organizations tend to focus their planning efforts on computer hardware, software, and networks, leaving critical social and behavioral questions unaddressed. On the other hand, a mutual adaptation model of successful implementation suggests that both social and technical factors should be given equal attention in the implementation process; their interlinkage means that if change processes address only half the relevant factors, a number of unplanned, unmanaged, and potentially deleterious consequences may well develop in the other half. Sociotechnical balance, then, characterizes successful planning for new computer-based systems (Pava, 1983; Tappscott, 1982).

### Supporting Change

Inevitably implementation is a people-based process. It turns on hundreds of choices made and actions taken on a daily basis by various actors throughout a process that can take months or years. This theme roughly includes the ways in which general implementation plans are carried out and the requisite changes supported. Prior studies of innovation had identified user involvement in implementation decisions as a major influence on the results of the change process (Bikson and Eveland, 1986; Bikson et al., 1983; Mumford, 1983). Current research on computer-based information tools has further reinforced the value of user participation in design and decision processes (Bikson et al., 1987).

Whether using or not using a computer-based tool for a particular task is a voluntary decision is one way of looking at the user participation theme (evidenced, for example, in RAND research as well as research by Lucas, 1978, and others). Since white-collar work is often susceptible to discretionary and variable procedures (Strassman, 1985), leaving the choice of how to accomplish it up to employees is one measure of participatory decision making. More often, however, user participation is represented by the type and extent of influence users have over the particular computer-based tools available to them. At RAND, for instance, we have studied the role of users in decisions about hardware, software applications, and new task procedures (Bikson et al., 1987). In contrast, user participation in system design has been the focus of much Scandinavian research. Finally, providing higher-level means for users to program or otherwise tailor the systems they use is a third avenue for user participation. While results of current research on user involvement in implementation decisions are not entirely consistent and conclusive, the preponderance of evidence to date suggests that it can be a powerful influence on success. It is, however, not trivial to arrange effective user participation and, even where it is well done, it is not a substitute for high-quality technical resources.

Next, supporting innovative change in an organization inevitably requires providing opportunities for learning (Berman and McLaughlin, 1978; Bikson et al., 1981). Training programs and other procedures for enabling employees to learn how to incorporate computer-based tools into their work should be regarded as central components of an implementation strategy (Bikson and Eveland, 1989; Bikson and Gutek, 1983). The importance of good training for effective computer use is often acknowledged but seldom enacted. The discrepancy between anticipated learning needs and common organizational practices led us to coin the term "humanware," designating the knowledge, skills, and technical resources necessary to take advantage of computer-based tools. Underinvestment in humanware, relative to hardware and software, is often responsible for the underuse of the latter.

When organizations provide training, moreover, it is typically for beginning-level use. Very little effort is directed toward users' continued learning, or even to providing back-up assistance while they try to come up to speed on new tools. Consequently, even high-level professionals may remain amateur users of tools closely implicated in the tasks for which they are responsible. Further, day-to-day technical help is likely to be generic and low in quality; thus users most often turn to colleagues who happen to be proficient users of the tool in question. But the availability of local "gurus" is by no means ensured, and often organizations do not encourage them to act as sources of technical help. Consequently, Kling and others regard the social infrastructure for computing support as a key implementation variable (e.g., see Bikson et al., 1985; Kling and Scacchi, 1982; Stasz et al., 1990).

## Commitment to Change

Historically innovation literature has emphasized the importance of attitudinal factors, chiefly addressing their role in adoption rather than implementation of new technology (Bikson, 1980; Bikson et al., 1981). However, as we have explained above, variables associated with adoption of computers for information work have not typically been able to predict successful implementation. On the other hand, attitudinal variables representing the nature of a work group's commitment to the change process itself have turned out to be more closely linked to implementation outcomes.

One attitudinal variable that has figured in recent research on computerization might be termed "diffusion status." It represents a group's conception of its role in spreading a technological innovation. That is, does the implementing group regard itself as a leading-edge model for the organization, as setting a positive example, or as having little or no directional influence? Recent innovation theory is unclear as to the consequences of early adoption of interactive technologies. On the one hand, early adopters tend to enjoy some advantages (the absence of formalized routines, the perception of being state of the art, and perhaps even the special "hand-holding" that an official prototype group enjoys). On the other hand, some features of this status are negatively correlated with implementation success (lack of a critical mass of users or lack of institutionalized structures to ensure the continued existence). Our research suggests that, from an attitudinal perspective, being at the forefront of a wave of diffusion is associated with success (Bikson et al., 1985, 1987). However, the larger the user community for interactive innovations—and especially for networked systems—the greater the advantage to all; so, objectively speaking, very late adopters may have more to gain from introducing the technology than early adopters did (Markus, 1984; Rogers, 1983).

A second critical implementation attitude is "change orientation": the extent to which participants in an innovation process view the change as a positive, problem-solving, and achievable goal—one that will benefit both management and employees alike. In one cross-sectional study of organizations introducing computerized information tools, this attitude was a highly significant predictor of success (Bikson et al., 1987). It is important to include here because of the widely shared belief that people are naturally resistant to change. More than 10 years of research on the computerization of information work at RAND have failed to substantiate this belief. On the contrary, resistance to change is more often observed in organizations than in employees. That is, organizations are notably resistant to recognizing new task demands and new competencies acquired by employees with commensurate changes in titles, job grades, pay, or career paths.

Employees are often justified in the belief that changes are being introduced primarily to achieve reductions in labor costs. While this has seldom been the actual result, there is typically a significant lag between change in employee performance and its formal organizational acknowledgment. A positive change orientation, then, taps the belief that the benefits of technological change will be fairly shared.

## IMPLICATIONS

Older frameworks for understanding innovation emphasized stasis as the mark of a successful transition. Technological innovation in general and the transfer of new computer-based tools in particular, however, are better understood as a dynamic and on-going process. The technology transfer framework provides a model.

First, the attributes of a technology itself have a distinct effect on how it will be transferred and incorporated into an organization (just as they reflect a number of properties of the developing organization). They also influence the kinds of decision-making processes and implementation strategies that may be invoked. The same attributes are not necessarily applicable to all computer-based tools. They are subject to widely differing perceptions among the participants involved, and they are susceptible to reinterpretation or reinvention. But they are a useful starting point for looking at what is and is not manipulable in technological innovation processes.

Second, several important conclusions can be drawn about relationships between organizational characteristics and successful innovation. In attempting to understand how new technologies are transferred and deployed in user organizations, it is important to distinguish between firm-wide and group-level characteristics. Moreover, it is wise to take into account the work groups and the design of jobs within them in planning for as well as predicting successful innovation. At that level organizational characteristics will be most closely linked to properties of the tools in relation to tasks to be performed.

Another point to bear in mind about organizational characteristics—regardless of level—is that they are not fixed or absolute, but rather are susceptible to shifts reflecting the state of equilibrium or disequilibrium in the system generally. Research models that treat such characteristics as "independent" variables for "predicting" technology transfer results risk missing this point. Technology transfer is an iterative and interactive process; throughout that period the organization is itself changed. Although features of the organization that characterize it before participation in the innovation process may initially bias the effort one way or another, it is much more interesting to think of them as "dependent" variables to be shaped and modified in the course of technology transfer.

Similarly organizational boundaries, originally thought to be rigid, are local and permeable. That is, they exist over limited parts of the system and for limited periods of time. While some boundaries are more permanent than others, the opportunity to achieve a competitive advantage may blur even the most longstanding of them. Any given part of an organization may be required to open a window to the outside in order to achieve an objective of interest, and it should structure ways of doing so that put the least possible pressure on those inside (March and Simon, 1958; Thompson, 1967).

Finally, the technology transfer framework includes the implementation process. Few of the properties found useful for thinking about the stages of innovation in previous literature are helpful for understanding the implementation of innovative computer-based tools in organizations. Perhaps it is better to regard an organization as being at a "mature" stage of computerization if its work groups take for granted that their information tasks will be done using interactive tools, even though the technology is undergoing continued change. Even relatively late stages in the implementation process cannot properly be understood in terms of approximation to stasis or completion of initial plans—especially when the base science is continuing to advance.

Rather, there is increasing evidence that the more important factors are properties of the implementation process itself: thorough planning that focuses on people as well as tools, user participation and training, and commitment to change on the part of managers and employees. A key element identified in implementation analyses is the role of "mutual adaptation" of tools and use settings. That is, new tools can and do change in the course of being integrated into particular settings, even as work groups must and do change in assimilating new technical capabilities (Bikson et al., 1981). The concepts of sociotechnical systems analysis (Trist, 1981) that emphasize the integration of the technical system of the organization (tools and procedures) with the social system (roles and relationships among participants) are particularly relevant. The important part is to recognize that such internal processes are both natural and necessary to the incorporation of new technology into organizations, and are short-circuited or overruled only with serious risk to the success of the venture.

Technological innovation is frequently said to be hampered by employees' resistance to change. Research provides little support for that view. There are countless examples of individuals doing old tasks in new ways and doing new tasks they would not have anticipated when they entered their current jobs. By self-report as well as by management assessment (Bikson et al., 1987), they tend also to be doing more work and meeting higher performance standards.

We suggest that resistance to change is observed more often in the organization than in its employees. For instance, organizations seldom acknowledge changes in employee skills, tasks or standards with changes in job titles, job descriptions or grades, or pay. They are reluctant to invest in training and learning resources that would better support employees' use of advanced tools. And they remain ambivalent about the need to facilitate technological innovation—only a minority see a continuing role for organizations in this area (Mankin et al., 1988). Given that there is no foreseeable end to the advance of computer-based tools, organizations will be involved in implementation processes for a long time to come. They would do well to aim at managing change successfully rather than at minimizing it.

## NOTES

1. To a large degree, the acceptability of automation in industry has been retarded by the belief on the part of managers as well as workers that it will lower employment costs, either by reducing the number of workers required or by reducing the skill levels needed. That these expectations were seldom borne out in fact has done little to alter the belief, which is frequently reinforced by official cost-benefit projections for successive new technologies.

2. Of course those few sites may well become highly advantaged by the tool—innovation is seldom an equal-opportunity process. And, if the sites are large customers, the developer may also do well.

3. User organizations as well often package technologies by creating highly complex procurements on which vendors are asked to supply specified mixes of products and services. The metaphors of procurement available to most organizations today bear only a dim resemblance to the real world of current advanced technology.

4. For the moment we will pass on the question of the critical role of self-knowledge, a commodity thought to be in less than overwhelming supply in most organizations. However, an organization's ability to learn about itself—and particularly, to learn from prior experiences with technological change—would be expected to play an important role in its ability to manage future change successfully.

5. There are also some mechanisms that operate in a quasi-market context. These include library-type systems (e.g., National Technical Information Service, DIALOG), research consortia (particularly those involving universities and industrial firms), publication in the open or not-so-open literature, and personnel exchange, either among developers, among users, or between developers and users. These arrangements are frequently part of other, more structured mechanisms.

## REFERENCES

Berman P., and M. McLaughlin. 1974. Federal Programs Supporting Educational Change: A Model of Educational Change. (R-1589/1-HEW). Santa Monica, Calif.: The RAND Corporation.

Berman P., and M. McLaughlin. 1978. Federal Programs Supporting Educational Change: Implementing and Sustaining Innovations. (R-1589/8-HEW). Santa Monica, Calif.: The RAND Corporation.

Bikson, T. K. 1980. Getting it Together: Gerontological Research and the Real World. Santa Monica, Calif.: The RAND Corporation, Report P-6447.

Bikson, T. K. 1987. Cognitive press in computer mediated work. Pp. 353–364 in Social, Ergonomic and Stress Aspects of Work with Computers, G. Salvendy, S. L. Sauter, and J. J. Hurrell, Jr., eds. Amsterdam: Elsevier.

Bikson, T. K., and J. D. Eveland. 1986. New Office Technology: Planning for People. New York: Pergamon Press.

Bikson, T. K., and J. D. Eveland. 1989. Technology transfer as a framework for understanding social impacts of computerization. Pp. 28–37 in Work with Computers: Organizational, Management, Stress and Health Aspects, M. J. Smith and G. Salvendy, eds. Amsterdam: Elsevier.

Bikson, T. K., and B. G. Gutek. 1983. Advanced Office Systems: An Empirical Look at Utilization and Satisfaction. Santa Monica, Calif.: The RAND Corporation, Report N-1970-NSF.

Bikson, T. K., B. G. Gutek, and D. Mankin. 1981. Implementation of Information Technology in Office Settings: Review of Relevant Literature. Santa Monica, Calif.: The RAND Corporation, Report P-6697.

Bikson, T. K., B. Quinn, and L. Johnson. 1983. Scientific and Technical Information Transfer: Issues and Options. Santa Monica, Calif.: The RAND Corporation, N-2131-NSF.

Bikson, T. K., C. Stasz, and D. Mankin. 1985. Computer-Mediated Work: Individual and Organizational Impact in One Corporate Headquarters. Santa Monica, Calif.: The RAND Corporation, R-3308-OTA.

Bikson, T. K., B. G. Gutek, and D. Mankin. 1987. Implementing Computerized Procedures in Office Settings: Influences and Outcomes. Santa Monica, Calif.: The RAND Corporation, R-3077-NSF.

Bikson, T. K., C. Stasz, and J. D. Eveland. 1990. Plus Ca Change, Plus Ca Change: A Long-term Look at One Technological Innovation. Santa Monica, Calif.: The RAND Corporation, WD-5032-USDAFS.

Calsyn, R., L. G. Tornatzky, and S. Dittmar. 1977. Incomplete adoption of and innovation: The case of goal attainment scaling. Evaluation 4:128–130.

Eveland, J. D. 1979. Issues in using the concept of 'adoption' of innovations. Journal of Technology Transfer 4(1):1–14.

Eveland, J. D., E. M. Rogers, and C. Klepper. 1977. The Innovation Process in Public Organizations. Ann Arbor, Mich.: University of Michigan.

Johnson, B. M. 1985. Innovation in Office Systems Implementation. Department of Communication, University of Oklahoma.

Johnson, B. M., and R. Rice. 1986. Managing Organizational Innovation. New York: Columbia University Press.

Kaluzny, A., J. T. Gentry, and J. Veney, eds. 1974. Innovation in Health Care Organizations. Chapel Hill, N.C.: University of North Carolina Press.

Kling, R., and W. Scacchi. 1982. The web of computing: Computer technology as social organization. Advances in Computers 21:2–60.

Lucas, H. C., Jr. 1978. Empirical evidence for a descriptive model of implementation. MIS Quarterly 2(2):27–42.

Mankin, D., T. K. Bikson, B. A. Gutek, and C. Stasz. 1988. Managing technological change: The process is key. Datamation 34(18):68–80.

March, J. G., and H. A. Simon. 1958. Organizations. New York: John Wiley and Sons.

Markus, L. M. 1984. Systems in Organizations: Bugs and Features. Boston: Pitman.

Mumford, E. 1983. Designing Human Systems for New Technology: The ETHICS Method. Manchester, England: Manchester Business School.

Pava, C. 1983. Managing New Office Technology: An Organizational Strategy. New York: Free Press.

Rogers, E. M. 1983. The Diffusion of Innovations. New York: Free Press.

Stasz, C., T. K. Bikson, and N. Z. Shapiro. 1986. Assessing the Forest Service's Implementation of an Agency-Wide Information System: An Exploratory Study. Santa Monica, Calif.: The RAND Corporation, N-2463-USFS.

Stasz, C., T. K. Bikson, J. D. Eveland, and B. Mittman. 1990. Information Technology in the U.S. Forest Service: An Assessment of Late Stage Implementation. Santa Monica, Calif.: The RAND Corporation, R-3908-USDAFS.

Stasz, C., T. K. Bikson, and J. D. Eveland. 1991. Assessing Benefits of the U.S. Forest Service's Geographic Information System: Research Design. Santa Monica, Calif: The RAND Corporation, WD-4590-USDAFS.

Strassman, P. 1985. Information Payoff. New York: Free Press.

Tappscott, D. 1982. Office Automation: A User-driven Method. New York: Plenum Press.

Thompson, J. D. 1967. Organizations in Action. New York: McGraw-Hill.

Tornatzky, L. G., and M. Fleischer. 1990. The Processes of Technological Innovation. Lexington, Mass.: Lexington Books.

Tornatzky, L. G., and others. 1983. The Process of Technological Innovation: Reviewing the Literature. Washington, D.C.: National Science Foundation.

Trist, E. W. 1981. The Evolution of Sociotechnical Systems. Toronto, Canada: Ontario Quality of Work Life Centre.

Von Hippel, E. 1988. The Sources of Innovation. New York: Oxford University Press.

Yin, R. K., K. A. Heald, and M. E. Vogel. 1977. Tinkering with the System. Lexington, Mass.: Lexington Books.

People and Technology in the Workplace. 1991.
Pp. 253–271. Washington, D.C:
National Academy Press.

# The Forest Service Information System

CHARLES R. HARTGRAVES

The Forest Service is the largest agency of the U.S. Department of Agriculture, its offices widely dispersed and frequently located in remote, sparsely populated regions. Increasingly, the work of Forest Service employees is information intensive. To enable its employees to perform their work more effectively, the agency is implementing a nationwide information processing system that provides advanced computer-based tools. Although many other organizations, in both the public and the private sectors, are also incorporating electronic tools into white collar work, the Forest Service implementation is notable—even unprecedented—in several respects. The system is very large (one of the largest in the country to date) and complex. It serves a great variety of users by integrating many functions within a single operating environment. This case study describes the origins and implementation of the Forest Service information processing system and explores the information environment that shapes its present and future use.

## THE ORGANIZATION

The Forest Service employs 29,000 full-time people, as well as 10,000 skilled temporaries who join the Forest Service during the summer months, to manage the nation's land and natural resources. Forest Service employees include about 5,500 foresters; 1,600 biologists, soil scientists, geologists, and other scientists; and 1,400 engineers. These employees operate from 653 district offices, 123 supervisors' offices, 9 regional offices, 9 research stations, 78 research project locations, 1 state and private area office, and the national office in Washington, D.C. What makes the Forest Service truly unique is that all employees and offices are tied into a comprehensive information management network. That network includes more than 900 computers and 18,000 terminals distributed over 45 states, the Virgin Islands, and Puerto Rico.

The Forest Service provides national forestry leadership and manages all National Forest System land, about 191 million acres of public lands (consisting of 156 National Forests, 19 National Grasslands, and 16 Land Utilization Projects). Its activities reflect diversified resource management activities, ranging from timber sales, fish and wildlife habitat improvement, recreation site management, land boundaries identification, to road and trail development and fire fighting, to name but a few (see Table 1). Forest Service programs, policies, and activities reflect both environmental protection and public needs, which are identified through public involvement. The guiding principle for use of the National Forest System land is "the greatest good to the greatest number in the long run." Because the Forest Service is highly decentralized, most day-to-day decisions are made at the local level.

The Forest Service cooperates with the states and territories, local governments, forest industries, and private landowners to promote good forestry practices on nonfederal forest lands and to increase efficient wood use. Most technical and financial assistance is provided through state forestry organizations for a mix of projects, such as controlling tree diseases, producing improved seedlings, reducing soil erosion, planting trees to conserve energy, and protecting against fire.

The Forest Service research organization provides national forest and rangeland research leadership. Forest Service researchers study the biological, physical, and social sciences, often cooperating with forestry schools and agricultural experiment stations. This research includes such activities as developing disease-resistant seedlings, mapping lightning fires, acid rain research, controlling forest pests, and improving wood processing efficiencies. Research results are made available through publications, films, workshops, computer programs, and other methods.

The Forest Service represents the United States in most world forestry matters, providing technical assistance to other countries through cooperation with the Department of State and the Food and Agriculture Organization of the United Nations. The Forest Service also participates in human resource and community assis-

**TABLE 1**  Forest Service Vital Statistics, 1989

| | |
|---|---|
| *Financial Ledger* | |
| Receipts | $1.84 billion |
| Expenditures | $3.19 billion |
| Permanent full-time employees | 30,500 |
| *Size and Scope* | |
| National Forest System | 191 million acres |
| National Forest System lands burned | 0.4 million acres |
| Wilderness | 32.5 million acres |
| Road system | 360,000 miles |
| Trail system | 108,381 miles |
| Wildlife and fish habitat improvements | 462,701 acres |
| National Wild and Scenic Rivers System | 3,338 miles |
| National Scenic Byways | 2,937 miles |
| Reforestation | 475.9 thousand acres |
| Watershed improvements | 39,190 acres |
| Timber harvested | 12.0 billion board feet |
| *Human Resources; Communities Served* | |
| Human resource programs | 95,608 persons served |
| Recreation use | 252.5 million visitor-days |
| Timber sold | 8.4 billion board feet |
| Grazing permits administered | 11,983 |
| Livestock grazing | 9.6 million animal unit months |
| Insect and disease suppression | 1.1 million acres |
| Mineral cases processed | 29,152 |
| Research publications | 2,078 |
| Woodland owners assisted | 153,855 |

tance programs to help improve living conditions in rural areas of the United States. Since the Civilian Conservation Corps of the 1930s, the Forest Service has participated in many human resource programs aimed at putting people to work and improving living conditions in rural areas. Currently it operates Job Corps Centers to teach skills to uneducated young people.

## EVOLUTION OF THE FOREST SERVICE INFORMATION ENVIRONMENT

Like many other large organizations, the Forest Service started using computers in the 1960s. These decentralized computers were located and used in several large regional offices. Remote data communications were nonexistent. The computers were used primarily for routine number-crunching applications such as accounting and engineering. The systems were very "unfriendly," and few employees knew how to operate them.

In the early 1970s, large mainframe computers and remote processing came on the scene when the Department of Agriculture established the Fort Collins Computer Center (FCCC). The Forest Service used this centralized computer system as well as some outside time-share facilities over the next 10 years to support a number of national business, engineering, and resource management applications. Remote access to FCCC was through "dumb terminals" and a low-speed data communication network. The applications were run mostly by trained specialists. Although word processing technology began to appear late in this period, typewriters, calculators, and telephones were still the predominate office tools.

It soon became apparent that there was a need for computer capability where the work was getting done. In 1971 a technical team wrote a long-term strategic document entitled "Blueprint for Action," which called for a national distributed computer system. This was followed in 1975 by a similar report written by the Systems Development Action Planning Team. This high-level management team, headed by a regional forester, and the subsequent report it produced, reinforced the idea of a distributed computer system.

Based on the recommendations of this report, the Forest Service had conducted a National Facilities Needs Analysis, comparing Forest Service requirements with the computer industry's ability to meet them. The Forest Service had decided early on not to think in terms of designing a custom system, but to look at what kind of technology the industry had available to fill its needs. From this analysis of needs, the Forest Service learned how to state its needs in terms of functionality and technology.

## SYSTEMATIC APPROACH TO AUTOMATION

With so much at stake, both financially and technically, the Forest Service refused to award a contract without ensuring that the vendor could fulfill it. In 1981 the Forest Service sent out a formal request for proposal (RFP) for a nationwide computer system, based on 32-bit technology and consisting of more than 900 general-purpose computers. These systems would be used for everything from collecting public comments on conservation issues to keeping track of the people and material needed to fight forest fires. The systems had to perform electronic mail, data base management, office automation tasks, and data entry, storage, and retrieval. Moreover, they had to be reliable enough for use on the forest level, where most of the resource management takes place.

The Forest Service provided the vendors with a comprehensive set of technical specifications based on the needs analysis and also provided functional specifications that were the result of actual workload measurements in the local offices. Based on those measurements, the Forest Service developed a series of benchmark procedures. Once a vendor passed the technical evaluation, the Forest Service visited the vendor and ran the benchmarks on several configurations of equipment. The Forest Service then dismantled the hardware to make sure it was configured as bid.

As the vendor selection process became clearer, so did the Forest Service's vision of what it wanted. Originally, the goal was to make computer power available to any field office that requested it. As time went on, it was decided to mandate a system for each of the field offices. Eventually, the Forest Service reached the point of wanting to move from paper to an electronic-based organization.

After a thorough examination that covered the capabilities, vendors, and costs of the various systems, the Forest Service chose Data General. When this decision had been made and accepted, the real work of implementing the largest nationwide distributed information network began.

As the time came to put the plan into action, the agency continued methodically. The first six months were spent working with Data General representatives preparing and establishing key standards and policy decisions. These included everything from site preparation requirements to administrative responsibilities. Small teams were formed to help install the systems and train system managers, who would in turn train their people.

At the same time, one ECLIPSE MV/4000 system and two MV/8000 systems were set up as test sites in offices in Washington, D.C.; Missoula, Montana; and Berkeley, California. Based on experience gained in these sites, the Forest Service established operational guidelines to take advantage of the system's ability to store and retrieve data and to communicate it from one user to another almost instantaneously. The first few systems were installed in September 1983. In January 1984 Data General began shipping systems to the rest of the Forest Service at a rate of seven a week and continued for almost three years.

Installing more than 900 computers throughout the National Forest System was not without mishap. One Data General computer fell off a ferry and is currently resting—or rusting—at the bottom of a lake.  Another time, a Data General systems engineer, en route one night to install a system, drove into a herd of buffalo.  Fortunately, he survived but his car did not.

Despite these delays, the process went smoothly.  In a 1986 independent report, the Rand Institute for Research on Interactive Systems noted that the implementation, installation, and initial training stage "appears remarkably successful; it has proceeded according to schedule, the systems have been reliable and use is high."

## THE FOREST-LEVEL INFORMATION PROCESSING SYSTEM

Currently, the Forest Service distributed processing system uses more than 900 Data General ECLIPSE MV/Family superminicomputers and 18,000 terminals.  The systems communicate with each other and with IBM mainframes located in New Orleans, Louisiana, and Unisys mainframes in the Fort Collins Computer Center in Colorado, over a Telenet X.25 public data network. The Forest Service also has more than 700 Data General/One portable laptop computers to extend its in-house data collection capability into the field.

At the forest and district levels, the Data General systems are used to perform a variety of tasks.  They help rangers generate memos and letters, produce reports, prepare budgets, manage office services, update mailing lists, and process forms and permits.  These systems also help rangers perform engineering studies of roads and facilities, maintain fire-control records, conduct environmental-impact studies, track timber appraisals, and print contracts.  One silviculture specialist uses the Data General system to prepare reports on various stands of timber.  Simply by changing the dates, locations, and figures, a 4-hour job was done in 30 minutes.

From the district to the national offices, the systems are called on to perform information collection and administrative tasks.  In many cases, the software for these applications was available "off-the-shelf."  CEO, Data General's office automation software, is especially useful.  In other cases, field and district personnel write their own programs using Data General's Command Line Interpreter and PROXI fourth-generation programming language.

Yet no matter what each system is used for, or where, the purpose is the same: to automate the collection, analysis, and exchange of information. The Forest Service tried to develop an understanding of information sharing and to turn all its offices into a single community of users.

## THE $120 MILLION INVESTMENT THAT SHOULD SAVE FIVE TIMES WHAT IT COST

Forest Service executives believed that switching from a paper-based operation to an electronic one would save money, but could not predict the amount. To find out, Labat-Anderson Incorporated, of Arlington, Virginia, and MetaResource Project of Santa Fe, New Mexico, were hired to perform an economic-benefit analysis. As part of the analysis, they surveyed 12 National Forest rangers and office personnel using the system and quantitatively calculated the financial benefit to the Forest Service.

The results were impressive. The analysis showed a 30 percent increase in productivity during the first 24 months, with almost a half-million hours saved. The time saved was reallocated to accomplish more work, improve resource management, organizational management, and public contact. Over the past eight years, the Forest Service has been forced to undergo a staffing reduction. However, in 1987, it still managed to increase productivity by 17 percent with 25 percent fewer people.

In dollars and cents, the study showed that the total value of the time saved reached $339 million in fiscal year 1987 alone. Based on these figures, the Forest Service is predicting a cost-benefit ratio of 5 to 1 for the life of the contract. In other words, the Forest Service saves $500 for every $100 spent.

Where did that cost savings come from? The electronic mail capabilities of CEO is one source. Using CEO, national headquarters can distribute letters and other information to any of its more than 800 offices in seconds. To prove how fast it is, a director in Washington can use CEO to send a letter to a forest supervisor, then try to call the supervisor over the phone. Nine times out of ten, the director will receive a note back on CEO before reaching the supervisor by phone. In 1987 the Forest Service saved more than $1.5 million in mail costs in the national office itself.

There are several other areas where the savings have been just as dramatic. Before the system was installed, the Forest Service communicated between local terminals and its Fort Collins Computer Center over dedicated lines. After installation, these communications were handled by the Telenet public data network. The telecommunications savings: $200,000 per month.

Another example of cost savings relates to time and attendance reporting for payroll purposes. Before the distributed information system was installed, each of the 30,000 Forest Service employees filled out time and attendance reports; every two weeks, 30,000 time sheets poured into the National Financial Center in New Orleans. About 1,000 people were required to process the paperwork, using optical character recognition readers to scan the time sheets. The error rate hovered around 30 percent. Once the system was installed, time and attendance reporting was done electronically. As a direct result, the Forest Service cut its costs for paper, postage, and handling by $3.5 million a year, or $300,000 every four weeks. In addition, the error rate dropped to less than 5 percent and is expected to continue to decrease.

There have been other benefits as well. Since the entire organization transacts much of its business electronically, the frustration of "telephone tag" has virtually been eliminated. Managers are also spending more of their time in running projects and less in handling paperwork.

The staff role has also changed. Instead of typing and filing, clerical personnel have become systems administrators who spend time managing file space requirements and making sure documents are routed efficiently. This has resulted in a definite increase in agency esprit de corps and productivity.

## THE FUTURE: MAKING AN EFFICIENT AND COST-EFFECTIVE NETWORK EVEN MORE SO

Currently, the Forest Service is upgrading many of the systems in the local offices. When the systems were first installed, there was initial reluctance to use them. But once managers and other staff members found how productive they could be, they quickly put more applications on the system until they outgrew them.

In addition to upgrading the systems, the Forest Service is also upgrading its field service capability. Originally, Data General worked with the Forest Service to provide installation, training, and field service. Now, as the result of a cooperative training program between Data General field service and the Forest Service personnel, Forest Service technicians have taken over many of the basic maintenance and repair services. They are also performing low-end upgrades and installations. This innovative program has served to lower maintenance costs and provide faster turnaround.

In the 1980s the information industry has shifted its attention away from helping to make administrative duties more cost-effective, toward helping executives, managers, and professionals—the "knowledge workers"—to achieve their business objectives. This important trend signifies a transition from the "computer era" to the "information era." It signifies a shift away from an emphasis on the "cost-displacement" benefits of automation and toward "value-added" benefits.

Cost-displacement benefits occur when an organization uses automation to perform a task more efficiently—produce the same output with less input. Value-added benefits are realized when automated information systems help an organization make better decisions and more effectively accomplish its mission. The value-added focus should lead us away from replacing people with computers, and toward giving people the tools needed to produce better business results.

Value-added benefits can easily exceed those resulting from increased efficiency. A manager with better information may earn his or her salary in five minutes with a single critical insight or decision. Perhaps more important, better decisions by executives, managers, and professionals have greater leverage on the success of the organization. The Forest Service believes that providing its "knowledge workers" with quality management information represents a significant opportunity to improve the agency's performance.

In summary, the nationwide distributed information network has made a tremendous difference in service to the public, and the Forest Service has learned how to manage information. In its mainframe days, the agency's appetite for equipment was insatiable, but it still was not getting the performance it required. Now the Forest Service has put itself in a position where it is doing more than it originally planned and is doing it better.

## LESSONS LEARNED IN SYSTEM DESIGN AND IMPLEMENTATION

The Forest Service recognized early on that it was not so much a particular technology that was needed as it was a set of integrated technologies. Those technologies must aid in organizing, manipulating, and communicating a large amount of data about resources, people, money, and other things. Much of that data is corporate, that is, it is data shared by people for various purposes to help meet the mission of the Forest Service. What they are striving to do is to transform the data processing environment, much as CEO made it possible to transform office functions. That implies a new order of business, a change in roles and priorities; it implies an environment in which all Forest Service employees can participate productively in the full range of collecting, managing, and sharing data related to their work. This is not just a Forest Service undertaking, of course, nor is it one unique to Data

General's line of products. It simply reflects the current state of the industry. The challenge is to get from "here" to "there" in a fast-changing world with some kind of order.

Data and information in the Forest Service are distributed over four levels of the organization (headquarters, regions, national forests, and ranger districts); and over three levels of architecture (mainframes, minicomputers, and work stations). The Data General system forms the backbone of this architecture at some 800 offices. Two Department of Agriculture mainframes are used for centralized accounting and personnel (on IBM machines at the National Finance Center) and for very large resource data bases and linear programming models (on Unisys machines at the Fort Collins Computer Center). Intelligent work stations will further disperse computing power in the not too distant future.

With the implementation of distributed processing in the Forest Service, a number of principles or axioms have been developed to provide the framework for the orderly design and integration of this new technology into the organization. The major principles are as follows:

- One community of users at each line office
- One information structure and interface at each line office
- Personal identity and accountability at all times when using information and technology
- Effective audit trail for interactive events
- Carefully constructed set of standards for information structure and the human interface
- Orderly framework for access to, and dissemination of, information in the interoffice environment

By focusing on these principles, the Forest Service has successfully implemented state-of-the-art information processing throughout the National Forest System. Forest Service managers at all levels have quickly integrated the tools of automation into their day-to-day business. The current goals of Forest Service information system include developing a commonality of purpose, information-responsive organization, effective use of scarce knowledge, and the implementation of standards for information structure and the human interface.

## One Community of Users at Each Line Office

The Forest Service's distributed processing system was designed to match the structure of the organization. The goal has been to fit the information technology to the work of the organization so that the technology does not constrain the ability of units of the organization to carry out their assigned missions.

The basic structure of the Forest Service is a line organization. The agency's internal structure has evolved over the past 80 years and continues to grow daily as it responds to new needs. The distributed processing technology will be adapted to the changing organization, rather than changing the organization to fit the existing technology.

Each line office is structured as a working unit to carry out its defined mission. Available human, financial, and information resources are used in the most effective way possible. As a participant in the distributed processing system, each line office has one set of priorities, one set of information structures, and one set of users. If the structure or mission of the line office changes, the technology support should be changed to match it. For example, for shared services between some of the research stations and regional offices, the technology should match this organizational approach.

### One Information Structure and Interface at Each Line Office

Organization of information through the distributed processing system permits the Forest Service to achieve its goal of having a single source that can locate any information needed within each office. Through implementation of information management standards, the Forest Service staff can index and classify the information needed to run an office to minimize duplication, inconsistency, and related problems.

Although the official records process creates a central repository of administrative and management information in each office, it does not account for electronic storage of information (e.g., in computer files or on tape) and informal knowledge held by individuals. The goal of the distributed processing system is to unify these three sources and make them accessible.

## PERSONAL IDENTITY AND ACCOUNTABILITY

The Forest Service is dedicated to securing the integrity of the information in the distributed processing system. The implementation of the distributed processing system drastically altered the configuration of the information processing environment from a small technical user community to a large-scale, end-user environment. Whereas in the past, trained data processing professionals handled information security on a routine and interpersonal basis, now many novice computer users work at distributed locations with no training in safeguarding information.

Under the circumstances, it is surprising that the Forest Service has had so few security problems. However, one incident several years ago highlighted the need for personal accountability, improved software and procedures, and training for security. An unauthorized individual gained access to a Forest Service system and then obtained further information on how to misrepresent himself as other valid users.

As a result of this security breach, the Forest Service has established user-name conventions and standards that do the following:

- Require unique personal identity at all times when using the system
- Require an individual to be a member of one and only one office
- Assign information management roles to individuals, not functions
- Link logs and other audit trails to individual actions, not functions
- Prohibit transferring personal identity between individuals for any reason

### Effective Audit Trail for Interactive Events

A key feature of the distributed processing system is a comprehensive audit trail that will ensure integrity and responsibility for actions. Each computer in the distributed network has a system log that has been designed to keep track of events by individuals, leaving an electronic record and other evidence of each individual's actions and allowing the events to be reconstructed. To ensure the integrity of the system, this logging function must be maintained in each office. On occasion Forest Service officcs have turned off the logging function because they thought it made their data processing less efficient, not realizing the security consequences of doing so. The Forest Service has stepped up a training and awareness program, emphasizing the importance of the audit trail as an element of the data security system.

## Standards for Information Structure and the Human Interface

With the implementation of the distributed processing system, the Forest Service has created a set of standards for organizing information within the system. Two goals of the standards are (1) to ensure an efficient means of navigating through the system to find a specific "information object," such as a spreadsheet, data base, data file, or document; and (2) to ensure that information in all Forest Service offices is organized similarly. In this way technical support can be provided from the central office, and personnel transfers will not require a complete retraining in use of the information system at each office.

The Forest Service uses a two-level organizational structure for large collections of information objects, employing the familiar office terminology of filing cabinets for names in the electronic filing system. The first level of classification is a "cabinet," of which there are three kinds:

- Public—information that may be made available to all users in the office.
- Staff or group—information that may be made available to a subset of local users in an office, generally by staff organization.
- Personal—information that is generally available only to an individual in an office, but may be made available to a limited set of others.

The second level of classification is a three-tier filing hierarchy, known as "drawers," "folders," and "objects" (or files). This allows a set of drawers to organize information in a level, and then to subdivide drawers further into a set of folders, in which the actual information files reside.

## Framework for Information Access and Dissemination

The Forest Service's distributed processing system is truly a network that facilitates interoffice transfer of information, thus improving speed and ease of information communication throughout the National Forest System. It ensures that more up-to-date management information is available, and it improves the agency's ability to function as a single unit rather than a geographically diverse group of offices. In an organization as highly decentralized (both organizationally and geographically) as the Forest Service, the benefits of this capability are far reaching, as are the costs in terms of organizational change.

Naming conventions were used to identify each office in the network, consistent with the organizational structure and, where possible, the hierarchical office relationships. One information structure (and usually only one computer) exists at each line office, although there are provisions for more than one physical computer at each office.

The creation, management, and maintenance of information in this structure have presented a variety of challenges to the Forest Service, as they require placing functions in each office that have no precedents in the Forest Service. The distributed processing system provides four interoffice communication capabilities: (1) mailing of documents from one individual to another anywhere in the network; (2) accessing a "home" office from another office in the network; (3) retrieving information objects between offices; and (4) using information held by one office without duplicating that information on another office system. Although these capabilities created exciting new opportunities, they also brought problems common to every distributed network, such as managing simultaneous updates of information and ensuring data integrity while allowing access to the data from outside the office. It is the goal of the Forest Service to provide careful guidance for the management of the processes of interoffice communication to maintain the integrity of the information while taking advantage of the tremendous capabilities of information dissemination and sharing offered by the technology.

### Trends Shaping the Forest Service Information Environment

There is a saying, "If you don't know where you are going, any road will get you there." A focused and well understood vision serves as a common goal for the organization to move toward.

One way to develop a vision of the future is to examine some key trends that will influence it. Certainly it will not be possible to address all of the trends that will affect the Forest Service. However, there are known or reasonably predictable movements, shifts, or changes in the Forest Service operating environment that are relevant to its future information environment. Some of these trends reflect forces in the external business world while others relate to forces inside the organization. Because these trends have implications for the Forest Service information environment, they help the agency to formulate principles to adhere to as it develops strategies to meet the challenges of the future.

## Trends—The Significant Shaping Forces

The following trends or forces will ultimately affect the characteristics of the Forest Service's future information environment. They are discussed in no particular order of importance.

Forest Service personnel will increasingly use computers as everyday tools to do their work—just like telephones, calculators, and typewriters in the past. Employees in all aspects of the organization will use computers to access the information they need to do their work. The computing skills of agency employees will continue to increase, and they will expect to have a wide variety of the "right" tools available to meet their needs.

The Forest Service will increasingly tap the "intelligence" of its professionals through the use of task groups, and the ability to network geographically dispersed specialists. Such task groups will be used increasingly to address management issues. Often, these teams will be assembled from selected individuals who are brought together from geographically dispersed locations, as well as from diverse professional and cultural backgrounds. The duration of these teams will range from days to months, and they will need to function as cohesive groups both at designated meeting sites and from geographically dispersed locations.

Commonly used data will increasingly be shared between public agencies and private organizations. The amount of program coordination, cooperative efforts, and information sharing between both public and private organizations will continue to increase. Effective computing networks of shared, commonly used information will emerge. The roles of some organizations will change to reflect their responsibility to provide quality source data to be shared in this networked information environment.

The public will increasingly demand more and better "consumer/ user" information about the National Forest System. The public will want to know how the management of the national forests will affect their personal lives, and they will want to know more about how to use and enjoy these public resources. By the year 2000, it is projected that 60 percent of the homes in the United States will have personal computers. There will be a more than commensurate growth in the public use of data communication networks and the public will interact directly with the federal government through electronic media. A few examples of the types of requests that the Forest Service's future information environment will need to support include the following:

• The casual forest visitor who needs information on recreation opportunities.
• The local timber industry representative who wants to see where future timber sales are located.
• A landowner whose property is adjacent to the national forest and who wants to see where future land exchanges are planned.

The public will increasingly be involved, both directly and indirectly, in influencing the Forest Service's management decisions and will demand to know more about the agency's business. Individuals and special interest groups will become more sophisticated in examining alternative ways to manage the national forests, communicating their desires, and influencing, if not helping to make, management decisions.

There will continue to be a great deal of political oversight of Forest Service programs. The issues surrounding the management of the National Forest System will be dynamic and complex. The agency's overseers will become more sophisticated in their use of computer information systems to do their jobs. They will expect to have direct electronic access to program monitoring information, and they will expect timely, consistent, and accurate responses to questions.

Information technology will continue to evolve and improve rapidly. There are many complex technological options from which to choose.

The Forest Service will likely have to operate with lower budgets and a smaller work force, but without commensurate reductions in the overall quantity or quality of expected outputs. Investments in information technology will be constrained by budget—there will be more competition for scarce dollars to accomplish the Forest Service's program of work.

### Implications—Refining a Vision of the Future

Some of the implications of the trends shaping the Forest Service's information environment are unique. Others are more general and pertain to more than one trend. The following summary of these implications is grouped into the three major components of the information environment: information, technology, and management.

*Information*

The future information environment will provide the information needed to accomplish the Forest Service mission. This information will

- be relevant and needed by the agency to meet its mission;
- be organized in some easy-to-understand structure so that users will know where to find it;
- be referenced using a language of standard terms, definitions, and codes so that internal and external users will be able to understand, use, and share it;
- be documented and referenced in a data dictionary or atlas;
- be accurate, consistent, and timely; and
- be secure.

*Technology*

The future information environment will provide users with "one-stop-shopping" for information by means of technology that is integrated, easy-to-use, and provides the state-of-the-art information delivery capabilities needed to help the Forest Service accomplish its mission. The information delivery system technology will

- support all essential information in an integrated, uniform; consistent electronic environment throughout the agency;
- be conveniently accessible to agency employees and the public;
- be easy to use by agency employees and the public;
- support a group working environment both at designated meeting sites and from dispersed geographic locations;
- support a mobile work force;
- be compatible with national and international industry standards;
- be state of the art and responsive; and
- provide a wide variety of "generalist" and "specialist" tools from which to choose.

*Management*

The future information environment will be managed so that it continues to help the Forest Service achieve its mission.

The agency's management will

- ensure the integrity and security of the information environment by developing policies and procedures that describe the roles and responsibilities of individuals and organizations to access, use, and update information;

   • ensure that the work force has the skills needed to help manage the information environment, focus on the high pay-off value-added opportunities, and make complex, high-risk decisions;

   • manage the change to minimize the potential instability and tension that can result from a rapidly evolving technological environment; and

   • manage for the "best" combination of organizational structure and information environment needed to accomplish the agency's mission efficiently and effectively.

## CONCLUSION

   This vision of the future information environment is a goal that the Forest Service will continue to strive for. It is critical for the Forest Service to understand the longer-term goal so that it can make better short-term decisions.

   Information is critical to success and managing information is an important aspect of the agency's business. The big payoff to office automation is the ability to distribute relevant, accurate, consistent, and timely information throughout the organization. The agency must focus on managing information also because it is expensive. The investments the Forest Service will make in information will far exceed any investments it makes in the technological components of its information environment.

   The key to maximizing value-added benefits is putting the right tools and the right information in the hands of the user. The "knowledge workers" in the Forest Service must have direct access to the information they need to do their work. They should not have to "filter" their requests through a technically oriented information broker. There is another important ingredient in the value-added approach. Users must be able to explore and experiment with new tools. The users of the information are best qualified to design systems and new procedures that fit both their needs and the needs of the organization. Instead of automating existing processes, the agency must allow the processes to change with the injection of new tools and better information. The Forest Service needs to focus not so much on the "technology as acquired" as on the "technology as needed."

   Finally, information environments have a significant influence on the structure and behavior of an organization. The technologies coming on-line will support the flexibility and responsiveness of a decentralized organization, as well as the integration and control of a centralized organization. The technology is providing management with the opportunities to blend the best combinations of organizational structures and information environment to achieve its objectives.

The vision of the future shows where the agency wants to go; strategies describe how it plans to get there. The Forest Service is not finished in describing its desired future information environment. In fact, the vision is not a fixed target. The principles on which it is built are relatively stable, but the characteristics of the future information environment will need to be responsive to changes in the internal and external forces that affect the operating environment. The agency also cannot expect to reach its ultimate goal with one giant leap; it will get there with many well thought out steps.

With each step the Forest Service will learn from past successes and failures. It will reevaluate and solidify the principles that guide it. It will need to reevaluate and take advantage of new technological opportunities. It should get closer to the goal of creating an information environment that delivers the quality management information needed to achieve the Forest Service mission—Caring for the land and serving people.

## NOTES

ECLIPSE, ECLIPSE MV/4000, CEO, DATA GENERAL/ONE and PROXI are registered trademarks of the Data General Corporation.

TELENET is a registered trademark of U.S. Sprint Corporation.

People and Technology in the Workplace. 1991.
Pp. 272–278. Washington, D.C:
National Academy Press.

# Introducing a Computer-Based Human Resource System into the United Way

ROBERT J. KRASMAN

The United Way for human health and social services is one of the largest fund-raising organizations in the country. Changes in technology and competition among philanthropic organizations over the last eight years have led to new ways of doing business requiring related changes in internal organizational structures. The United Way of Allegheny County, located in Pittsburgh, Pennsylvania, provides an innovative example of introducing a computer-based human resource system to meet the needs of the changing environment, while overcoming strong staff resistance related to fear of obsolescence and budget constraints. In this case study, a computer system is introduced to an office with three people having many years of experience with the old system. This study highlights the importance and complications of technological change not only for large organizations, but for small ones as well.

## THE ORGANIZATION

Most United Ways throughout the country function in a similar manner. There is a great misconception, however, about what they do. The funds raised, usually on an annual basis, are allocated to agencies providing human health and social services to their local communities. The allocation is done by volunteers who also live and work in these communities. The same volunteers also work to identify new and emerging issues that affect their communities. The task facing each United Way is how to raise funds and act as a catalyst within the community to bring the necessary resources together to help solve these problems.

The competition among philanthropic organizations over the last eight years has increased. In the past, the United Way held a special place in most companies because they had a payroll deduction program. Recently, with the cutback of available funding for nonprofit health and social service agencies, the competition for the use of payroll deduction has increased. Increased competition and changing markets have forced most United Ways to restructure and refocus. They are doing strategic plans, organizational assessments, and environmental scans. They no longer talk about donors, but about markets. Technology is facilitating the use of telemarketing, credit cards, and direct mail campaigns in ways that were not used 10 years ago to raise funds.

When a strategic planning process was started in the Allegheny County United Way, one of the most valuable resources was information. The process of gathering, storing, and disseminating information to the users provided one of the most interesting challenges. By making use of technology, it was hoped that resources could be more efficiently used in this process.

## MOTIVATION

One of the weaknesses of United Way fund raising was the unavailability of donors' names. The use of payroll deduction as a primary method for raising money eliminated the need for gathering names of donors. If donors work for a corporation and contribute through payroll deduction, their names are not known to the United Way. To communicate more effectively, United Way began to collect the names of donors.

How to get the names and what to do with the information became a major question. Over the past four years, United Way placed great emphasis on the use of technology to answer this question for fund raising: for learning where the donors are, how to reach them, how they want to be reached, and how to solicit them for funds. This emphasis placed a strain on some of the internal functions of the organization, particularly the human resource system.

Until the mid-1980s, there was a manual system for tracking employee information, including a job application and the forms needed for benefits, government requirements, retirement plans, and training activity. The employment base in the organization was stable. There was an organization of about 50 employees, and during the course of the year, 8 to 10 of those people would leave. It was relatively simple to look through these forms for particular information that was needed.

The telemarketing program, however, along with several other ventures, more than doubled the size of the organization, to about 120 employees. The telemarketing program also had extremely high turnover of 4 to 6 people a week because of the nature of the work. In addition to the internal requirements for tracking employees, there were also a number of external requirements for retirement plans under the Employee Retirement Income Security Act (ERISA) and the Consolidated Omnibus Budget Reconciliation Act (COBRA) laws enacted in 1989. The paper system was no longer useful in providing the necessary information. The results were missed deadlines, internally inaccurate information, and inability to make good decisions. It became necessary to introduce new technology.

The problem was how to design a system and train people that had no experience, and did not want any experience, with technology. One staff member provides an example of how new technology is viewed. She wanted a fax machine; it was embarrassing to pass out business cards and not have a fax number. Yet she was very resistant to a new computer system. It was the buzz words and things that could be shared with friends that were important. The harder task was to bring her into a project within the organization and actually get her to use new technology.

## STRATEGY

In the administrative area of the business, the employees had from 22 to 36 years of experience. Computers were something they did not want to hear about, and they began to find numerous reasons why the old paper system would work. They felt extremely threatened. It was important to get them to explain how and why the current system was used, what was needed, and what they were not getting. The first thing that came to their mind was that they were to be replaced once this information was put on the computer. Yet these people knew the most about the system, the flow of paperwork, and what results were needed. They had to open up so that a functional system could be designed.

An alternative in trying to introduce technology into an organization is to bring in new people who are familiar with computers and their applications. There are two problems, however, in an organization the size of the United Way of Allegheny County.

Not only is there less flexibility because of limited resources, but also the individuals who have this computer literacy do not know the operations of the organization. You cannot replace the skills, knowledge, and dedication of staff with new technology. The goal was to marry the two, resistant staff and new technology, and to do it in such a way that people did not feel threatened.

A complementary strategy was introduced in 1986. Within the organization, individuals were identified who seemed to be adapting best to technology. For example, several people working as clerks were taken out of that environment and put in the Management Information System (MIS) department. Salaries and position titles were upgraded, and they began working with the departments as trainers in a much less threatening environment. They are now beginning to develop as mentors in the departments.

## THE SYSTEM

The human resource system was designed by seven students at Carnegie Mellon University under the direction of Sarah Kiesler at a total cost of $5,700. A successful system for desktop publishing was already being used. Students built on this system to keep the standardization that had developed, even though it may change in a few years, and to create a more low-key, nonthreatening situation. They were dubious about the system's capabilities but worked with the staff to develop a system with a Tandy 3000 personal computer, a word processing program, a relational data base, and other software.

The system was up and running and all the data entered in late December 1988. Some of the basic reports were available in January for year-end closings. Other people in the organization not directly involved in the human resource system also had informational needs that the system could provide. The next stage of success was reached when the staff was able to provide useful information. The staff members who wanted no part of technology began to feel pride when they realized that they were providing useful information to their peers. When they were able to feel this sense of accomplishment, they started to feel an ownership of the system.

## THE PROCESS

This success was achieved by students and employees undergoing a very tedious process. They began by defining what the problems were with the paper system. After the initial staff meeting, the students met with the director. They reported that according to the staff there were no problems with the system, only with the director. If he would quit asking some of the questions that had not been asked in the past, there would be no need for a new system. Given that the questions were asked, however, the second problem—time—was the most difficult. The employees would say a suggested change looked great, but they did not have the time to work on it. After the problems were defined, it was a constant push for employees to make the time necessary to work with the students. Without making the time, they were never going to succeed.

In addition to meeting with the staff, the students met with representatives of the MIS department. Initially the MIS staff resisted going outside the organization to design and implement a new human resource system. They reported that they could not support the project and that if there were problems they could not be pulled off another project to help. The alternative was to let the MIS staff design the system, but they did not have the time.

We could have used professional consultants, but there was a very limited budget. The students were ideal. They were patient with the users in the development and training stages, and their time was not a critical factor, because we were not paying for the service on an hourly basis. Not having a deadline ensured a great deal of success. The MIS department was given the opportunity to be part of the process and to select the hardware that they could support.

Once the problems were defined, the students worked on solutions with the hardware that had been selected. Again, they came back and went through the process and the application of the system to define the design. At each step of the design stage, the staff found excuses not to meet; usually a lack of time was the reason given. Testing was also done by the students. There were many mornings when they began work at 7 o'clock and did testing and revisions at night based on what they were hearing from the staff.

After the system was designed, the students made a presentation and then began training the staff. Training was the key to successful introduction of the system. Success was due to the one-to-one relationship between the experts who designed the system, and the employees who would use it. Through that slow process they began to develop a trust. Considering the obstacles, the patience and the dedication of the students working with the employees was phenomenal. The students wanted the system to succeed and spent at least 18 hours working with staff members, just to get through the basic menus.

Again, lack of time was the major complaint from employees because their jobs included duties not related to the personnel system, and they still had to maintain the old paper system. But when their workloads were reviewed, the biggest problem was the avoidance of the assignments given to them by the students. As obstacles were removed and workloads reduced, it seemed that they were afraid that they would not be able to learn the system. They were afraid of failure.

Patience was the greatest virtue needed. Following a training session that did not go well, students were able to maintain enthusiasm. They began to hear from the staff all of the things that did not work with the system, but they resolved problems in a nonthreatening environment and they got the staff members involved. For example, after the system was about 90 to 95 percent completed, the staff decided that this was very inefficient. To access an employee's personal record, his or her Social Security number was necessary. Under the paper system, records were filed alphabetically in six or seven binders or files depending on the subject. One Social Security number seemed easier. Staff members developed a phone directory with all employees' names in alphabetical order and right beside that their Social Security number. One of the users went into the system and made a directory.

An important factor in student success was the structure of the program. Most of these students were experts, with jobs in industry before they worked on this project in summer school. Their grades depended on the value of the system that they built, not on the time they put in or whether they attended classes. They did not have to take tests or write papers. The course was designed so that students would care about and internalize the goals of the organization they were working for. They now work for Microsoft and IBM and management consulting companies that are leaders in the field of management information.

The students were in fact teachers. In addition, there was some success in training staff members by using games on the computers and also cassette tapes for PC applications. People could sit, listen to a tape, and work on the terminal. In another approach, some of the secretaries who were resistant to change were asked to design programs to teach somebody how to type. They became interested because their typewriters were real security blankets to them; making comparisons between the typewriter and the personal computer helped to overcome their fears.   One of the most counterproductive things a manager of this process can do is to become frustrated with staff members. Rather, remind them of other changes they have made in the past, and they respond.

After two months of operation, the three staff people began a new problem identification process in which they could make changes to this system.   Some of their ideas are good and are being considered for application at a later date.   Although there is still some resistance to the new system, the hesitation and the fear are gone.


## THE PAYOFF

There were two major payoffs from the computer-based human resource system.  People accept innovation and it helps them and the organization.  The system is functional and provides information.  For example, the system is very useful in tracking benefits and their costs.   There was probably no other way to get these results in the short term.   Another example is that because of the changes throughout the organization over the past years, the training budget has been upgraded.  As a part of the new system, training programs are being tracked with individuals' interests. Employees are asked during the evaluation process about what training opportunities they need, and this information is correlated with information about workshops and training programs in local universities.   This is a functional part of the system that greatly helped the human resource department because there was no other way to provide this service.

The system will soon outgrow itself, or the organization will soon outgrow the system.   That is not a concern in terms of the investment, however.   There is no way to put a dollar value on taking three employees who had their feet dug in and their stakes in the ground, saying they are not going to change, and then demonstrating that they are capable, that it is not hard, and that it helps them to perform their job more efficiently.  This is particularly valuable to others in the organization who will soon have technology introduced into their jobs.  The real value of the technological changes discussed here is not measured in dollars, but in the value to the organization of retaining the experience of the staff members affected.  The major factors contributing to success were the skill and patience of the students and the training they provided.

People and Technology in the Workplace. 1991.
Pp. 279–295. Washington, D.C:
National Academy Press.

# Telecommunication in the News Industry: The Newsroom Before and After Computers

WILSON R. LOCKE

The newsroom at the *Los Angeles Times* is supported by one of the largest news editing systems in the world. The computer system is unique in that writers, editors, and others with a news background designed it and are now responsible for its management and development. The successful integration of electronic technology into the manual world of the newsroom, illustrated in this case study, is attributed to extensive staff involvement, cooperation across departments, simultaneous development of the appropriate technology, and management's commitment of time and resources.

## THE SYSTEM

In the days before computers, video display terminals, and downloads, there was a primitive instrument in the city rooms of America known as the typewriter: slow, noisy, and unreliable. Often it ran out of a thing called a ribbon, jammed, and always required excessive manual effort. The typewriter was a primitive tool, often battered beyond recognition by reporters and editors venting their hostilities by using excessive force on the keyboard. It was appropriate for a place where reporters smoked, photographers kept bottles of alcoholic beverages in their darkrooms, and editors were forever spitting in the wastebaskets—a practice not only condoned but encouraged, since it kept them from spitting on the reporters. This was a terrible time in the history of American journalism, and I am pleased to report that times have changed. Today we are blessed with computers that are both silent and efficient. They have helped change the newsroom from a noisy, smoked-filled hovel into a quiet, air-conditioned room with indirect lighting. The new systems are not without problems. The technology is accused of causing blindness, sterility, and carpal tunnel syndrome. People still batter keyboards, are not above spitting in wastebaskets, and vent their hostilities by sending electronic messages to each other. Yet the physical changes are suggestive of more fundamental changes in decreased costs, improved communications, and greater flexibility. These three elements have been critical to the newspaper industry's ability to benefit from entirely new methods of information gathering and dissemination brought about by technology.

At the *Los Angeles Times*, the Editorial Computer System, shown in Figure 1, is the core of a network of computers that supports more than 1,200 terminals and more than 1,500 people. It is used to write, edit, and publish news stories and to communicate with a staff around the world. Each day, as many as 25,000 messages move through the network and hundreds of stories are written, sent, and received. More than 100,000 stories are stored on the system.

The network is composed of 24 Tandem computers in four systems. The main system and a small portable one—called the road show—are located in Los Angeles. The others are located in a plant in Orange County (40 miles south of Los Angeles), and in the *Times'* bureau in Washington, D.C.

The main system supports many local news bureaus, receives incoming stories from news agencies, backs up the Orange County system data base, and is used to produce copy for daily publication. The road-show system is used to cover news events outside of Los Angeles, such as political conventions and the Olympic games, and to test and develop new programs.

The system in Orange County is a smaller version of the one in Los Angeles and, like the L.A. system, supports a host of local news bureaus and is used to produce type for publication in the newspaper. This system also serves as a backup for the L.A. system and can operate independently, duplicating incoming wire service stories, communicating with the "outside world," and composing stories for publication.

The Washington, D.C., system supports the news bureau in that city and acts as the communications center for all *Times* bureaus outside of California, including those in other countries.

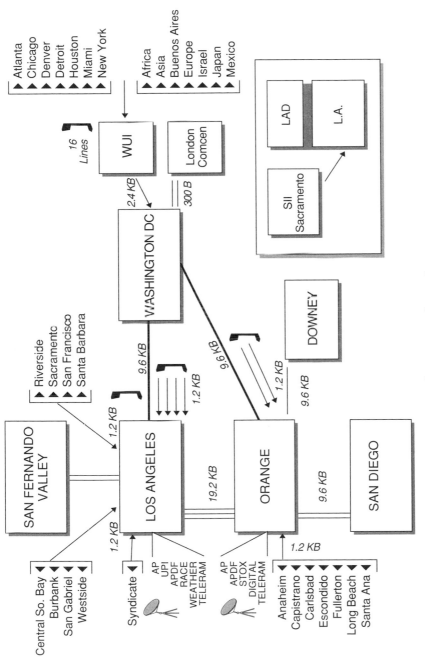

FIGURE 1 *Los Angeles Times* editorial computer system.

Although the D.C. system is capable of setting type, it is not used for that purpose because there are no production facilities or type-setters at the bureau.

The technological change was not achieved easily. The motivation and the process required for this successful project demonstrate the importance of planning, staff involvement, patience, and resources.

## MOTIVATION

In 1974, managers in the *Times'* Editorial Department identified three reasons for considering computers in the newsroom: economics, communication, and flexibility. Computers offered the potential of a more efficient way to produce the newspaper by reducing costs and speeding up production at deadline, thus maintaining a competitive edge while also increasing editorial control over the production process. Computers could facilitate rapid communications among writers and editors as well as intelligent, high-speed connections to the larger world of developing information technology. Finally, computer technology offered alternatives in case of emergencies such as power failures in a geographically diverse organization.

### *Economics*

Historically, the number of dollars given over to the correction of type is almost beyond comprehension. But more meaningful to the news department have been the hours upon endless hours spent waiting for type to be reset, and the drudgery of overseeing it replaced in the paper. This chronic necessity for correction, it should be said, did not stem from lack of diligence or competence in one department or another. It is traceable to a shared accountability between two departments (Editorial and Production) and a score of intervening nuances, right down to the age of brass mats in Linotype machines.

One potential saving of a computer system was to avoid retyping stories. The buzzwords were "save the original key stroke." Rekeyboarding stories introduced errors that cost thousands of dollars in proofreading and corrections. If news type was more accurate it would lead to smoother production and a decline in the number, and thus the cost, of corrections. Also, the increasingly insistent production demands had to be more readily accommodated.

As part of reducing costs and improving efficiency, an editorial system would also lessen the problem of shared accountability by making those who write and edit words also set them into type. The day the first scribe laid down his quill pen in behalf of flexible type, he unknowingly put into the hands of others the responsibility for validating what he had written. The by-product of this transition was not apparent in the measured pace of early typesetting. However, as the tempo of newspaper printing increased, there arose among writers and editors a sense of frustration in converting their words faithfully into type. The computer would return the English language to the control of the Editorial Department and, at the same stroke, place in the department's hands a tool to vouch for the integrity of type, a prospect that gave its users new inspiration.

## Communication

Just as the integrity of a reporter's thought and research should be preserved from its original keystroke, stories from reporters based outside Los Angeles must move to the central office with speed and reliability. Experiments with portable terminals already demonstrated the benefits to be accrued from technology. Stories were transmitted quickly from any telephone anywhere in the world.

Terminals in all local and national bureaus, as well as portable terminals for those traveling on assignment, brought dramatic changes in news gathering for the *Times*. Before these machines were introduced, news copy was delivered in a variety of ways: hand carried by messengers, by dispatch truck from suburban offices, by facsimile machines, by telephone dictation, by Telex, by mail, and in one instance by carrier pigeon. In each case the time between completion of a story by a writer and delivery to an editor was measured in hours and sometimes days. This had the sinister effect of sacrificing the decision-making process to the demands of setting type.

Electronic technology, as it was practiced in the editorial bureaus, reduced this writer-to-editor segment to minutes. When necessary, a writer could move a story to his editor in installments, transmitting his lead and succeeding parts to Los Angeles, while simultaneously writing the remainder of the story. A news editing system could refine this capability, increase the speed of transmission (making two-way communications more feasible), and provide more time for thoughtful writing and editing.

## Flexibility

The facility in Times Mirror Square is a complex structure made efficient by centralization of elements required to produce the daily newspaper. In recent years satellite plants and bureaus outside downtown Los Angeles expanded the newspaper's production and news-gathering capabilities. At the same time, the communications required for this diversification created a vulnerability to the need for continuous electrical power and telephone service. In case of a disaster, publication would be extremely difficult because of space limitation in any one *Times* plant, the problems of moving people and equipment over difficult terrain, and the loss of essential information. In the instance of failure in one location, a more extensive and integrated computer system would provide backup capabilities in another location.

## THE PROCESS

The creation of the *Times'* news editing system started in 1974 when the decision was made to explore electronic technology. Because the Data Processing staff did not seem to understand the needs of the Editorial Department, management decided to use editorial staff to develop the system. A research team was formed. It consisted of two news editors and a composing room foreman. A "fourth member" of the team was one of seven writers, editors, and clerks who worked with them on a two-week rotation. This group made all recommendations and basic system decisions. A larger advisory group of 23 staffers also was formed. This group met once or twice a month with the research team, to apprise each other of progress on the project and changes in the news room. Their efforts were coordinated by an assistant managing editor who kept senior management informed, approved expenses, arbitrated disputes, and kept the project on course.

In the seven-year odyssey that followed, the staff learned a new language of bits, bytes, baud, and buffers; they learned the difference between needs and wants; found out how much they did not know about their own operations; and established department objectives. The process was divided into three distinct parts: planning, development, and implementation.

## Planning

The first year was spent orienting the editorial staff and defining needs. A small editing system consisting of a computer and two terminals was leased from the Hendrix Company. In a period of six weeks, more than 400 members of the Editorial Department—in groups of fours and fives—were shown how an electronic system operates. After the demonstration, each participant prepared a detailed job description and discussed with the team the problems faced every day.

Specifically, each person wanted more control over the words written and the words edited. In the wider view, the staff asked for improvements in the amount of time it takes to get a news story into the office and set into type. Uniformly, all said they wanted new tools to be fast, accurate, and dependable. Based on these discussions, the following six major objectives were identified:

• Maintain editorial integrity over the written word and its translation into type.

• Produce a near-perfect newspaper at an hour more acceptable to the Editorial Department, but simultaneously more acceptable to the Production and Circulation departments.

• Receive, route, write, and edit news stories with flexibility and at a speed compatible with the anticipated changes in typesetting equipment.

• Create an indefinite memory of news and an indexing capability responsive to any reporter or editor's command.

• Establish standing formats for tabular copy, such as earnings reports and box scores, which could be called up on a terminal, filled in, and released to type upon receipt of the data in the Financial or Sports departments.

• Dramatically speed up news communications, whether from the Civic Center office across the street or the *Times* bureau in Moscow.

The second year was devoted to studying the existing production methods, preparing specifications for an editing system, and surveying how other newspapers were using electronic technology. Copy flow charts were prepared for every department, and conferences were held with the Production, Information Systems, and Telecommunications departments.

Particularly valuable were interviews with editors, writers, and production people at more than 15 newspapers around the country that already had electronic newsrooms, for example, the *Louisville Courier-Journal*, the *Tucson Citizen*, the *Houston Post*, the *Vancouver Province and Sun*, the *New York Times*, and the *Long Beach Press Telegram*. Criteria for these interviews included the users' experience and evaluation of their system; their evaluation of the vendor's competence, size, and stability; how their system software worked; and if the vendor seemed to understand their system objectives and requirements.

Universally, the data processing people and technicians were happy with their system; editors and writers were either very proud of it or dissatisfied because of the amount of computer coding required to do their jobs. Valuable insight was gained into the relationship between buyers and sellers (ranging from good to poor, but improving) and what could be expected after contracts were signed. More important, it appeared that no system on the market would come close to accomplishing what was needed at the *Times*. A new system would have to be developed.

Study of the *Times'* production methods continued in the third year, along with rewriting the specifications, conferring with vendors, and preparing a return-on-investment statement that justified the cost of an electronic system. A major decision point that emerged was whether to do the project in-house on an existing, centralized mainframe computer or to hire an outside vendor and use minicomputers in a distributed system.

A software house was commissioned to study and report on the options. They sent a team to Los Angeles to spend a month interviewing editorial, data processing, and production people, reading the specifications, and probing the operations. The report said that neither a centralized nor a distributed approach was inherently superior. Different aspects of each system seemed best suited to specific requirements.

The main item of controversy was whether the mainframe computer could handle the increased work load and at what cost. The Data Processing Department wanted to use the existing computer to implement the editorial system and argued that the existing computer was underused. In addition, the Data Processing Department planned to install a second computer, primarily for another department, which they said could also handle the sudden impact of the greatly expanded computing requirements. In the Data Processing Department's view, the mainframe would easily accommodate the local terminals, as well as those in Orange County and the bureaus. They argued that a centralized system was also feasible since the news editing system requirements were more straightforward than those encountered in most applications because the editorial sub-departments operated on similar information. The Data Processing Department approach would create a separate file management system for Orange County on the computers in Los Angeles.

Editorial argued there would be no local processing capability in Orange County, and that the plant would be totally dependent on Los Angeles for its operation. Editorial wanted a system in the Orange County plant that would be configured with a smaller subset of the Los Angeles system, use identical software, and be able to operate independently.

The report by the software house went on to address the Editorial Department's desire to program, maintain, and control the news editing system. It said that implementation of either system was likely to result in split leadership in the area of data processing. It warned that "If, indeed, a situation involving split leadership should remain after system completion, it would make an integrated system impossible, seriously impacting such long-range company goals as pagination."

The evolution of information systems also provided some insight into the advantages of functionally specialized distributed systems. After several years of frustration with attempts at centralized systems, the trend changed, and the predominant model became a set of information systems modules, each designed to accomplish a relatively small task. Thus, the systems are designed proceeding from the small to the large, not conversely.

The success of the modular systems elsewhere has been attributed to several factors. First, the information needs of a single department are better defined. Second, when the system is developed in the department where it is to be used, it is natural to involve the ultimate users in the design decisions. Thus, cooperation is fostered from the beginning, and the system is tailored to its environment. Third, since the job is more circumscribed, the system can be brought into use and tested relatively early, while there is still enthusiasm. Thus, the system can evolve in use. Fourth, it is more practical to arrange for backup of a distributed system. Finally, new systems can be developed without affecting those in regular operation—which is simply not true of centralized systems.

The report concluded that the following substantial advantages were to be gained from a distributed design:

- Inexpensive and effective backup could be easily provided.
- Pieces of the system could be easily and safely modified, developed and tested in virtual isolation from the production system.
- Functional specialization could easily be achieved, for example, special facilities provided for the sports desk or the editorial page.

• Users' involvement in the ongoing implementation could be encouraged and simplified.

Managers in the Editorial Department decided to develop a distributed system along these lines recommended in the report:

• Prepare a management plan for a news system and provide a clear definition of system goals. Develop milestones, establish areas of responsibility and concepts of operation, and set future goals for pagination and backup.
• Revise the specification to address a Phase I news editing system, including specific design criteria and building blocks for the full system, particularly full editing capabilities, communications input, printer subsystem, and basic story file maintenance.
• Initiate a study of story file and directory-handling requirements to enable data base management functions and performance criteria to be specified for Phase II.
• Issue a specification for Phase II development after a high degree of confidence is attained in the performance of the Phase I building blocks, so that full system functions can be specified.

The report laid a solid foundation and brought the project into focus. The third year ended as it had started, but with renewed staff vigor and a new perspective.

In the fourth year a return-on-investment (ROI) statement was completed and a contract signed to build a news editing system. The ROI statement listed all savings, from paper clips to long distance telephone toll charges, and all costs, from programmers to taxes. It showed a 12.5 percent return and a payback of approximately six years and four months on capital expenditure. The need to move forward was reinforced by the *Times'* growth, a vastly expanded program of news coverage, increasingly stringent deadlines, and growing press runs. The conversion in 1974 to photocomposition (abandoning hot metal in favor of film), required the Editorial Department to execute an increasing number of intricate procedures in a narrower time span. Photocomposition in particular, and the knowledge gained by talking to other newspapers, made it clear that the Editorial Department could and would begin to set its own type.

## Development

A standing joke in the newsroom was to ask people working on the project when they would have a system, and the stock reply was "next year." This did not change in the next few years.

Years five and six were spent building the system and refining requirements (finding out what was possible and what was not). Several major events occurred after the contract to build the system was signed.

The first event was that the Data Processing, Editorial, Production, and Telecommunications departments, following months of vigorous debate, united with a common goal. Task forces were formed to attack the problems, and weekly conferences kept each team abreast of what was happening with the others. One group worked on the terminal, another on printers and communications, another on the data base and user applications, and another on typesetting. Each group brought to the effort an impressive expertise.

An implementation schedule was drafted, discussed, and adopted. An acceptance test plan was devised. Acceptance tests were to be performed at established milestones in each stage of development, with a final performance test when the system was completed.

The next event was an alliance of "systems" people at the *Times* and the other newspapers we had visited. When applications questions arose, we started contacting the experts at those newspapers. For example, to resolve typesetting questions before a test system was in place, electronic copy was sent to staff at the *Vancouver Sun* or the *San Francisco Chronicle* to be set into type on their systems and returned by mail. Soon they were calling back to ask how we were handling a problem they faced. This group shared insights, exchanged information, and developed new concepts. This alliance has continued through the years and become a valuable resource in the daily battle to make things work.

The third event that had an impact on the project was the confederacy formed between vendors and the alliance of systems people. The annual American Newspaper Publishers Association Technical (ANPA/Tec) conference brought together newspaper people and most of the major vendors of newspaper equipment.

ANPA committee meetings, such as the one on wire service communications, were attended by vendors and systems people. In 1977 the wire service committee was struggling with the transition from teletypesetting (TTS paper tape) to electronic transmission of copy and the coding to allow computers to recognize and interpret it. It was a complex problem because one bit of information out of alignment would turn a fine news story into garbled trash. The main objective of the wire committee was to establish communications standards.

Systems users and system vendors talked to each other about

standards and solutions to mutual problems. This dialogue resulted in systems, using different computers, being programmed to communicate with each other or at least being able to transmit to each other. It also opened the door for vendors to discuss and resolve problems concerning word hyphenation and to develop mutually satisfactory applications.

It was not uncommon for the people who were building the *Times'* news editing system to discuss a problem with established, competing vendors. A difficulty with this candor and openness, however, was that innovations would lead to renegotiating the system being built. This and the complexity of the job led to delays, missed deadlines, and cost overruns in the project.

Building the system was slow and complicated. As programs were written, tested, and revised, the blocks fell into place. The terminal functions for typing, scrolling, defining and moving copy, inserting, and editing were progressing; the printing devices were being driven by the main computer; the typesetting programs were nearing completion—kerning tables, hyphenation algorithms and type-font tables were being refined; the communications programs were receiving copy from Associated Press and United Press International; and the data base programs were beginning to come together. As each segment was completed it was integrated into the main system.

Then we were plagued with a rash of delays. The typesetting program was not working, and an expert was hired to resolve the problems. Next a glitch developed in interfacing the terminals. Every time one fire was put out, another would start. In the latter part of the sixth year, amid feelings of despair and desperation, it was no longer funny when someone asked when they would have a system. The publisher, managers, and editorial staff were losing confidence and interest in the project. Then, by mutual agreement, the project was abandoned because of the delays and mounting costs.

At the same time, however, a second generation of systems had arrived. The search was resumed. The *Washington Post* had embarked on a similar project and that system was studied. They had a beautiful terminal with a very readable screen display. The computer met the *Times'* criteria for a redundant system (in which every element has a backup), and the applications software was first rate.

Although the *Post's* system was still under development, it was the first system that addressed the needs of a large newspaper (400 plus terminals) without compromising performance and functionality. Concern about the time the system took to process requests was resolved. Changes made to the communication software, however, forced the *Times'* team, reluctantly, to reject the system because the change would have made the required communications links to Orange County unworkable.

During this period information was gathered on ergonomic issues such as lighting, radiation, seating, keyboards, and workstations. The newsroom was rebuilt to accommodate the new technology, anticipating the future.

While the staff had been working on a unique system for the *Times*, an off-the-shelf product was developed that met 99 percent of the requirements. It was real and it worked. In 1981 the Editorial Department purchased and installed a small development system that was to grow into the current sophisticated news editing system.

## Implementation

The Editorial Department would have been naive to undertake these new responsibilities with anything less than great care Nothing was more sobering than the contemplation that we were to have a key role in the very complicated process of setting type. The editorial staff sought and received counsel and help from the Production, Information Systems, and Corporate Management Services departments. A phased approach was used, starting small and building block by block.

After the news editing system was installed, there were clear signs of success. The network united writers and editors around the globe, and there were immediate savings in production. Failures were few and, for the most part, insignificant. Goals were achieved in terms of economics, communication, and flexibility.

Typesetting savings included better ability to cope with the late changes in stories and late advertising changes that force revisions in page layout. Lost or misplaced type and the need for setting and storing large amounts of type before pages are ready for makeup were reduced. In addition, there was a means to check the proper placement of the elements of composition such as bylines, subheads, windows, box inserts, and jump lines.

Writers and editors gained almost instant communications with one another, whether they were in the same building or separated by a continent. Wire service stories, as well as stories and messages from staff writers and editors in remote locations, were automatically sorted as they arrived and were delivered to the appropriate department, desk, or person. An unlimited number of editors and writers had simultaneous access to stories coming into the system, thereby eliminating a sometimes long waiting period for delivery of hard copy from the wire room. Appropriate editors were notified immediately of wire service bulletins or urgent copy through special "alert" software provided with the system.

The system constantly monitors communications lines in the *Times'* network. Under normal conditions the system sends stories and messages to the various *Times'* offices over preselected routes. However, if a line is disabled, the system will automatically reroute the transmission over the next best path, even if that includes sending it through another set of computers in Orange County or Washington. Through a process of software searching, the system also scans incoming stories for specific words and from this makes topical compilations of stories into files such as Economics, Oil, Space.

For the Editorial Department, the sophisticated communications abilities of the system make feasible such flexible alternatives as operating from the Orange County plant in a backup mode. The computers' communications program and the *Times'* fiber-optic link with Orange County unite two elements of the news editing system. Coupled with satellite dishes in Orange County for wire service reception, writers and editors in either Los Angeles or Orange County can produce all or part of the editorial portion of the daily newspaper. If, for example, the Los Angeles production facilities were inoperative but the news editing system was intact, this software would allow the Editorial Department to write and edit in Los Angeles while setting type in Orange County.

The news editing system also extends the reach of either operating plant to encompass other facilities, bureau offices, temporary offices, or mobile stations—any location where at least one terminal and a telephone can be set up. In effect, one telephone call turns Ventura or Riverside or San Diego into one corner of the newsroom. As an extreme illustration, in an emergency editors, copy desks, and production facilities could be set up in the Orange County plant while most of the reporting staff operate from suburban bureau offices closest to their homes or in their homes using personal computers.

Finally, the news editing system becomes its own savior, helping to maintain its own integrity as well as that of the daily and standing news file in Los Angeles. As stories reach critical baskets in their evolution, the system automatically, or at a staffer's direction, sends a copy to another system for safekeeping. Magnetic tape is also used for storing backup copies of the text and system files.

In either case, essential information and the foundation of a news file are available in duplicate and in widely separated locations. With its speed and communications intelligence, the news editing system is a positive response to single-point failure and, in spreading the *Times'* resources, eases the threat of vulnerability.

Staff acceptance of the news editing system was almost total with very little resistance, although there are still several people who would rather use pencil and paper. Comments from writers and editors illustrate the positive impact of the system. For writer Martin Bernheimer there were professional benefits once he overcame his resistance:

> I was the last convert. I didn't want to join the 20th century. I liked torturing my prose to death on paper. I enjoyed rewriting each sentence a dozen times and driving typesetters crazy with penciled overscores, with special instructions scribbled in margins and with arrows connecting sentences a mile apart. I gave up my battered friend only with a fierce struggle, and some gentle, patient coaxing. Who needed these fancy new-fangled contraptions anyway?
>
> I did. It took me about three hours to discover the joys of clarity and flexibility as the contraption actually made me work better, not to mention faster. Contrary to expectation, the computer did not make me a slave to technology. It may not have made me free, but it certainly did make me a more efficient, more professional, more accessible writer. My trusty new Coyote (the name given to the terminal) has changed my professional life—and changed it for the better.

Editor David Blume wrote about professional and personal benefits beyond speed and efficiency:

> In terms of general use, of course the Coyote when it arrived provided speed and efficiency. I am much swifter now that I ever was at a typewriter, even though I am not a formal touch typist. But in my case, to use it in an ordinary way was insufficient and noncreative. At first, the method generated more interest than substance. The ability to create shortcuts became an end in itself, and I spent every idle moment creating new user keys. About a third of them turned out to be extremely useful. The rest were ideas that weren't so good in execution as

*they were on the drawing board. Usually, finding out where I went wrong was a humbling experience. The mistakes were almost universally stupid ones.*

*Another side effect was the interest working on the Coyote generated in electronic music devices. Since I started using the word processor, I have bought six electronic keyboards, including the latest, a very intricate sampling machine. All of them have required a great deal of homework and practice, but the rewards are substantial in terms of creative results at increased speed.*

There were five key elements in the successful implementation of the system:

- Planning
- Constant interaction with the staff, from clerks to editors
- Resisting the temptation (and at times it was tempting) to select a system that did not meet our needs
- Development of appropriate technology
- An enlightened management that allowed time and funds to achieve the objective, with some mistakes along the way

## THE FUTURE

The news editing system also introduced a language expressed in digital form. This digital transformation makes available an entirely new field of information gathering and dissemination. Foremost among the prospects are a computer-based library system, pagination, and exchange of stories and information with such organizations as wire and weather services, government agencies, and cable television.

In the short term, the typeset version of a news story is also the preliminary library version. The Editorial and Information Systems departments are working on a program of full-text retrieval. This program allows librarians to call up stories through the news editing system for indexing and enhancement in order to make these stories available to editors and writers through a central data base. It also provides an information bank of *Times* stories that are a marketable commodity. Repackaging of news for distribution by such agencies as Times Mirror Cable is also an obvious consideration.

The next large step in news technology is news pagination, which involves the electronic composition of news pages. This includes text, ads, graphics, and pictures as well as integration of all production aspects from editing to distribution and billing. It is practiced today by several newspapers, and while the *Times* has pioneered in display ad layout, full-page classified ad and stock page makeup, this competence is only a first step.

The next generation, or fourth wave, holds promise of even more sophisticated equipment, such as voice recognition computers, and facsimile devices that convert documents into text files. This equipment will allow us to communicate and produce our newspaper with even greater speed and accuracy.

Many pieces of the puzzle are in place and working. The task is integrating all the pieces into one homogeneous unit that satisfies the requirements of the *Times* and, especially, the people who produce the newspaper.

People and Technology in the Workplace. 1991.
Pp. 296–308. Washington, D.C:
National Academy Press.

# A Business Approach to Technology: Shearson Lehman Commercial Paper Inc.

SIGNE A. VON VERDO (WEBER)

Shearson Lehman Commercial Paper Inc. (SLCPI) is a primary dealer in money markets and in mortgage-backed and government securities. SLCPI first opened its doors in 1963 as a wholly owned subsidiary of Lehman Brothers (subsequently acquired by Shearson/ American Express). At that time, SLCPI's business focused on a limited number of products, all of which were easy to understand and easy to process. Starting around 1979, however, a number of innovative fixed-income securities were introduced into the marketplace, and business took off. There has been a tremendous growth of product types, product complexity, and transaction volumes since then. Today SLCPI is a low-margin, highly competitive business with a broad range of complex products. It is a profitable and powerful organization that accounts for a significant profit for its parent company. In 1986 SLCPI was using a set of manual processes and struggling to catch up with the business. It has since become an organization on top of the industry's tremendous growth. SLCPI has consciously cultivated a partnership between technology and business, resulting in redefined work flows and replacing manual processes with automated systems.

## THE ENVIRONMENT

Looking at SLCPI rather simplistically, the organization has two basic functions, referred to as the front office and the back office. In fact, because this structure is found across the entire industry, competitors such as Goldman Sachs or Salomon Brothers look fundamentally the same as SLCPI. The front office is made up of the sales force and traders, who deal directly with the client base—typically large institutions such as AT&T and IBM. The sales force maintains the ongoing client relationship, focusing on investment requirements and short-term financing needs as well as providing a key contact for error resolution. In SLCPI it also includes a number of "quants," or quantitative analysts, who perform analysis on trade data, pricing information, and economic data in an effort to support traders in evaluating market directions. Traders are authorized to execute the trades both for SLCPI's client base (per instructions of the sales force) and for the "house" account (SLCPI's money). Traders and the sales force are typically compensated on the amount of revenue they generate, and annual earnings of six figures are not uncommon. Back office personnel include clerical and professional staff who ensure that trades executed by the front office are processed correctly, accounted for accurately, and reported in a timely manner. It is important to note that many SLCPI products require settlement on the same day they are traded. This leads to a sense of considerable urgency in the back office to stay on top of its work load. Back office personnel are usually on straight salary and paid a bonus based on the overall performance of the organization.

## THE ORGANIZATION AND THE TECHNOLOGY—
### 1986 TO 1988

In 1986 the SLCPI environment was characterized by processing backlogs, high error rates, and overtime. SLCPI had 650 employees handling about 4,000 transactions a day in 28 major products. The daily trade total was $50 billion or roughly $12.5 million per trade. Because the dollar amount of any trade was so large, associated processing errors or backlogs became significant. As one SLCPI manager put it, "All the money made in the front office can just as easily be lost in the back office." Challenges due to high growth and increasing complexity of the business were compounded by predominately manual operations that had been put in place to handle the products of 20 years ago. It was a constant game of catch up, and senior management was becoming increasingly concerned over managing the inherent risk of SLCPI's high dollar trades. Management reporting was limited as was the time to assess where the problems were. Furthermore, support personnel were spread out across SLCPI and had limited opportunity to share ideas.  A few enterprising individuals had attempted to streamline their units where they could and were working with stand-alone personal computers.  There were perhaps 10 or so of these units across various departments where spreadsheet applications were being used.  Those individual efforts were uncoordinated, and ineffective.  Apart from the few personal computers peppered throughout the organization, the bulk of data processing support was provided by a central management information systems (MIS) function.  Requests for data processing support were made to the central MIS group, which also provided design and programming.

Today SLCPI has grown to 950 people and trades more than 40 major products plus an additional 100 derivative products.  The business has grown more than 50 percent since 1986 and currently trades $85 billion on 5,500 transactions every day.  Despite the high rate of growth, SLCPI has successfully eliminated the processing backlogs of 1986 and reduced error rates to a manageable level without increasing the number of back office personnel. (Sales and trader positions together with the addition of systems professionals accounted for the overall growth in personnel).  Morale is high and overtime is down.  Most of the manual back office processes have been automated across five major micro-computer-based networks linking more than 500 terminals and running 100 unique applications.  Figures 1 and 2 show a work flow that was transformed from manual to automated processes.  Systems support has been wrested from the central MIS unit and moved under the control of SLCPI management.  SLCPI has further decentralized systems and programming support, pushing it into individual business functions in the organization.

## THE PROBLEM

SLCPI's transaction processing and back office operations (i.e., securities clearance and accounting, which take place once trades have been executed) were developed years ago for a different type and breadth of product line.  Work flows were manually intensive and simply not able to handle the increasing product complexity and growing volume of trade activity.  The clerks and line management who staffed these functions were also rooted in the past.  The reactive and urgent nature of daily operations left little time or energy to step back and assess how the operations could be changed and improved.  Not surprisingly, there was a limited awareness of systems or technology in general such that potential opportunities that could have helped were not explored.

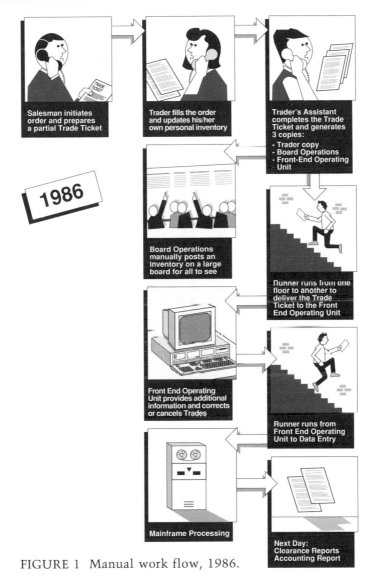

FIGURE 1 Manual work flow, 1986.

Of all the problems facing SLCPI in 1986, management's inability to manage the risks posed by processing errors was the most critical. The size of SLCPI's individual trades meant significant revenue loss when errors or processing backlogs occurred. The interest lost on $12.5 million (the average size of a trade in 1986) came to thousands of dollars a day. When several trades were in error suspense or backlogged, the revenue loss multiplied.

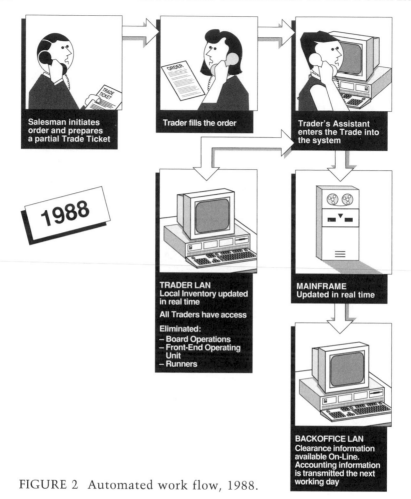

FIGURE 2  Automated work flow, 1988.

Existing management reports did not provide sufficient timely information to determine the firm's position accurately. Consequently, SLCPI found it difficult to manage problems or even to know if there was a problem. Limited management reports became more of an issue with passage of the Securities Act of 1986, which required companies to demonstrate they were maintaining an acceptable ratio of liabilities to assets.

Ongoing requests for improved management reporting were primarily directed to Shearson's central data processing (DP) organization.  Shearson, not unlike any number of other firms, was highly centralized in its data processing support and maintained a large group of systems professionals who ultimately reported to the chief financial officer. Also not unlike other centralized DP shops, Shearson maintained a hefty backlog of programming requests. In addition, systems that were developed by DP and delivered to SLCPI were not finding acceptance with the people who requested them. Despite the increasing urgency of SLCPI's system needs and the number of resources the DP shop was willing to commit, system support was generally considered sluggish and not responsive enough by SLCPI management.

Thus SLCPI was faced with backlogs and processing errors, increasing regulations from the Securities and Exchange Commission, lost revenues, low morale, and a never-ending chase to complete the day's processing and book all trades before being ready to move on to the next day's business. All of these conditions existed in an increasingly competitive environment requiring streamlined and accurate processing and reporting.

## THE SOLUTION

Two key moves in 1986 began the transition that was to allow SLCPI to gain control over its operations. First, Steve Gott, a senior vice president from the First Boston Corporation, was recruited to clean up SLCPI's processing problems. Second, under Gott's direction SLCPI consolidated key processing areas—back office operations and accounting—into a new organization called Trading Services. The idea was to create an identity for previously far-flung operations and develop a synergy across the newly formed organization. Nearly 80 percent of Trading Services' 100 or so managers were asked to step aside, and a new team of hand-picked recruits was brought in to replace them. The new organization then set about the task of defining the problems. Each of the Trading Services functions was scrutinized. Work flows were analyzed, skill levels assessed, and bottlenecks identified (see Figure 3). Associated reporting requirements were defined. All of the work was done in-house with the philosophy that line managers should be as close to their problems as possible.

During the analysis, Trading Services determined that effective information systems would be the key to achieving SLCPI goals. As a result, Trading Services proposed to pull MIS support entirely away from the central DP shop and put it under the direct control of SLCPI where it was hoped problems and solutions would find themselves more quickly. Vigorous discussions between SLCPI management and central MIS management ensued,

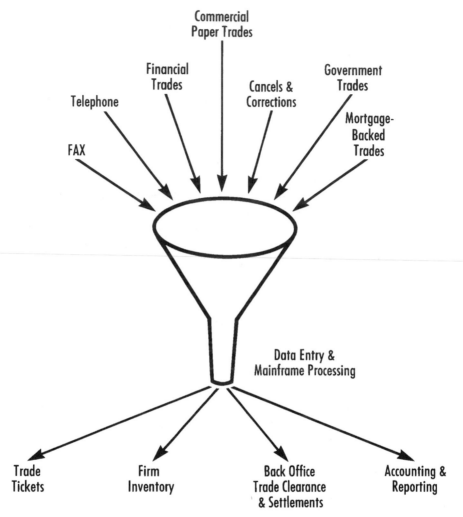

FIGURE 3  A major bottleneck in 1986 was having one central data entry
function support all of SLCPI's data entry requirements.  Mainframe processing also was not segmented to allow concurrent updating by product
area.  The bottleneck was eliminated by distributing data entry to each
product area and processing across five separate local area networks.


and in October 1986, data processing support moved over to SLCPI
and was added to the responsibilities of the Trading Services organization.

   The analysis included a close look not only at each function in
Trading Services but also at the people staffing each function.

There was a general assessment of each person's abilities and potential, with the result that more than 100 people (in addition to the 80 departing managers) were replaced. The urgency to resolve quickly a number of critical problems pressed the need to bring in a higher level of technical and business professionals and replace those perceived as requiring time to come up to speed. A formal program was established for those asked to leave, and efforts were made to assist them in finding new positions either within Shearson or outside the firm. As new talent was brought on board, the emerging organization began to solidify. Teamwork was emphasized, and individuals were encouraged to develop a general understanding of SLCPI's business. Formal training was established to further this end, and each SLCPI employee was expected to sign up.

Top-quality systems professionals were recruited to staff the data processing support function that Trading Services had assumed. In an effort to ensure that these resources were close enough to the business problems that needed to be addressed, the organization was structured such that the systems professionals reported directly to the Trading Services department they supported. This highly decentralized structure provided an opportunity for business and systems people to work as closely together as possible. Adding a new twist, business and systems professionals (not including traders) shared equivalent job levels, base compensation, and bonuses determined by SLCPI's performance. Another innovation was to make the responsibility for developing successful systems an explicit role of the business manager rather than an implicit role of the systems professional.

The emphasis on a partnership between systems and business professionals worked both philosophically and from the standpoint of compensation to build a strong team environment. The further emphasis on SLCPI's performance not only helped in team building but also encouraged individuals to look around outside their immediate scope of responsibility. The result was an organization whose members had a good understanding of SLCPI's business in general and the freedom and encouragement to establish contacts as needed across the organization.

In addition to bringing in high-quality recruits, instituting team-building efforts, and winning the fight for local systems support, the head of Trading Services also introduced a new style of planning to the organization. It spelled out activities and expenditures for the coming year as well as the short-term system deliverables and paybacks expected in each quarter. Senior management was presented with the Trading Services plan for 1987 and asked to review and approve the project list and associated expenses. Since the issues at hand were generally understood and payback periods were short, approval of the plan presented no particular obstacles. However, the capital acquisition process dictated by SLCPI's parent company raised problems by slowing acquisitions of computers and related equipment and software to about two months. In light of the aggressive nature of the Trading Services projects and associated commitment to short-term payback periods, an exception to Shearson's existing acquisition policy was necessary. This policy exception pushed the authority to make decisions for all technical expenditures within the approved budget down to each budget center manager and significantly accelerated the acquisition cycle for hardware, software, and approved personnel requisitions.

A new style of system development was also introduced and encouraged a certain degree of experimentation. Instead of the traditional phased approach to applications development often adopted by central MIS organizations, a more iterative, pilot approach was frequently employed to test a proposed system. Pilots typically incorporated roughly 80 percent of known requirements and anticipated changes from the start as the design evolved during use by the business community. As the pilot was moved into production, the iterative process for identifying changes and refinements continued. In fact, it was not unusual for the original requirements to undergo a total revamping as the business process was explored collectively by the design and user teams. Changes continued until the department determined that further modifications would not provide sufficient payback or that there was a more pressing priority. Because both business and technical resources were "business smart" and operated as a partnership, priorities for spending limited programming resources were rarely disputed.

From the start, five separate local area networks (LANs) were defined for each of the four primary product areas and the back office. The networks were designed to do the bulk of SLCPI's trade entry, back office processing, and accounting functions. Selected information locally stored on SLCPI's networks was in turn transmitted daily to the mainframe to update the firm's central books and records. Figure 4 shows a schematic of the SLCPI network structure. SLCPI believes that development components as well as development time are more manageable in a microcomputer environment than in a mainframe environment. Precisely

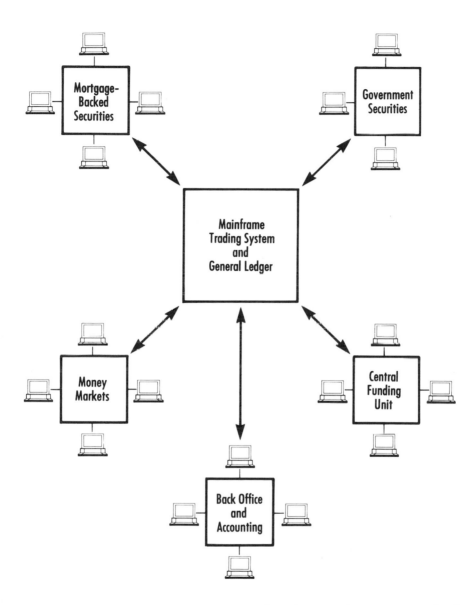

FIGURE 4 Five major microcomputer-based networks support each of SLCPI's four product areas and the back office function. The networks link more than 500 terminals and run 100 applications. Information going across SLCPI networks uses the mainframe as an exchange hub.

because SLCPI was so far behind in systems support, the firm was eager to select a solution that would allow the fastest development time possible for concurrent development efforts.

The technology SLCPI adopted was primarily microcomputer based. From the middle of 1986 to the end of 1988, more than 500 workstations were installed on five separate LANs, and more than 100 applications were developed. Specifically, SLCPI installed a 300-workstation Novell/Proteon LAN, an 85-workstation 3COM optical fiber LAN, and three Sun LANs supporting 80 workstations. The Novell LAN is installed in the back office and supports updates to SLCPI's income statement, balance sheet, and client accounts—all of which are maintained locally. The 3COM LAN is installed on the money market trading floor and is used by traders to enter trade information directly into an automated system. This system both captures data for transmittal to the Shearson mainframe (as well as subsequent updates to SLCPI's locally maintained accounting information) and updates a real-time securities inventory file accessible by each trader. The money market LAN also provides a number of analytical tools to assist traders in their assessment of market direction. Government securities, mortgage-backed securities, and the central funding desk are product areas supported by the three separate Sun LANs. The government securities system is similar to that used on the money markets trading floor. Trade information is captured and transmitted to the Shearson host, and the LAN provides a real-time inventory of government securities. The Sun LAN supporting mortgage-backed securities hosts an expert system that facilitates the calculation of complex mortgage-pool allocation algorithms. Finally, the central funding desk Sun system tracks the short-term finance contracts created by this product area. Each LAN installation represents a separate set of departmental functions with a limited exchange of information across networks.

Although most of SLCPI's systems were developed on microcomputers, there was also a sizable amount of work with mainframe systems. Unlike microcomputer equipment, the mainframes were not owned and operated by SLCPI. The high-end hardware was resident at Shearson's central data center and maintained around-the-clock by MIS operations. Mainframe systems and programming efforts, however, were clearly under the direction of SLCPI Trading Services.

SLCPI established few technical standards during this time to avoid limiting its solution alternatives. SLCPI adopted a high-level computer architecture using UNIX as the standard operating system, C as the standard programming language, and MIS-sanctioned telecommunication protocols for data going to and from Shearson's mainframe. Information going across SLCPI networks used the mainframe as an exchange hub.

In addition to the applied technology described above, SLCPI began work on a number of pilots that could reasonably be considered "cutting edge." Voice recognition enabled traders to enter real-time trades orally. Image processing was implemented for storage and retrieval of back office information, and an expert system was developed to assist in highly complex and time-critical mortgage allocation calculations.

## CLIMATE FOR ACHIEVEMENT

Apart from specific management actions, such as realigning the organization and changing the approach to system development and planning, a number of environmental factors helped to set the stage for success. For a start, Steve Gott was a strong, aggressive leader. He was charged with turning around a highly visible set of problems that were clearly on the priority list of SLCPI's senior management. The SLCPI organization was profitable and powerful enough to ensure that funding was available for required capital and personnel expenditures. As a result, Trading Services was able to recruit systems people familiar with the microcomputer technology base best suited to solving SLCPI's processing problems quickly. They were also able to recruit line managers with demonstrated abilities and familiarity with pertinent data processing tools and techniques. The adage "you get what you pay for" is clearly supported by SLCPI's results since 1986.

SLCPI's processing problems of 1986 were fertile ground for immediate payback opportunities. The problems were real and the return on investment was quick and high. For example, lowering the transaction error rate through system validation and reporting techniques reduced the receivables balance and translated into significant savings. Likewise, eliminating a bottleneck of data entry by distributing the work from a central site to user areas reduced overtime demands. Project results could be defined in the short term, and there was a sense of achievement. Senior management could see results almost immediately. The poor perception of central MIS support was also firmly implanted and provided the impetus to bring systems and development in-house to SLCPI operations.

## RESULTS AND FUTURE DIRECTIONS

SLCPI has successfully made the transition from a firm struggling to keep its doors open to one that is viable, profitable, and poised for future growth. The firm has supported a 15 percent annual rate of growth each year between 1986 and 1988 without adding additional support personnel, and it projects that it can handle at least three times the current transaction volume with minimal errors. In addition to accommodating industry growth, the organization has eliminated processing bottlenecks through the combination of changes in work flows and the simultaneous addition of automation. Structured, reliable information is now available to ensure monitoring of such things as backlogged transactions and to manage the firm's balance sheet. The product development cycle has also been significantly shortened, and new products are brought to market within one to two weeks of product definition. The formerly error-prone, tedious, and labor-intensive processing has been replaced by streamlined, redefined procedures and automated support tools. Overtime has been significantly reduced, transaction backlogs—once a primary concern to senior management—have been brought down to a manageable level, and aged receivables are no longer relevant.

SLCPI's systems installations have been both comprehensive and successful. The organization came from a point where it had limited systems support, no PC development, and no user-driven requirements. The organization shared a limited understanding of systems. Since then, more than 500 terminals across five separate local area networks have been installed and are in use. The major system development cycle from project inception to production (including both hardware and software) has typically been between 3 and 10 months.

SLCPI's general long-term direction is to move toward a completely electronic environment that provides high-quality, real-time information and is insensitive to daily fluctuations in volume. The microcomputer-based technology now installed provides a stable hardware platform on which to build the new applications and move them closer to the objective of total automation. SLCPI also has made considerable headway in exploring the potential of emerging technologies such as imaging, voice recognition, and artificial intelligence. It has approached the evaluation of these technologies in much the same way as when it began to use microcomputers. The firm is primarily concerned with business problems and how each proposed technology translates into a solution.

# Contributors

**Paul S. Adler** is assistant professor of engineering management at Stanford University. He received a doctoral in economics and management in France while working as a research economist for the French government. He has also worked with the Brookings Institution, Columbia University, and the Harvard Business School. Dr. Adler's research interests are in three related areas of management: implementing automation, managing the design/manufacturing interface, and developing technology strategy.

**Tora K. Bikson** is a senior scientist in the Department of Behavioral Sciences at the RAND Corporation. Her work has emphasized field and experimental research designs related to the investigation of cognitive and psychosocial behavior. She has also worked on the changing organizational structures in implementing new office technologies. Dr. Bikson holds A.B., M.A., and Ph.D. degrees in philosophy from the University of Missouri-Columbia, and M.A. and Ph.D. degrees in psychology from the University of California, Los Angeles.

**Milo L. Brekke** is president of Brekke Associates, a Minneapolis-based group of consultants specializing in research and evaluation concerning health services, education, and religion.

**H. Robert Cathcart** is president of Pennsylvania Hospital. He has served as chief executive officer since 1952, and president since 1970. The hospital, the first in the nation, includes the 435-bed Department for Sick and Injured and The Institute of Pennsylvania Hospital, a 234-bed psychiatric hospital. Mr. Cathcart has presented and published papers on health care and management issues, and has served in leadership posts with the American Hospital Association and other professional medical organizations. He holds degrees from the University of Iowa and the University of Toronto.

**Thomas Choi** is associate professor in the School of Public Health at the University of Minnesota, teaching in the Division of Health Services Research and Policy. His courses encompass organizational theory and the measurement of complex variables used in social and organizational research. Dr. Choi's research in health organizations focuses on the organization and delivery of health care.

**John M. Driscoll, Jr.,** is professor of clinical pediatrics at Columbia University's College of Physicians and Surgeons and has been director of the Neonatal Intensive Care Unit at Babies Hospital for 19 years. His current research focuses on the developmental outcome of infants from the NICU. Dr. Driscoll also serves as director of Columbia Presbyterian Infant Bioethics Committee, which reviews difficult clinical situations at the request of staff and parents and serves as a consultative body in the resolution of these issues.

**J. D. Eveland** is currently visiting associate professor of organizational psychology at the Claremont Graduate School and consultant to the RAND Corporation. His interests involve organizational uses of technology, particularly information technology, and their relationships to organizational communication and effectiveness. In addition to RAND, Dr. Eveland is a regular consultant to the National Aeronautics and Space Administration, the National Science Foundation, and the National Institutes of Health. He received a B.A. degree in history from Reed College, an M.P.I.A. from the University of Pittsburgh, and an M.P.H. and Ph.D. in administration and organizational behavior from the University of Michigan.

**Bruce Gissing** is executive vice president-operations, directing the Continuous Quality Improvement program in the Boeing Commercial Airplane Group. In this position, Gissing supervises activities that include the Continuous Quality Improvement Center and the Boeing organizations of Human Resources, Planning, and Quality Assurance. Gissing is also chairman of Boeing Canada and is the Operations functional executive of the Commercial Airplane Group. Among his previous positions at Boeing, Mr. Gissing was vice president-general manager of the Renton Division, where he directed the design and production of the Boeing standard-body 737 and 757 jetliners. He also has held a number of other management positions, including director of operations for the 747 Division and the joint 747/767 Division and vice president-general manager of the Boeing Engineering Company. Mr. Gissing earned a B.A. from City College, New York, and an M.A. from the University of Denver.

**Charles R. Hartgraves** is associate deputy chief for administration with the Forest Service of the U.S. Department of Agriculture. His responsibilities include computer sciences and telecommunications, property and procurement, accounting, law enforcement, and information systems. Before assuming this position in 1983, he was director of the Forest Service's Land Management Planning Staff. Mr. Hartgraves holds degrees from New Mexico State University in range management and from American University in public administration.

**James R. Hettenhaus** is vice president of manufacturing and technology for International Bio-Synthetics USA. In more than 20 years of experience in the process industry, he has participated in and directed the establishment of semiautonomous work teams in both union and nonunion plants as a supervisor with Monsanto, as a plant manager with Anheuser-Busch, and in his current position, where he has accomplished part of the job redesign by concurrently installing centralized process control systems. Mr. Hettenhaus has a B.S. in chemical engineering from the University of Wisconsin and an M.S. in servomechanisms from St. Louis University.

**Joseph C. High** is executive director of human resources for Cummins Engine Company and was formerly director of human resources for Consolidated Diesel Company, where he has managed a joint venture between Cummins and Case IH in manufacturing diesel engines. He has held management and human resource positions with TRW and Union Carbide. His work in adopting new technologies is concentrated on flexible benefits and the establishment and maintenance of high performance work systems in a manufacturing environment. Mr. High holds a B.S. degree from the University of North Carolina, Chapel Hill, and an M.A. in human resources management from Central Michigan University.

**Helen Jameson** is a nurse consultant with Rochester Methodist Hospital in Rochester, Minnesota, and St. Luke's Hospital in Jacksonville, Florida, and has conducted operations research in nurse scheduling. She received her registered nurse's diploma from Mounds-Midway School of Nursing and holds bachelor's and master's degrees in nursing and administration from the University of Minnesota. Before assuming her role as nurse consultant, she was associate administrator at Rochester Methodist Hospital and head of the nursing department there.

**Rosabeth Moss Kanter** is the Class of 1960 Professor of Business Administration at Harvard University and editor of the *Harvard Business Review*. She has conducted pioneering research in the study of organizational change and corporate entrepreneurship, served as a consultant to several corporations, and authored 10 books, including *The Change Masters* and *When Giants Learn to Dance*. Dr. Kanter has also taught at Brandeis and Yale universities, Harvard's Graduate School of Education, and MIT's Sloan School of Management. She received a B.A. from Bryn Mawr College and a Ph.D. from the University of Michigan.

**Robert J. Krasman** is senior vice president of administrative services for the United Way of Allegheny County. Before being appointed senior vice president, he served as manager of accounting and finance and vice president for the United Way. Prior to the United Way, he served as business manager and board secretary in a public school system in the Greater Pittsburgh area. He serves as a member of the National Professional Advisory Committee for the United Way of America in the area of information and technology. Mr. Krasman holds a B.S. degree from the University of Steubenville.

**Edward O. Laumann** is professor of sociology and dean of social sciences at the University of Chicago. His research interests include urban and political sociology, network analysis, formal organizations and the professions, and society and AIDS issues. Dr. Laumann received a B.A. from Oberlin College and a Ph.D. in sociology from Harvard University.

**Wilson R. Locke** is editorial systems editor for the *Los Angeles Times*, responsible for the operation of the *Times'* new editing system network of computers. Over the course of more than 30 years in the newspaper industry, he has worked as a manager, news editor, and reporter. In his capacity as assistant managing editor of the *Oakland Tribune*, he was instrumental in installing the newspaper's first computer-based editing system. Mr. Locke attended Stanford University.

**Gerald Nadler** is professor and chairman of the department of industrial and systems engineering at the University of Southern California. Previously, Dr. Nadler taught at Washington University, the University of Wisconsin-Madison, and several universities in Europe and Japan. His related research focuses on developing interdisciplinary systems planning and design methodologies, and designing and implementing technical literacy programs for nonengineers. He received his B.Sc. and Ph.D. in industrial engineering from Purdue University.

**Brigid O'Farrell** is a senior associate at the Center for Women Policy Studies and formerly study director for the Committee on Women's Employment and Related Social Issues at the National Research Council. Her research focuses on the change process in organizations in general and, more specifically, on the implementation of equal employment opportunity policies for women. Her most recent work includes pay equity, child care policy, and work and family issues. She holds an Ed.M. in social policy from Harvard University and a B.A. in political science from Kent State University.

**Charles J. H. Stolar** is an associate professor of surgery at Columbia University's College of Physicians and Surgeons and has been the director of the ECMO program at Babies Hospital since its inception nine years ago. He is also chairman of the Registry Committee and charter member of the Steering Committee of Extracorporeal Life Support Oxygenation and national representative to the American Society for Artificial Internal Organs.

**Andrew Van de Ven** is 3M Professor of Human Systems Management in the Carlson School of Management and director of the Minnesota Innovation Research Program in the Strategic Management Research Center of the University of Minnesota. His research has focused on the development and testing of group decision-making processes, organizational planning and problem solving, and instruments that measure and evaluate the performance of jobs, work units, and organizations based on structural designs and environmental situations. Currently, he is leading a major longitudinal research program on the management of innovation.    Dr. Van de Ven taught at the Wharton School of the University of Pennsylvania and Kent State University after receiving a Ph.D. from the University of Wisconsin-Madison.

**Signe A. von Verdo (Weber)** joined Intellinomics Corporation in early 1990 as manager of the company's New York office and is currently in the San Francisco office.  Intellinomics is a San Francisco-based firm that markets software products developed using breakthrough design technology and tools.  Formerly, Ms. von Verdo held the position of vice president of Quality Metrics— Information Services at Shearson Lehman Hutton responsible for defining data processing service levels and product quality that directly impact Shearson's external client base.  Before this, she headed the company's Office Systems Group, overseeing the support of more than 2,000 personal computers and 1,000 minicomputer users.  She also worked with Xerox Corporation in a number of internal consulting positions in the United States, the United Kingdom, and Western Europe, and on a special assignment with the Grace Commission.  Ms. von Verdo holds B.S. and M.B.A. degrees in math and accounting, respectively, from the University of Rochester.

# Index

## A

Accountability, 263–268
Activity mix, 23–24
Adhocracy, 112, 113
Adoption. *See* Innovation adoption
Ambulatory care unit case
    diagnostic technology in radiology and pathology in, 168–169
    establishment of short procedure unit in, 162–165
    health care cost payments in, 159–160
    key points raised by, 153–155
    and laser use in outpatient surgery, 166–168
    obstetrics and gynecology technology in, 166
    and payment system changes, 160–162
    results of new technology in, 169–170
Argyris, C., 149–150
Arthroscopic techniques, 161–162
Attitude, 246–247
Audit trail, 264

Authority, employee, 95
Automated Nurse Scheduling System (ANSOS) computer program, 197

## B

Bernheimer, Martin, 293
Blume, David, 293–294
Boeing, William E., 90
Boeing Company
    future steps in organizational design at, 100–101
    lessons learned by, 99–100
    organizational redesign within, 90–92
    overview of, 89–90
Boundary phenomena, 240–242
Boundary spanners, 242
Breadth strategy, 148
Bryson, J., 150
Bull's-eye concept, 95–96
Business mix, 20–23